Justice, Human Nature, and Political Obligation

Justice, Human Nature, and Political Obligation

Morton A. Kaplan

THE FREE PRESS
A Division of Macmillan Publishing Co., Inc.
NEW YORK

Collier Macmillan Publishers
LONDON

The Free Press
A Division of Macmillan Publishing Co., Inc.
866 Third Avenue, New York, N.Y. 10022

Collier Macmillan Canada, Ltd.

Library of Congress Catalog Card Number: 76-8145

Printed in the United States of America

printing number

1 2 3 4 5 6 7 8 9 10

Library of Congress Cataloging in Publication Data

Kaplan, Morton A
  Justice, human nature, and political obligation.

  Includes bibliographical references and index.
  1. Justice. 2. Natural law. 3. Ethics.
I. Title.
JC578.K34   320'.01   76-8145
ISBN 0-02-916890-2

Contents

Preface

Justice, Human Nature, and Political Obligation is one of two closely interrelated books, the other of which is *Alienation and Identification.* Although each elucidates the other, each is designed to be read independently.

My objective in this book is to examine the character of the good and the just. I shall attempt to show that these concepts are not merely arbitrarily personal or idiosyncratically cultural. I believe that they are related to human nature as it manifests itself in different conditions. However, human nature is not something that can be defined in the abstract, regardless of the social and political setting within which it flourishes. If it were, the human variability we find in different societies could not be explained. Human nature is dispositional. It responds differently in different settings.

On the other hand, if the differences between societies or between men were determined merely by historical experience or by upbringing, the historicist argument, which I reject, would hold. Each society or each man would be *sui generis.*

I shall argue that conceptions of the good and the just are no more determined by environmental conditions and past history alone than they are by an abstract human nature. There is a continual interaction between man and society and environment. During these interactions—in our responses to each other within institutional settings—we develop a sense of justice that is related to our identifications with other men and with institutions. This matter of identification—which I analyze in *Alienation and Identification*—is central to a conception of justice, for it establishes an objective interest in society and its rules that goes beyond more narrowly conceived notions of the good.

I shall attempt to show that justice is related to the systems of identification that bind men to social or political groups. These identifications, therefore, are incomplete and in partial conflict. As a consequence, a concept of justice that is timeless, independent of circumstances, and uniform regardless of membership—and some variant of this position is currently dominant in philosophy—is inapplicable to the predicaments in which men often find themselves. It fails to do "justice" to conflicting interests as they arise among men, between man and society, and among competing societies; and, thus, it deals with problems of political obligation only superficially.

Although my position is consistent with the naturalistic tradition, which includes such modern writers as Morris R. Cohen and John Dewey, it conflicts sharply with the dominant current beliefs. The contemporary rejection of the naturalistic tradition in part responds to what are believed to be insoluble problems that confront that tradition, including a meaningful treatment of human nature. In part it rests upon the current notion of what science is and what objective knowledge consists of: a domain that is believed not to include values. These conclusions, which are generally, although not exclusively, accepted by moral philosophers, have led to a variety of positions. Existentialism attempts to fill the void created by the denial of objectivity in values by a leap of faith. Relativism in ethics assumes a unique solution for each culture. Hence, either explicitly or implicitly, it denies a moral critique of that culture from some different or wider perspective. Others believe that a single set of moral norms can be applied directly to any society regardless of its institutional or environmental features. These, therefore, treat justice independently of—or as exclusively determinative of—the good. John Rawls, for instance, as in the case of most other contemporary moral philosophers, develops his theory of justice prior to consideration of what the good is. I shall attempt to show in contrast that (1) the argument against objectivity fails (the distinction between first- and second-order frameworks of reference that is developed in chapter 3 will elucidate how ethical relativists misunderstand the problem of relativity in ethics); (2) the conception of justice as a transitive and closed system misrepresents its character; (3) justice is a field in which different rules, goods, conditions, and consequences coexist in a loose equilibrium and jointly govern decisions.

The question of procedure in establishing these positions is one that seriously concerned me. One might argue the case independently of the literature. However, as the opposing position is dominant, this would lead many to believe that my position is not responsive to accepted arguments. One might quote the arguments of various writers for the opposing positions and attempt to refute these. However, arguments torn out of context are easily misrepresented. I chose a third procedure: to search for the most distinguished and systematic works of moral philosophy that argue the positions at issue and to show how and why their arguments fail. I have, therefore, chosen my adversary positions—Stephen Toulmin's *Reason in Ethics* and John Rawls's *A Theory of Justice*[1]—with care, for they must be representative of the best statements of what I wish to dispute. And I need to carry out the task of analysis with fidelity both to aid in the elucidation of my own position and to assure those readers who are not specialists that my task has been undertaken adequately and fairly—an effort that may be particularly useful to students.

Stephen Toulmin's *Reason in Ethics* rightly is regarded as a modern classic in ethical theory and includes the best statement of the case against the objectivity of values. It contains a summary of the major contending positions: the objective, the subjective, and the imperative, as well as Toulmin's alternative to them. In the process, there are discussions of the positions of such classic philosophers as Aristotle, Hume, Spinoza, Kant, and Hegel, as well as such modern writers as Jeremy Bentham, C. D. Broad, John Dewey, G. E. Moore, Karl Popper, C. L. Stevenson, John Wisdom, and Ludwig Wittgenstein.

My treatment of Toulmin on objectivity is far more concise than Toulmin's own statement of his position. Yet it remains faithful—and can be seen to do so—to both his conclusions and his mode of argument. As he has made the most celebrated attack on the objectivity of values, the reader—who, experience leads me to believe, will favor Toulmin's position over mine—will have his doubts removed before the positive exposition begins. Thus, although I rarely use what philosophers call technical argumentation, I will have better prepared the way for my own discussion of objectivity. Moreover, by showing how Toulmin misconceives the character of ethical argument, I prepare the way for my critique of Rawls.

Although Rawls, I believe, does not mention Toulmin, he implicitly accepts, as do almost all writers on the subject, Toulmin's argument that values are not objective—and thus believes that justice can be analyzed independently of, or at least prior to, the good. However, unlike Toulmin, he recognizes that this causes a problem with respect to obligation, which he attempts to solve by developing further the Kantian ethical position. In doing so, he has achieved the most powerful, general, and consistent expression of the great contractarian approach to a theory of ethics. Thus an analysis of these two works will play a significant role in this presentation of my position.

Each of the four chapters of this book has a specific function in the presentation of my position. Because it was the systems framework of analysis that enabled me to find a way to meet the objections to a contention that values are objective, a statement concerning systems analysis is important to my task.

Chapter 1 is designed to outline those features of systems analysis that are useful for clarifying problems of value and justice. In this chapter, I shall distinguish systems and system levels. I shall show why laws employing terms for which there are generally appropriate measures do not exist for homeostatic systems—a category that includes all social systems. Thus, general theories of politics or of ethics are excluded. I shall also show that the absolute distinction between induction and deduction breaks down: a position that is implicit in the pragmatist philosophies of Charles Peirce, Morris Cohen, and John Dewey. The best recent expression of this position is in Willard van Orman Quine's "Two Dogmas of Empiricism," a précis of which is presented in appendix 2. Many readers will find this technical exposition useful to a fuller understanding of my position. Others may be satisfied with my briefer statements concerning it in this preface and in chapter 1. In chapters 1, 2, and 3, I shall examine important differences between the realms of theory and praxis. The former contains all particular theories and the latter consists of the entire body of knowledge, the loose equilibrium of which predisposes us to accept certain axioms and standards of evidence over others. That ethics is an area of praxis will have important consequences as we shall discover in chapters 2 and 3 and in appendix 3.

One other aspect of chapter 1 warrants discussion here. Much of the discussion consists of speculative hypotheses

xii   *Justice, Human Nature, and Political Obligation*

concerning the human personality system. It hardly needs to be stated that our understanding of these matters is in its infancy. Mathematical students of brain structure and functions have moved well beyond Ashby's early work.[2] Their work utilizes exceptionally complex theoretical designs that are difficult for the layman to understand. However, the level of generality employed in chapter 1 is sufficient for our purposes.

Chapter 2 has three functions. First, drawing upon the systems concepts of chapter 1 to show that Toulmin's arguments against the objectivity of the good are faulty, it specifies what is meant by the objectivity of values and shows both its similarities with and differences from other types of assertions concerning objective features of the world. Second, it states the iterative procedures of the test in principle that permits an ordering of ethical rules that is not restricted to the existential "givens" of particular human or social situations. This is the method that permits us to move beyond historicism and absolute ethical relativism. Combined with the concept of first-order synonymity of values that is developed in chapter 3, it permits a conception of justice that is not univocal or transitive and closed. Third, by showing how the restriction of ethical analysis to a system of rules misconceives the problem of ethical analysis, it prepares the way for a discussion of Rawls and justice.

In one sense, chapter 2 may appear to make chapter 3 irrelevant. If the good can be treated in objective fashion, and if ethics or justice cannot be restricted to the confines of a system of moral principles, Rawls's enterprise might appear to be neither necessary nor possible. However, a demonstration that the good can be treated objectively is not sufficient by itself to show the relationship between the good and the just or to prove that an independent theory of justice is impossible. Moreover, although the reasons given in chapter 2 against treating ethics as a system of moral principles will be seen to provide a general explanation for the failure of John

Rawls's neo-Kantian enterprise, it would be merely frivolous to accept this conclusion without critical examination of so major an achievement.

My extensive discussion of Rawls's generalization of the Kantian approach to ethics permits me to show that no mere circumstantial defects that greater ingenuity might avoid defeat the neo-Kantian position. The defect is radical and results from Rawls's violation of a crucial principle that is expounded in chapter 1, where distinctions are made between mechanical and homeostatic systems of equilibria and between theory and praxis. The latter, within which social systems and their moral rules are included, require qualitatively different treatments for different types of systems rather than submission to a single theoretical framework or covering law. The appropriate rules for any social system depend upon both the character of the system and the conditions of its environment. This is not an equivalent to a determination of the initial conditions of a system: a procedure necessary for the application of any theory or law, as in the case of atmospheric friction for the calculation of a falling body, the propensity to save in Keynesian economics, or the state of public opinion in Kaplan's "balance of power" theory when explaining late-nineteenth-century discrepancies from the essential rules of the system. No single system of logic applies, for instance, to members of such seemingly similar pairs as "balance of power" and bipolar international systems; extended and nuclear family systems; or modern and traditional economic systems. And any effort to make such applications will produce vacuous generalizations rather than genuine covering laws.

Although this conclusion from systems analysis is absolutely fundamental to an understanding of theory in the social sciences, its application to particular cases requires demonstration. Thus, as I have indicated, the extended discussion of Rawls in chapter 3 will show that his premises do not permit choices between contradictory rules of justice and that this is a radical difficulty that reappears at each juncture of his argument and not merely a particular oversight, an error subject to correction, or a consequence of a failure to state initial conditions.

Although my test in principle hypothesizes a weak moral ordering that determines preferences for moral rules in particular societies and preferences for one society over another, this assumes a coding of the organism and not an independent rational rule or set of rules. The choice of one rule or set of moral rules from among others depends upon the outcomes of the choices the individual sets of rules produce in different social environments. Even this is not sufficient to determine appropriate moral rules, however, without additional hypotheses about the nature of man. The discussion of Rawls will demonstrate that his attempt to abstract from such considerations vitiates his conclusions and their contradictories as well.

These conclusions directly follow from systems analysis as expounded in chapter 1. One other important consideration applies that also vitiates the conclusions reached by Rawls. Because the information required to assess ethical rules is, in Quine's sense, at the periphery of knowledge, ethics is best treated as an area of praxis rather than as a strictly theoretical discipline, at least in the deductive sense of the term. In chapter 1 and appendix 2 the discussion of Quine's "Two Dogmas of Empiricism" will elucidate the point that systems of moral rules and of good outcomes are loosely interdependent parts of a field, within which neither the good nor the just can be given absolute priority. Moreover, statements about this field depend upon boundary conditions. Statements are not reified "absolutes" that can be detached from contexts.

In chapter 2, I shall show how the test in principle permits detachment from one's embeddedness in social roles and how it thus casts a different and more rational light on the relationship of the intellectual to social class and alienation than that stemming from the Marxian tradition.

One further task remains for chapter 3: to distinguish between first- and second-order objectivity—the problem of relativity and frameworks of reference—with respect to the good and the just and to show how these are related to the perceiving and valuing individual. Important aspects of objectivity that would have diverted the flow of argument have been removed to appendix 1. Appendix 1 deals with philosophically important topics that are concerned with the differences between knowing and communicating. I shall show that objectivity in the classical sense—that is, of a one-to-one correspondence between a representation and an external reality—is not meaningful but that the concept remains useful if appropriately employed.

Chapter 3 makes clear the futility and even the potential harm of absolute, transitive, and closed univocal systems of ethics; it shows how they neglect legitimate, but conflictful, existential interests and yet how relativism in ethics, at least as it is ordinarily understood, can be avoided. It permits us to state how an appropriate conception of the just can be formulated and why, in its very nature, it is likely developmental in character. It also indicates the hypotheses concerning man on which it is likely dependent.

This prepares the reader for chapter 4, in which I apply these conceptions to the problem of political obligation and show how they permit a richer and more appropriate "theory" of obligation than does the restrictive neo-Kantian framework of John Rawls. However, an actual examination of questions of justice requires extensive empirical investigation. Answers cannot be derived from a single theoretical schema for what are essentially matters of practice. For this reason, in a work that is essentially metatheoretical, I have attempted only to delineate some of the more general characteristics of an account of political obligation. I am aware that this will prove disappointing to those readers who would have preferred a detailed discussion of obligation under contemporary conditions. However, the primary purpose of this book is to show that such a worthy enterprise must respond to the contextual features of the contemporary world and that this history-related task is possible without a retreat into either subjectivism or historicism. This is surely the prior task, or at least so it seems to me. Moreover, to develop a theory of ethics for a particular society requires an analysis of that society and of its prospects as well as of the nature of men and their identifications with one another. In Quine's terms, however, these considerations are at the periphery rather than the center of knowledge. To use a classic distinction inexactly, they deal with opinion rather than with knowledge. To focus upon the content of moral behavior in a particular society would be to divert attention from an examination of how to go about such a task in any society.

With these foregoing comments in view, I can provide a preliminary statement of my position, which is taken from *System and Process in International Politics:*

> The general concept of man involves an abstraction from the circumstances that individualize specific men and from the environments which set specific problems for individual men. However, at a more pragmatic level, appeals for cooperation will fail if they are phrased in an exclusively instrumental fashion. And individual men who think in such terms will become unfit for society— as Aristotle said, they will be either beasts or gods. Even if such men are biologically possible, natural selection will tend to breed them out.
>
> All societies are based upon a concept of justice. Justice . . . depends upon rules that are independent of particular personalities. *Noblesse oblige* is an obligation of all nobles. Decorum and restraint are expected of all judges in Great Britain, not just of Judge Jones. All veterans wounded in war have the right to free medical treatment, not just Private Smith.
>
> Social systems can maintain themselves only if the rules according to which they operate are independent of labeling. Society—which men need to survive—constrains men to communicate, even to think, in terms of

just relations. Those who cannot conform tend to be eliminated. Others adapt to the concept of justice, and it becomes an intrinsic and autonomous need of their personality systems.

The very stuff of tragedy occurs when vital needs of a particular individual are in irreconcilable conflict with the needs of society. Must life be sacrificed for honor? Should one commit treason to save one's life? Secondary or unimportant conflicts may be resolved one way or another and forgot. But the great conflicts are inherently insoluble. . . .

There is only one escape from this dilemma. That escape is to modify the environment in such a way that the two sets of needs cease to be irreconcilable. Thus, in most social situations, there is an underlying strain toward social change. But as change occurs, the society itself changes. As society changes, statuses, roles, and social values change. The ways in which man and his needs are viewed change also.

To the extent that change reduces or eliminates irreconcilable cleavages of interest between some men and society or between some men and some other men, individual interests converge and become compatible. What is good for individual men becomes good also for society. The society becomes so regulated that it produces good for all men.[3]

Rawls provides a statement of a universal set of norms. I regard this position as faulty and deny that a theory of justice can be formulated in that manner, although I do provide a methodology for arriving at warrantable moral judgments. The reasons for this difference can be succinctly stated. We both agree that justice depends upon abstracting from the circumstances of men. However, whereas Rawls wishes to base his solution on a hypothetical contract made in an original condition of great paucity of information, my solution is based upon extensive comparative knowledge of different roles in alternative political and social systems.

Whereas Rawls's theory appears to produce a single transitively ordered and closed univocal system of rules for justice —although, as chapter 3 will show, he cannot succeed in this, even within the framework of his own assumptions—my solution does not assume univocality or transitivity of possible competing rules, regardless of circumstances.

Justice, in my view, is not something that exists but that must be created. The systemic interests, based upon ontological identities, that produce wider spheres of justice depend upon the interactions of man with society and nature. Rawls calls his system neo-Kantian. Without taking those terms too literally, my system in contrast could be called neo-Hegelian or neo-Marxian. Although it dispenses with the Hegelian Absolute, the reader may note the analogies in methodology as the test in principle brings the individual to moral awareness. However, these differences cannot be made clear in a short introduction. It is the function of *Justice, Human Nature, and Political Obligation* to elucidate these remarks.

Finally the reader will note that I call "human nature" meaningful and yet say few things about it. Rather than constituting a problem, this follows directly from the character of the analysis. Because human nature is meaningful only in context, few general statements can be made about it, for meaningful statements would be concrete and richly contextual. Thus, to say much about human nature, I should have to examine its manifestation in a rich set of circumstances. That would have entailed a book quite different from the one I chose to write, as would have a systematic analysis of obligation—the subject of chapter 4—in a modern society.

Acknowledgments

I wish to thank Leonard Linsky for his comments on the first two chapters of this book. Donald Wittman was helpful on the discussion of utilitarianism in chapter 3 and Uwe Nerlich made a contribution with respect to the same chapter. Ira Katznelson made some useful suggestions. I am particularly grateful to John Nelson for detailed and incisive criticisms of a late draft of the manuscript. It would not have been feasible to finish the manuscript without the devoted and efficient services of my secretary, Kersti Thompson.

Chapter 1

Systems Analysis

We begin our inquiry into the good and the just with an examination of the concept of "system." This choice of a beginning recognizes that goodness and justice are attributions made by thinking beings whose actions are motivated. Thus, inquiries concerning goodness cannot exclude examination of the characteristics of purposeful, motivated human systems. Justice involves rules for settling motivated claims; and thus an inquiry into justice also requires reference to the characteristics of motivated systems. Therefore, we must understand what motivated, purposeful systems have in common with other types of systems and how they differ from them.

THE SYSTEMS CONCEPT

The concept of system in many respects is as ambiguous as it is obvious. The often used term "systems theory" predisposes some to believe that a systems theory either does or can exist in the same way as mechanical theory in physics.

Yet no theory of systems exists—or can exist—that will permit derived predictions of human behavior in the way in which Newtonian theory, for instance, can be applied to the solar system. Neither is systems "theory" genuinely a methodology. If one speaks of the methodology of titrating chemicals, he can specify a set of procedures to be applied to the process. In playing games of chance, there are statistical methods for determining the best strategy to employ. No particular methodology belongs to systems theory.

Is systems analysis a metatheory in the sense in which scientific method can be called a metamethodology? In a broad sense scientific method involves the use of public methods for validating—or for invalidating—hypotheses within the framework of knowledge of a time. The specific methods for accomplishing this are learned through experience. Our beliefs concerning them change over time and are validated, in turn, by praxis, which will be explicated later in this chapter. Moreover, the methods may differ from subject matter to subject matter. Thus, the methods employed in macrophysical theory, in high-temperature physics, in particle physics, in various forms of chemical theory, in biology, and in some of the softer sciences differ, although they do have in common the attempt to employ more or less precise measurement and various techniques of quantification. If systems theory as a metamethodology or metatheory implies only this, then it adds nothing to scientific method in general. Yet, if it implies something beyond this, what can that be?

The term "system" is one that has been used historically by scientists and that is coming into ever increasing use with the popularity of systems analysis. For instance, "atomic system" and "solar system" are well-known examples of use of the term. If we examine the best-known example—the solar system—the term at first appears to be purely descriptive. It refers to the pattern of the orbital paths of the planets around the sun. The term "system" in this case implies an ordered patterning of elements, the explanation of, and predictions concerning, which are supplied by Newtonian theory, although Kepler's laws earlier provided a partial explanation involving not a general theory of gravitation but a special explanation of one particular empirical solar system.

In the case of Newtonian theory, the concept of system "told" the scientist not to treat planetary motions as independent events, unrelated to the complex of sun and planets. (Later it became clear that for certain purposes the solar system could not be treated as a closed system.) As contrasted with the experiments of Galileo, which were concerned only with the path of a falling body, Newton's theory was more dependent upon explicit recognition of the existence of a system.

Technically this is incorrect, for the Galilean problem could be considered a classic two-body problem in which the movement of the earth toward the smaller body is negligible. The assumption that wind resistance does not affect the velocity of the object specifies the assumed system boundary for purposes of scientific explanation. However, despite the formal similarity, conceptually the Newtonian problem requires greater awareness of the existence of a system. Whereas for Galileo the earth and the falling body were obvious objects of inquiry, the astronomers had to distinguish the rapidly moving circles of light as planets from the relatively stationary circles of light as suns and to recognize that the planets bore a relationship to a particular sun. Although the Newtonian mechanical laws apply to all solar systems, the discovery or perception of such laws arises only from an awareness of such systems qua systems.

Scientific theories may be considered systems in another sense. The concepts employed in a set of laws, mass, for instance, and the functions relating them may be considered the internal elements of the system. The assumed conditions under which they operate, for instance, a vacuum, constitute the boundary conditions of the system. This is no longer a descriptive system which gives rise to a problem that science seeks to solve or to explain. It is a theoretical system or, in more ordinary language, a theory and provides a framework for explanation. Although theories have a hypothetico-deductive form, their interpretation and application—as is true of any analytical system—require information not contained in the formal specification of the theory, a subject to which we shall return in the discussion of praxis.

Presumably every theory employing laws contains a complete specification of boundary conditions. However, we can never be sure that we know all the relevant boundary conditions. Thus, we often learn that what we regard as universal is in fact applicable only under a specified set of boundary conditions. We were not aware, for instance, of superconductivity until certain elements were examined under conditions of extreme temperature or pressure. It is possible, even likely, that what we believe to be the most general laws of the physical universe will require a radically different statement under some changed parameter of which we are now unaware. (Of course, it is also true that our explanations sometimes lead us to look for previously unobserved events.)

For the scientist, however, these are relatively minor problems. Even those scientists who are relatively unsophisticated in methodology, and who would be unable to articulate verbally the procedures they are applying, know that they must specify the conditions under which the experiment takes place and the variables upon which the experiment is to be performed. Thus, despite the increasing propensity of scientists to talk about scientific systems, there would probably be no great loss if the term were not used. The standard laboratory procedures of science guard against the most egregious mistakes and minimize the dangers of misconception. Those scientists who hypostasize the results of particular experiments would probably make this mistake anyway even if they used a systems terminology.

The problems that the physical scientist can afford to ignore because they are taken care of by standardized laboratory techniques infest the social sciences and mandate a systems orientation, not for all problems of social science but for those where conscious recognition of the interrelationship of some elements within a complex whole is essential to a correct statement of the problem. One might argue that the requirements previously stated are obvious in the social sciences also. However, the literature of the social sciences is filled with examples of research that do not respond to this methodological orientation. In his chapter in *Diplomatic Investigations,* for instance, Martin Wight chooses examples from two thousand years of history to illustrate certain principles of statecraft. That the international systems in which these actions took place may have been radically different is not a question that occurred to him. That the numbers of states, their weapons systems, their economic potentialities, their patterns of alignment, and so forth, may have produced different types of systems within which the cited examples functioned differently was foreign to his analysis and indeed foreign to any analysis before the middle 1950s when systems concepts made their entry into the international relations literature. He is far from alone.

Ironically it is precisely in the area of mind as a system that modern systems analysis had its origins, for it was designed to distinguish between the operations of neurological systems and of other systems treated by science. Although the concepts of systems analysis have not yet been sufficiently developed for a fully satisfactory explication of human purpose, they at least have permitted an effective inquiry into the ways in which the activities of the mind involve processes that are distinctly different from those of other behavioral systems. (The discussion of ultra- and trans-stability later in this chapter will provide some insight into this question.) Systems analysis thus had its origin not in an attempt to develop a methodology but in an attempt to solve a particular type of scientific problem that required an explicit orientation to systems qua systems.

There is also an explicit focus to this inquiry: to investigate those aspects of human behavior relevant to ethical inquiry. This investigation will not be derived from systems analysis, but it will provide an assessment of a system (human) to which problems of ethics are relevant.

I shall not here anticipate the discussion of chapter 2 except to note that much of the confusion in ethical inquiry results from a failure to ask in what respects systems for which values are relevant differ from other types of systems. I do not pretend to give a complete or exhaustive explanation of these differences but aspire only to make some relevant distinctions and to gain some insights into the basis of ethical behavior.

No type of behavior exists in the abstract. Physical behavior does not consist of symbols and equations. Concepts such as force and mass may be abstract, but only bodies possess force and mass. Physical behavior involves bodies; however, physical behavior is explained by laws that employ the concepts of force and mass. Valuational or ethical behavior also involves bodies—in this case, human beings—and an explanation or assessment of this behavior should be given in terms that are as related to human being as are the explanations of physics with respect to physical objects. Until we have discovered the relevant variables of the system and the functions by means of which they are related, valuational behavior will remain a mystery. The problem is not one of distinguishing facts from values but of determining what type of fact a value is. We determine hot and cold by touch but temperature by means of a thermometer and on the basis of an "absolute" scale. The accessibility of a particular type of fact to knowledge depends upon identifying the type of fact that it is and upon determining the procedures by means of which it can become known.

WHAT A SYSTEM IS

Systems analysis instead of being considered a theory, should be considered an approach that calls for the development of theories or the elucidation of propositions oriented to those aspects of reality for which the explicit recognition of systems characteristics is useful. Thus, our initial task in this inquiry is to determine the characteristics to be attributed to the term "system."

A system is a set of interrelated elements sufficiently distinguished from their environment by certain regularities to serve as a focus of inquiry. The elements of a system may be concrete in the sense that they are physically distinguishable or they may be abstract in the sense that they are conceptually distinguishable. Thus a system may consist of points, of numbers, of roles, of persons, of organizations, or so forth. The elements of a system need not be of the same type. These may include, for instance, people or roles. These elements may then be related in terms of authority, wisdom, wealth, strength, or any other relevant characteristic of the persons or roles. We may include as parts of the system characteristics such as economic capabilities or information. We may also distinguish as part of the system the behavior that accords with the other elements of the system under specified parameter conditions.[2]

Systems include both elements and functions. Thus the heart pumps blood and the lungs process oxygen air. Priests provide absolution, legislatures pass laws, courts apply law. An input into a system that changes its characteristic behavior is called a step function. Thus opium changes the characteristic optic behavior of the biological organism. A successful revolution changes the characteristic behavior (and the characteristic values and normative rules) of a political system. (This is a schematic explanation of the principle that invalidates the search for a universal set of rules that applies to a system regardless of its internal characteristics or boundary conditions. It applies to normative and also to other behavioral aspects of system functioning.)

The choice of a system is, in effect, a choice of a subject matter. There is no "absolute" single system in the concrete world. In principle, the same reality may be analyzed by a variety of systems models. It is an empirical or at least a praxical—rather than a theoretical—matter whether this is useful. This also applies to the choice of which variables are internal and which are external to the system. Later in this chapter, we shall see that a similar analysis applies to the choice of axioms, theorems, and the other elements of theories.

THE CONCEPT OF EQUILIBRIUM

Systems approaches make wide use of the concept of equilibrium. By equilibrium, we mean that two sets of properties are in an unchanging relationship with respect to each other. A parked car on a flat surface, for instance, is in equilibrium with the surface, for it will not move even if the brakes are released (unless it is pushed). Equilibria are normally classified as stable, static, and unstable. One may think of a ball in a valley, on a flat surface, and on top of a narrowly peaked ridge as metaphors for these concepts.

Whether an equilibrium is stable or not depends on our perspective. Thus, biological life on earth is stable from the standpoint of men with short lives, and even of nations with longer lives, but unstable from the standpoint of eternity; for eventually the sun will nova. The Roman Empire was stable from the standpoint of a Roman of the first century A.D., but unstable from the standpoint of some historians. There is no contradiction here—or retreat into subjectivity—for, given an adequate statement of the character of the inquiry, there are objective—that is, publicly communicable standards—to determine their accuracy.

Political Implications
of an Equilibrium Approach

There has been a widespread view that scientific concern with equilibrium produces a bias toward conservative politics. Regardless of some mistaken uses of systems analysis, this is absurd. The best safecrackers are those who understand the mechanisms of the safes they burglarize. The best assassins know the weakest parts of the human anatomy, that is, those particular links in the system that are at the same time essential to the equilibrium of the biological organism and vulnerable. By the same token, the best doctors understand the workings of the human organism. And the best defenders of a political system are also aware of its most vulnerable elements.

Every human being wishes some equilibria to persist and some to change. Most healthy but poor people wish their health to persist but their fortune to change. The revolutionary wishes the system he intends to install to persist although he wishes the system he intends to overthrow to disappear. One is always for particular changes and against particular changes; and if he believes differently he is merely being foolish.

However, an important distinction needs to be made. Systems analyses, as they apply to particular systems, have neither conservative nor liberal—neither reactionary nor radical—implications for the reasons already given. However, systemic pragmaticism—which infuses Peircean pragmaticism with a systems perspective—has distinct political implications, depending upon factual conditions. Whether these are liberal or conservative, evolutionary or revolutionary, depends on the state of affairs. But the long-term effects of the philosophy are at least evolutionary. As man comes to fuller awareness of the meaning of his own existence, the insights gained from this knowledge produce a disposition to change the world: to leave the realm of necessity and to enter the kingdom of freedom, in Marx's words. (The basic methodology, of course, is Hegel's and is developed in his *Phenomenology*.) To show how and why this is so is the subject of this book.

The Rationale
for Equilibria-oriented Approaches

There is a reason for an interest in studying equilibria. The reason, however, is pragmatic rather than ideological. The biologists tell us that mutations are bad, by which they mean that most mutations lack survival value. On the other hand, the existence of man is a consequence of mutation. Presumably we consider that good. However, whether we consider it good or bad, the fact is that there are fewer workable combinations of genes or of economic, social, or political elements than there are unworkable ones. Thus our scientific task is made more manageable when our inquiry starts with equilibrium. In the first place, there are fewer systems in (relative) equilibrium than in disequilibrium. In the second place, equilibrium is a precondition for recurrent behavior. Therefore, systems in equilibrium provide us with a better opportunity to study them than systems in disequilibrium. In the third place, systems that persist usually must overcome disturbances and, therefore, we likely can acquire detailed and systematic information about their vulnerabilities.

In trying to construct models or theoretical sketches, we have enormously narrowed the range of permutation if we attempt to explain systems in equilbrium. If we can do this, we can then learn about the vulnerabilities of a system to disequilibrium produced by particular changes at the boundary of the system. As it would be an unmanageable task to attempt to do this for the complete range of possible disturbances—at least for complex systems in complex environments—our task is simplified by restricting our inquiry to those possible disturbances that we believe more likely.

Although in principle we could construct dynamic models in disequilibrium, there are so many different ways in which we could do so that the *a priori* probability that we would have hit upon a model useful for any actual system in disequilibrium would seem to be remote. Thus, equilibrium is a useful focal point for inquiry into the operations of systems. Beyond this, however, and even more important, the differences in types of equilibria manifested by different types of systems provide us with information concerning important aspects of the behavior of systems. The study of valuational behavior is intimately linked to the equilibrial processes of purposeful systems. Thus, it is this aspect of the systems approach that is particularly appropriate in the investigation of problems of values.

Mechanical Equilibria

The best-known type of equilibrium is the perhaps inaptly named mechanical equilibrium. We say that a car resting on a flat surface is in mechanical equilibrium. By this we mean that the forces that might move it are canceled. These forces are not merely inferred from the resting state of the car. They generally can be measured independently. And their cancellation in this instance can be derived from Newton's laws.

A law is a universal relationship between sets of properties. We shall call a law a covering law when it can be expressed in a set of equations the terms of which are independently measurable and generally invariant for all systems of application. In this limited sense, all mechanical equilibria can be explained by covering laws. Although the concept of mechanical equilibrium in physics does not convey much significant information—far more information is conveyed by the other specifics of particular theories—it is more than a label and thus conveys more information than a label normally conveys.

Homeostatic Equilibria

When we move to homeostatic systems, such as thermostat-controlled heating systems or the mechanism that controls the temperature of human blood, this is no longer true, although all homeostatic systems operate within boundaries set by some mechanical system: for instance, one can determine how much energy is required to raise the temperature of a room a specified number of degrees if one knows the volume of the room, the thermal qualities of the energy source, and the efficiency of the heating mechanism.

No such independently measurable system of equalities applies to the thermostatic system, however. Thus, in this case, an explanation of the temperature equilibrium of the room requires reference to the way in which a thermometer operates within a system of relays designed to turn the heater on and off. In this case, "homeostatic equilibrium" is a label designating the type of system and conveys only the amount of information that a label can convey, whereas the explanation of the behavior of the system is not linked to a concept of equality. The label merely tells us that the system is one in which changes in certain specified elements of the system maintain one or more particular elements of the system within a "requisite" range.

This is one reason—the other, and related, reason being the degree of complication of the system—for an important distinction between theoretical analyses in the social and the physical sciences. Many common terms are used in mechanics, thermodynamics, optics, and astrophysics. And their measurement in experiments in each, in general, is made according to a common scale. Generally we can define and identify these terms independently of more complex system variations. And we can, therefore, employ them in covering laws.

The units of social and political analysis cannot be experimented upon in isolation, either in principle or in practice. We cannot define them in a way that employs terms for which there are common measures independent of some varying system contexts and according to which "equality" is empirically meaningful. Because this is so, we cannot develop a measure of system efficiency in processing such variables as we can for engines that use fuels. "Demands" and "supports," for instance, do not exist in the same way as physical units, for their scale lacks meaning independently of the character of the political or social system that processes them,[3] whereas the energy contained in fuel is measurable independently of the efficiency of particular engines. For this reason, covering laws of the type available to physicists are not available to the social scientist.

Because no common measure is available for variables in homeostatic systems, important information is lost as attempts are made to apply common generalizations across different types of generically similar systems. Thus, although "Democratic systems require popular support if they are to function" is a truism, it conveys little information about conditions for support in any democratic system. Moreover, democratic systems often function well without much support; and the proposition tells us nothing about how to distinguish between these cases. Indeed, even non-democratic systems require support.

As the level of abstraction is raised to statements that apply to all political systems—for instance, "Political systems are in equilibrium when demands and supports are in balance"—we no longer even have a weak truism. In the absence of independent measures that are generally applicable, the statement is vacuous. This does not imply that demands and supports are vacuous concepts but only that their qualitative manifestations in concrete circumstances differ in major ways from system to system. The strength of these manifestations does not have a measure that is independent of experience, either practical or theoretical, with particular types of political systems. Therefore, if statements are to be relatively meaningful, their range of application must be restricted to subtypes of systems. When lower-level generalizations function in a qualitative theory or theory sketch, with specified boundary conditions and specified actors, as in my international systems models, they do convey useful information. Later in this chapter, I shall indicate how comparative analysis enables us to develop useful information about political systems that can be specified in propositional form.

In chapter 3, in the discussion of J. C. C. Smart, we shall see how the attempt to find an ethical rule that is independent of system differences turns a rule into a definition of rational behavior. The rule, therefore, ceases to serve as a proposition that can function within a theory. We also shall see how a similar error invests attempts to generalize economic theory to primitive economic systems. Rawls's attempt to find a single set of ethical rules for all societies will be seen to fall victim to this error also. Later in this chapter we shall see that comparative evaluation is required for cross-system generalization.

In an interesting parallel case, the only game-theoretical area for which there is a general solution is the zero-sum game. In this game, the same physical payoff is evaluated identically by all relevant players, thus establishing a utile value for the payoff that is independent of context for purposes of the analysis. In this sense, the general solution to the zero-sum game requires a kind of equivalent to the independently measurable properties that are essential to the applicability of covering laws in physics. Where this is not the case—the non-zero-sum game—no general solution has ever been found; and particular solutions apply only to particular types of non-zero-sum games.

The failure of rules or common formulations to apply

across different types of homeostatic systems is sometimes misunderstood by incautious students of so-called general systems theory. They note, for instance, that the growth curves of populations within city limits and of bacteria within enclosed cultures may be similar. They then infer that general trans-system "laws" have been found.

Their mistake is that of reference. The growth curve in this case is a constant that applies to systems with certain characteristics. To the extent that these specific characteristics are dominant—and this will be true only for some concrete realms of application of the mathematical formulas and within specified boundary conditions—the particular interpretation of the formula will provide an explanation for only the relevant facets of the real world. It will not explain other closely connected facets of behavior in the real world.

Thus, such formulas may explain certain features that some political units have in common with some non-political units, whether social or biological. They do not explain either the differences between different types of political units or those aspects of political or ethical behavior that are not relevant to these variables. They are thus not general theories but particular theories, such as theories of population growth in an enclosed area. And they function only as parameters in studies of political systems qua political systems or of bacterial systems qua biological systems. That is another reason why general theories cannot explain the behavior of different varieties of the same general type of substantive systems. And, where they appear to do so, they will be either vacuous or consistent with contradictory applications, as we shall see in succeeding chapters.

Ultrastability

In the case of both mechanical and homeostatic equilibria, the systems have resting states; and, in the latter case, although ordinary homeostatic systems might be called goal seeking, they obviously are not purposeful as that term is ordinarily used. The system change is completely determined by the environmental change, although unlike the case of mechanical equilibria, parts of the internal system vary with the external changes while maintaining an unchanged value of a particular internal variable.

Let us, therefore, carry the inquiry one stage forward with the concept of ultrastable homeostasis that was developed by W. Ross Ashby.[4] Consider an ordinary homeostatic system such as an automatic pilot in an airplane. If the plane deviates from level course, the automatic pilot senses this and corrects for it. Suppose, however, that the automatic pilot has been incorrectly linked to the ailerons of the plane so that the correction imposed by the automatic pilot removes the plane even farther from level flight. Conventional automatic pilots would continue to engage the same damaging "correction," thus throwing the plane into a spin. However, it would be possible to build an unconventional automatic pilot that could take note of the fact that its correction only worsened the drift. It could then attempt, either on an ordered or a random basis, some other patterns of activity until it found one that was corrective. This kind of system can change its own mode of response to environmental disturbances. This system is ultrastable.

Purpose

The ultrastable system exhibits some of what we mean by purpose. Let us look at another machine and then at some hypothetical human behavior to see if we can determine what we mean by the term and how we determine its content.

Consider a device with a gasoline-powered motor and a battery-driven set of headlights. When its gas supply begins to run down, it moves itself to a pump and fills itself up. When its batteries begin to run down, it moves to an electric circuit and plugs itself in to recharge. If obstacles are placed in its path, it moves around them to seek either gas or an electric outlet. Perhaps we do not yet wish to call this behavior purposive, but, as in the case of the ultrastable machine, this machine does things that seem to be among the signs of purpose.

Consider how we might infer contrasting purposes from the behavior of two different men. One man holds down two jobs. Is he seeking extra money to support his family? Is he merely compulsive? Or does he fear the future? Another man, although proclaiming his desire to work, does not apply for work often and fails in his applications when he does apply. Is his verbal claim insincere? Does he fear rejection?

How do we choose among such competing hypotheses? Consider the case of the man who has failed to find work in the example above. Further investigation reveals, for instance, that he is bright but did poorly in school except with teachers who were very supportive of him. Despite his intelligence, he avoided demanding classes. We incline toward the hypothesis that he feared rejection. Perhaps we do not have high confidence in it, but we base our conclusion on his observed behavior. We may even make this observed behavior count strongly against his assertion that he does not fear rejection but is merely waiting for a better opportunity than has yet appeared.

Another man tells us that he gambles because he enjoys the thrill of winning, but we notice that he almost always loses. A patient on a psychiatrist's couch makes a Freudian slip and perhaps gains insight into a motivation of which he or she was previously unaware. The insight, if it is such, is reinforced by behavioral observations that in many ways the patient's behavior was more consistent with the motivation indicated by the Freudian slip, although perhaps not in any straightforward way, than with the motivation that he had accepted as an explanation of his own behavior. A salesman may reason with a customer about his products. If this fails, he may develop an "aggressive" sales pitch. Perhaps in some cases the goals are transformed in the process of achievement. A suitor may switch from the pursuit of beautiful women to pursuit of any woman. A man unsuccessfully seeking the love of his mother might become an artist and seek acclaim instead. We hypothesize that the latter is a substitute for the former.

Let us briefly examine these examples and see what we mean when we attribute purpose to them. In each case there is an attributed resting state: the consequences toward which the motivation would lead. In each case obstacles were overcome to achieve this resting state. Our mobile machine had this characteristic. Our ultrastable pilot mimics part of the behavior of the salesman who changed his "pitch." Neither machine "mimics" the behavior of the suitor or the painter.

Obviously conjectures about purpose require a great deal of supporting evidence before we place any confidence in them, but they all possess a consistent form: a conjectured resting state of which the concrete result is a manifestation. These resting states usually are identified through transformations by complicated procedures of inference involving criteria. These resting states are regarded as purposeful because the actor overcomes obstacles to achieve them. Moreover, they have a more or less persistent relationship to his character and personality. That is, they have some (not necessarily fully or transitively) ordered relationships. A man's own statements to what his purposes are have evidential value but are rebuttable by other aspects of his behavior. Even in those cases in which we believe that he is consciously telling the truth as he knows it, and not attempting to mislead us, we may believe on the basis of other evidence that he is misleading himself.

The case of the individual who learned through a Freudian slip what were his unconscious or preconscious motivations was mentioned earlier. This example is stated not to imply that a preconscious purpose is a fundamental purpose, for bringing it to consciousness may reveal childish and irrational linkages that are useful in eliminating it from the system of purposes. It does, however, illustrate graphically one of the essential aspects of human learning about human character. Our purposes are not presented to us on mental demand. We learn about our purposes from our behavior in a variety of situations. Some people may live through an entire lifetime without learning that they are potential cowards as a consequence of good fortune in not being presented with situations that would produce cowardice in them.

We often say that our purposes change over time, but what may happen more often is that we gain a more sophisticated understanding both of the external world and of ourselves. Alternatively an individual may be subjected to such environmental distress that his learning about himself, which helps to shape his character and his behavior (this is a positive feedback situation), is unfortunately extremely one-sided. In other words, we are dealing with an extremely complex system which learns well or poorly about itself in part by observing itself in behavioral interaction with others and with the environment. Few of us have such a variety of experiences under a variety of circumstances that we can have more than a glimpse into our human potentialities. Usually anyone who believes that he "fully knows himself" will be an extremely truncated compulsive/obsessive type who secures "certainty" of knowledge at the expense of fullness of being.

Differences between Types of Homeostasis

Let us now note the differences between these last behaviors and the earlier example of the unconventional automatic pilot. The latter is an example of relatively simple conduct in a relatively simple environment. It is capable of changing its own behavior in the same environment in order to achieve a constant goal and of overcoming obstacles to do so. A relatively small number of observations would exhaust the potentiality of such machines and permit us to reconstruct the codes that determine their behaviors.

The ultrastable automatic pilot has a one-to-one correspondence between environment and flight path. The ability of the system to "reprogram" itself distinguishes it from ordinary homeostatic systems. However, alternative goals cannot be chosen, even as a substitute in reaching some higher-order goal.

The informational elements to which such systems respond are small in number, highly explicit, and not subject to ambiguity. Goal transformation through symbolic identification does not apply to them. Nor do the systems control their intake of information as an essential part of their process of goal pursuit. Consciousness and its distinguishable mental operations do not play a role in their "choices."

The human system is conscious and can substitute alternative behaviors in the same environment. It can pursue identical behaviors in the same environment. It can pursue identical behaviors in different environments. And it can transform its goal structure, presumably in terms of some higher-ordered comparison. I call this type of process transfinitely stable.

The Mind-Body Problem

Some mechanists attempt to dismiss conscious behavior as epiphenomenal. Behavior according to this view is physiological. Thoughts merely accompany underlying physiological processes. The fundamental error involved in this position can be elucidated by turning to a non-conscious entity: the computer. We cannot derive the behavior of the computer, including the content of the output tape, from its circuitry unless we know the content both of the internal code of the computer and of its input tape. If we know these, we can then predict the output from the input plus the internal coding. Knowledge of the particularities of the wiring of the computer would be unnecessary for this prediction, although some form of appropriate wiring and memory system are necessary for the computer's operation. The sequence of operations of the computer depends upon the internal code as well as upon the wiring, so that the activated coding element actually triggers the next flux of energy within the system.

However, the problem is more fundamental even than this. If we knew the content of the coding of the computer, then, given the input, we could predict the output. However, even this depends on the computer's ability to compare the symbols on the input tape with its code and to recognize their identity. Thus, even at this presumably non-conscious level, the computer "knows" the "meaning" of the symbols. However, we still do not know how to relate the output tape to any observation we can make external to the computer unless we know how to identify the output symbols with observations.

To accomplish this, we must have knowledge of their meaning. Thus, at every level of analysis, whether symbolic or referential, meaning is essential. Quine was able to demonstrate that the absolute distinction between the synthetic and the analytic cannot be maintained, that extra-systemic meaning is always required for the interpretation and use of formal analytical systems.

Nor is extra-systemic meaning derived directly from sensations. As John Dewey argued, our knowledge of "red" is not derived from a red sensation. Instead, the theory that perceptions are produced by sensations depends upon experience. Yet physiology reveals the inadequacies of naive empiricism as adequately as does epistemological theory. Because the normal eye pupil is in continual motion, no set of sensations could present a stationary object as stationary to the brain. Instead the brain must transform the sensations and this can be confirmed by experiment. Thus, experience always requires the active participation of the perceiving system. And meaning is an essential element without which the process cannot occur and not simply an epiphenomenal derivative from sensations.

Moreover, as Quine pointed out, Carnap, the leading exponent of purely analytical procedures, was forced to abandon his beliefs in the one-to-one translatability of statements about the physical world into statements about immediate experience.[5] As Quine says, statements about the external world face the tribunal of sense experience not individually but as a corporate body.[6]

However, we do not start with an invariant set of meanings. Our initial understanding of meanings is subject to change with experience and is variant as changes occur in the realm of praxis. We learn about meaning as we use terms, theories, and logical forms. It was the inability of Aristotle's logic to account for such knowledge as "If horses are animals, the heads of horses are heads of animals" that led to the development of inferential logic. Every form of inquiry involves meanings that are validated by use.

"Meaning" has several aspects. "Meaning" is fully conveyed neither by verbal definitions nor by "pointing" denotations. No complex sentence has a one-to-one correlation with perception; and "pointing" merely identifies a case and, therefore, assumes meaning.

Meaning is related to the coding employed by the organism. However, this coding does not link a discrete coding element to a discrete perceptual element in any simple fashion. Stimulus/response theories assume such discrete elements. For a sufficiently stable world and a sufficiently simple organism, or for simple aspects of a more complex organism, this mode of explanation may be sufficiently good, even though not fully accurate. As we shall see in chapter 2, this conception of "coding," as in the case of color, for instance, reifies concepts.

It is more likely that coding is field-dependent—that it is dependent upon many of the characteristics of the experiential and of the neurological fields. As these shift, the codings acquire different experiential and volitional meanings. In higher organisms this involves the developing and modification of concepts, changes in their relationships, and changes in relations between different levels and types of abstraction. In higher organisms, the method by which different "fits" are tried may not be strictly deterministic and the equilibrium that occurs may not be optimal. However, the field and its codings are stabilized by their complex fit with the experiential world. And, although the pathways to a "fit" may not be determined, the equilibrium of a complex of codings is determined by its "fit." Indeed, the resistance of a person to an intellectually better "fit" may depend upon its inconsistency with other elements—for instance, volitional—of his larger field. The "freedom" of the organism in developing concepts within the field is the source of creativity. And its existence probably can be explained by evolutionary advantage.

System Decoupling. We have already shown that physiology and thought are independent systems. Thought is not a mental version of synaptic energy flows and cannot be predicted from physiological theories. Thought is a system that requires analysis in terms of its explicit and implicit grammars and logics and its content or meaning. And it can no more be understood without an assumption of prior knowledge, that is, of meaning, than can the events or things to which thoughts refer. There is no such thing as purely formal knowledge.

The theories that account for physiological and logical or mental behavior are not parallel, nor is one fundamental and the other derived. Each offers an explanation of different aspects of behavior. Physiological theory requires an understanding of the operation of neural networks and of their relationship to other physical behaviors. The theory of reasoning requires an understanding, among other factors, of logic and inference, as well as of content or meaning. The system of logic and inference may be treated in the abstract, in which case the meanings of its symbols are treated as if they are formal only. Or it may be employed in an empirical theory, in which case its derived propositions are linked to observations of behavior by a process of identification that, however, does not imply a one-to-one parallel linkage between the symbols and observations. Neither theory accounts for insights or creative thought, for which we require a theory of preconscious behavior.

The general reasons for the existence of different levels of explanation are not hard to discover. Ashby's demonstration, for instance, of the great power—indeed of the mathematical necessity—of decentralization in systems in which partly independent or decoupled part systems perform control functions[7] is merely a special case of the more general phenomenon. The behavior manifested by subsystems may be compatible with a wide—but not unrestricted—range of component systems and design variations, as in computers, for instance. At some limit, the particularity of an individual system of explanation may affect behavior as predicted from some other framework. For instance, the theory that the atomic weights can be expressed by integers holds except in the case of extremely fine measurements. However, short of this, explanations of behavior, whether of the physical or informational variety, are naturally decoupled according to systems and system levels. The failure to recognize this is the fundamental flaw in all reductionist theories. And it explains the fallacy in the attempt to explain complex real-world events only from the standpoint of one particular theory. It is superfluous to add that some theories may be extremely sensitive to variations in component subsystems and, in some cases, so sensitive that the macrosystem explanation becomes "swamped" (extreme subsystem dominance). The opposite case (system dominance) is also possible.

Conscious and Preconscious Mind

Earlier examples that we used, for instance, Freudian slips, imply non- or preconscious mental processes. Consciousness is obviously linked to the sense of identity and apparently involves some degree of self-reflexive thought. We are aware that it involves certain portions of the cerebral cortex of the human brain and that these portions are directly associated with the higher mental activities. Moreover, we know that most thought processes are triggered by preconscious mental processes and that human inventions, including the discovery of important theories, have this characteristic also. This means that there are pre- or non-conscious search procedures and perhaps reasoning processes.

John von Neumann speculated that the language used in this process was less precise but more reliable that that employed in ordinary language.[8] Whether or not his speculation is correct, the reasons for this division in mental functions (other than the evolutionary) are fairly obvious. The extent of the search procedures required for the operations of the human brain would interfere with and overload the precise analytical capabilities to which conscious attention can be turned.

Is consciousness an essential element in purpose? That is a difficult question to answer. We know to some extent how the process of purposeful choice occurs in humans. There are both preconscious and conscious elements. Preconscious judgment makes fine discriminations that are essential to identification. Consciousness validates or otherwise utilizes this information through potentially exhaustive analyses and comparisons; and it does so in a fashion that can be publicly communicated to other minds.

Although in principle computers could be programed to carry out all the logical operations of mind even more efficiently than the conscious human brain, the creative fertility of the brain depends upon a constant interchange between preconscious and conscious processes. Is this merely a defect in current computers? Is consciousness necessary? Or would these operations at a self-reflective level produce a conscious computer? These are not problems for which I pretend to have an answer.

The Relevance of Judgment

We have not yet learned to program computers to perform recognitions that small children can perform. The problems facing human beings usually require far less in the way of reason than they do in the way of recognition and "fit." Thus the statesman must recognize similarities that govern the applicability of policies in political situations. Yet he can articulate these only partly in communicating with other people. They will understand him only if their framework of experiential knowledge is sufficiently similar. Otherwise they can only reject his advice or take it on faith. The bridge expert with wide experience in playing tens of thousands of hands implicitly recognizes differences in the texture of hands that the most precise bidding systems cannot communicate. The expert tea or wine taster can train others in his art through empirical drills, but his verbal attempts to explicate what he does are insufficient except for the most obvious differences.

Although the sense of recognition one experiences upon a correct identification is obviously not self-validating, it emphasizes the fact that the conscious belief in the identity is triggered by a preconscious act of recognition. This preconscious capacity of mind is open to a variety of experiences and to modes of being that the conscious, reasoning mind can only adumbrate. Yet the reasoning aspects of mind apparently also possess substantial control over the preconscious, imposing logic upon it, and sometimes perhaps a logic far too rigid for the world to which the human system must adapt.

The process of recognition applies to more than observables. Complex scientific and mathematical theories and musical and artistic forms have their origins in such recognitions. And much of our practical orientation to the world is dependent upon our capacity to intuit the presence of form and relationship. Intelligence tests are poor in determining the presence of this capacity, and this may provide part of the explanation of the fact that some individuals who score extremely well on these tests do not behave with intelligence or, as one distinction would have it, with wisdom.

If the preconscious mind identifies, recognizes, and invents, the conscious mind formalizes, organizes, establishes, and implements. It is the governor that steers the system through the disturbances and tribulations of its environment. This reasoning governor employs the powerful tool known as generalization—a tool that gets its power from its capability ruthlessly to ignore details, with the result that generalizations fit individual cases with imprecision, and often with great imprecision.

The conscious mind has only limited access to the information in the mental system. There are limits to its ability to gain access to information the suppression of which is not under conscious control. We know little about the processes of repression that block out certain types of recognitions. Yet few, if any, of us are unaware of little sparks of recognition that quickly get damped. Just how this gateway process operates and whether there are perhaps two independent scanning processes pushes our speculation beyond any reasonable limits. In any event, such precise knowledge is inessential to the few broad points I wish to make that are relevant to the chapters on the good and the just.

Although the conscious mind employs rather than generates intuitions, it also synthesizes knowledge and examines the consistency and "fittingness" of the realm of knowledge. These two categories of generalization and analysis (explanation) on one hand and synthesis and selection (assessment) on the other represent the distinction between theory and praxis. This distinction, which will be employed throughout this book, has great importance for all applied intellectual endeavor and particularly for understanding problems of law and ethics.

Theory and Praxis. The distinction between theory (explanation) and praxis (assessment) is not absolute, for even the well-confirmed theories and covering laws of physics depend upon substantive assumptions that may later be modified by other information. Assessment and praxis, however, do not obtrude, at least not obviously, in the cases of those theories that are able to treat their parameters as "givens" for practical purposes. Assessment and praxis come to the fore in those cases in which the interdependence between assumptions concerning the boundary conditions of a theoretical area and the determination of how to formulate theory is so strong that choices among identifications of subject matter, boundary assessments, and theoretical formulations become problematic in practice.

The Hempelian deductive covering law model gives the best account of how theoretical scientists state particular theories, of how they confirm or disconfirm them, and of how they reason from them—including sometimes the prediction of surprising results. Thus, the covering law model is not merely an ex post facto formalism, although it is not a complete account of scientific inquiry. It comes closest to practice with respect to the formal derivation of a consequence from theoretical assumptions under specified and relatively non-controversial boundary conditions. It begins to diverge somewhat more as "non-obvious" interpretations are required in the actual use of scientific tools and methods, including but not restricted to the assessment of experimental results as confirmations of prediction sentences.

In theoretical physics, new information, for example, the Michelson-Morley experiment and non-Euclidean geometries, or new observations, may lead either to a reformulation of a theory or to a replacement of one theory by another. Among other differences, this replacement may involve shifts in concepts, for example, mass; changes in axioms, for example, the constant for light; or changes in theorems, as in the geometry of space. Both Newtonian and Einsteinian theory were able to treat their concepts and parameters as "givens" for significant periods of time. The methods of praxis come to the fore during periods of transition in which alternative theories are compatible with experimental evidence. In these cases, choice is determined by consistency with other confirmed elements of science; range, economy, and "centrality" of explanation; "fittingness"; and so forth.

The social and physical sciences share the characteristics noted above. However, because of its complexity and the rich interconnectedness of its elements, especially with respect to socially or politically relevant and important factors, social science is predominantly, but not exclusively, a realm of praxis. This is particularly true of ethics within which the identifications of particular ethical systems, of rules within a system, and of applications as relevant are necessarily contextually determined to a great degree.

Later in this chapter we shall examine cases in social science in which no single theory provides enough of the variance to account for observations, predictions, or explanations. In this case, the reasoning within each relevant theoretical framework has explanatory form; but its adjustment to other frameworks in accounting for actual events is dominated by a different form of reasoning in which consistency plays an important role. Along with the identification of the relevant theories, this assessment occurs in the realm of praxis.

The identification of a theory with a relevant realm of application is crucial. Even in physics, we must be able to distinguish between electrons and planets; otherwise we could not know whether to apply general relativity theory or quantum mechanics. Yet in the social sciences the reification of words such as "state" or "international system" lead us to assume an identity that may not exist for theoretical purposes.

Use of a theory involves explanation. Decisions concerning its superiority over a competing theory involve assessment and fall in the realm of praxis. Both theory and praxis employ reasoning, but that reasoning process takes different forms in each. Theory in its formal phase closes the system of explanation at its boundaries simply. Praxis, in addition to the evaluation of the elements of theory, of boundaries, and of evidence, may involve at least partly independent chains of reasoning that are related to different theories. In the latter case, each part of the reasoning process operates within tentatively assumed parameters. However, these tentative parameters usually will differ for the different theories. There is a segmented series of adjustments in which less "fitting" theories are replaced by more "fitting" theories and in which the surviving theoretical influences are estimated in assessing the case. Thus, in their analytical aspects, explanation and assessment use different but closed forms of reasoning. Closure characterizes the formal aspects of science. Yet the real world is obdurately open. This is one reason why reason can never exhaust particularity.

"Theory" is a term that is both used and abused; and I am aware that much of what I call praxis is merely a somewhat stricter form of what some people call theory. Those elements of praxis that set constraints on how theory may be formulated but that are consistent with substantively different theories might perhaps be called metatheory. Much of the reasoning in this book is, in fact, a very loose form of praxis in which assessments are made discursively rather than rigorously. I regard this kind of "metatheory" as legitimate, and even necessary, for the treatment of the broadest forms of reasoning that deal with matters that are problematic and only loosely connected.

As the realm of praxis is explored in the succeeding chapters, the reader will observe that transfinite stability centrally involves the reinterpretation of experience as inconsistencies are revealed in the realm of knowledge by experience and its active analysis. In *Alienation and Identification,* we shall see how this manner of treating the realm of experience permits a reinterpretation of the concept of ideology. It also avoids methodological dualism, for it intimately links mental activity to the rest of existence in one experiential realm. And, in this respect, it is central to the problem of justice, for it links ethical or moral rules to the existential conditions that make them relevant while permitting a moral hierarchy of sets of rules by means of a test in principle—a concept that will be explicated in the next chapter.

Praxis and Meaning. Meaning is intimately involved in reasoning in the form of praxis. It is involved in a highly structured rather than in a vague sense. Praxis primarily relates "objects" and "processes" in a coherent fashion. Of course, the distinction between object and process is no more absolute than that between analysis and synthesis or theory and praxis. As information theory tells us, structure is merely more slowly changing process.

These distinctions are not absolute. They are related to use and they change with both the instruments and purposes of use. Newton's "absolute" system was conceived as if it were independent of instrumental techniques. Einstein's system incorporated an essential instrumental aspect in "C," the constant for light, which is a major element in the "relativity" of his system—a subject to which we shall return in chapters 3 and 4. Nonetheless, the Einsteinian equations are determinate with respect to relations among non-instrumental aspects of macrophysical "objects" within inertial systems, and they produce similar but transposed predictions for independent inertial systems. With respect to quantum theory, the relationship between instrument and system of reference is more intimate, with consequences for determinate outcomes that are well known.

In both cases theory refers primarily to the "objects" of inquiry and not to the instruments and operations of inquiry. These are taken into account only insofar as necessary. Science and philosophy of science are not concerned with operational "games" and would not have progressed to the extent they have if they had been so concerned.

Of course, instrumentation cannot be ignored. In chapter 2 we shall see that reference to the physiological human instrument of inquiry is required to deal with the question of the "objectivity" of the good. Language is also an instrument of inquiry, and the analysis of language, including the use of concepts, is essential to certain aspects of inquiry. No more than in the case of instrumentation, however, can the analysis of language become the object of inquiry, at least with respect to non-linguistic problems.

Let me repeat; the language of inquiry, even—or especially—if important to an inquiry, cannot be divorced from the substance of inquiry without serious failures in analysis. It is not good enough to assert that language "points beyond itself" and to make a comparison of uses that are abstracted from the "object- or process-like" features of the system within which they are used. Comparative analysis is important for certain purposes, and we shall return to that subject in this chapter. However, as we shall further see in chapter 3, there are no necessary universal meanings for concepts, even in the sense of family relationships. Meaning is generated within the circumstances of systemic "closeness" at the "object-level" of inquiry. Attempts to discuss or to analyze comparatively meanings that are divorced from intra-systemic "object-level" analysis will soon rise to a level of abstraction that is sterile. It is therefore no accident that the inquiries of so many adherents of the ordinary language school of philosophers are sterile and boring. "Language games" are "games" in the pejorative sense of the term as it is used by these philosophers. Despite their recognition of the lack of isomorphism in the "use" of language, language is hypostasized by them. The analysis of language is essential to certain stages in inquiry—particularly inquiries concerning human behavior—but the philosophy of ordinary language analysis, at least as most of its exponents use it, is the converse error of Wittgenstein's earlier position—an error that he, if not many of his followers, likely did not make.

INFORMATION AND BEHAVIOR

The fact that the system we are talking about contains multiple feedback loops, including informational items, is essential to understanding the characteristics of certain types of facts about this type of system. Ratiocination about its behavior is a fact of this type of system. This type of fact is usually called subjective, but that term is troublesome. A belief is subjective in the sense that it is about something else, presumably something external to it, although there are also beliefs about beliefs. Whether or not one holds a particular belief is a factual matter and presumably is subject to objective test.

The Problem of Information Control

Let us see if we can place this process within perspective. Locke's tabula rasa is rejected. It never could acquire any information. When we see a stationary table, for instance, the brain has imposed an order on the incoming sense data, for the pupil of the eye is in continual motion, unlike the stationary lens of the camera. The brain interprets the incoming "signal" and human knowledge is dependent upon its ability to do so, as the earlier example of the computer also makes clear.

Information is possible only for systems that start with knowledge, although negative feedback may aid them in correcting and improving upon the knowledge they start with. Thus a system starts with knowledge and it learns with experience. Much of its "learning" may be mistaken. For instance, much Freudian theory—including portions of it that are not dependent upon hydraulic metaphor or other dubious aspects of Freudian theory—relates to incorrect identifications made in infancy or early childhood. This system of identifications apparently affects later perception and understanding in ways that are not entirely logical.

Even, however, were this not true, the system requires controls for sorting information flowing in from the environment. Distinctions must be made between the important and the unimportant, between those items that must be reacted to immediately and those to which further study may be given.

It is an evolutionary advantage to reject exploration of pathways that are statistically dangerous. The mother fox slaps those of her cubs that proceed in dangerous ways. Optimal design choices increase some risks and minimize others. Air-raid systems that emphasize protection against false alarms pay a price in terms of detecting actual raids and vice versa.

The Problem of Dysfunction

What is optimal in one environment may not be optimal in another; and if an environment is poor enough, the system may be driven to so-called secondary gains. Thus, for instance, a nation that has been under attack for a hundred years may neglect information about internal decay as a drain upon, and indeed as a threat to, its defensive capability. Yet the structures designed to implement this important function may continue after the external threat has diminished, thus resulting in a suboptimal input of information into the system. A child confronted by a hostile mother, and unable to win her love, may become difficult, seizing upon punitive attention as a substitute for loving attention and thereby becoming attached to this neurotic secondary gain and the information distortion upon which it depends.

Dysfunction and Self-evaluation

The previous conclusion deserves careful examination, for it will be central to our examination of the good in the next chapter. Information is essential to the operation of the type of system we are talking about. The information it has constitutes a factual element of its existence. There are techniques for learning about the information that is possessed by a system, however faulty they may be, just as there are techniques for learning about other factual aspects of the system. However, the beliefs a system has are partly the consequence of the situation it finds itself in and of its history up to that point. They may be the product of less than optimal information-regulation characteristics and less than optimal environments. Its behavior, including its beliefs, are information-dependent; and independent evidence may establish that its information acquisitions are defective in certain respects.

The human physiology behaves differently under conditions of vitamin deficiency than it does under conditions of vitamin sufficiency. It behaves differently in warm climates and in cold climates. We can establish that under some conditions its information-adjusting mechanisms operate inefficiently. Therefore, just as we can compare how the physiological behavior of a system under conditions of vitamin sufficiency would differ from that under conditions of vitamin deficiency, in principle at least we can compare how behavior will differ under conditions of information optimality and under conditions of information deficiency.

The argument for the objectivity of the good will be made in chapter 2 and for the just in chapter 3. It is important to understand how the current discussion establishes the foundation for those discussions. We are claiming that the human system is capable of misperceiving the environment and its own motivations for reasons and in ways that are subject to objective analysis. Information-handling mechanisms can continue to operate under circumstances in which they have become dysfunctional; and secondary or substitute gains may be sought by the system.

Because of the complicated nature of this system, we should be cautious about statements we make concerning it. But, in principle at least, objective determination is possible. In this sense, whether our interpretation of a system's goals warrants high or low confidence, in principle it is not determined only by the beliefs of the observed person about himself; it treats his beliefs as one factual element in a complex of system elements in a complex environment.

For instance, in our earlier example of a community subject to external attack which thereafter represses information concerning internal disturbances as a threat to its defensive capability, the functionaries who carry out this censorious task may be motivated to do so because their life styles and promotional prospects depend upon this. Their effectiveness in carrying out such tasks may inhibit other citizens from conveying information about domestic shortcomings. Thus, the ongoing system loses in adaptability in a way that becomes dysfunctional if later the external threat diminishes.

This process may be as difficult to correct as many neurotic defense mechanisms. Yet, those who establish such a process likely do not intend this consequence. Even if a particular system becomes "locked in," we can recognize this as a case of system dysfunction. Its adaptive mechanisms are not adequate for the problems with which the environment confronts it.

That this is a reasonable conclusion can be subjected to a hypothetical but interesting test. Suppose that the decision makers of the indicated system at the time of the first external attack are confronted with two different mechanisms for mobilizing defensive energies against that attack. By access to a new scientific breakthrough, they can project onto a screen a rapid history of circumstances after adoption of each of the mechanisms. Each is equally effective for mobilizing their defensive capabilities; but one, and not the other, proves readily adaptable to the new tasks faced by the system after the external threat diminishes. Does anyone doubt that the latter system would be preferred? If one agrees with this, then essentially what one is saying is that with sufficient information and enough system capacity, one would make choices that would not result in the fate of the described system.

In short, this process is objective in the following sense. We attribute the behavior to an independently determined "deprivation." We show that in optimal circumstances the preferences previously associated with the deprivation disappear and that the "optimal" circumstances are optimal in the sense that they would be chosen in preference to the "deprived" circumstances. Thus, although the statement deserves only low confidence, it points to a universality of behavior under adequate test conditions. To the extent that these observations are about good ends and good rules or rules of justice, they indicate the objectivity of the latter. Other problems connected with objectivity will be discussed in chapter 2.

Design Problems of Self-evaluating Systems. The complex character of this process renders the human system subject to certain design difficulties that have already been adumbrated. The (limited) capacity of a system of this type to attend to tasks requires it to withhold responses and to delay "gratification." Precisely because of the wide range of choice patterns available to this type of system and the wide variety of objectives among which choices may be made, and the uncertainties involved in forecasting, the possibility of indecision and anxiety is increased. Because the coding process employed by this system entails ambiguities that are holdovers from early experience and the utilization of identifications that cannot be fully articulated within the framework of conscious thought, anxiety may also be produced.

The ability of the transfinitely stable governor of this kind of system to program its behavior depends to some extent upon self-reflexive thought. At this level, the sense of identity of the system is bound up with the verbal grammars and the conscious logics that it can articulate. These are inadequate for the range of discriminations open to it. Moreover, the generalizations it employs usually do not specify the boundary conditions under which they are appropriate; and they therefore occur within thought as unqualified absolutes. Many of our common language reifications (chapter 2 will discuss these) such as, for instance, "This leaf is green," result from this process. As the system identifies itself with a set of "absolutes" that is not applicable in a variety of situations it may meet, the sense of identity, which is required for coherent behavior, may be "defended" by the censorship of information or by self-transformation. This brief account of these phenomena reinforces our earlier discussion of the mechanisms of dysfunctional regulation as they affect our discussion of the objective nature of statements about the character of information-utilizing, transfinitely stable systems. The concept of dysfunction is objectively applicable because we can specify with reasonable clarity what we mean by it.

Implications of the Self-evaluation Problem.   Let us now clarify what we are not stating. We are not stating that with sufficient information and sufficient environmental opportunity all systems would seek the same resting states. We do not have enough information to assert that. (Chapters 2 and 3 discuss weak value orderings.) We are not stating that in the same circumstances and with the same information all individuals would make the same decisions; for, apart from situational, biological, and personality differences, we do not know to what extent choice is dependent upon partly random processes that cease as soon as a reasonable accommodation occurs. However, the life histories of some individuals or societies may "lock" them into patterns of activity that are recognizably different from those they would have chosen under fuller conditions of information or environmental opportunity.[9] Note how the process upon which these assertions depend differs from that of ordinary ultrastability. The complexity of the process makes for enormous permutational possibilities among values. These permit widely different sequential operations. Thus systems of this type could display the same behavior in different environments and different behaviors in the same environments. No simple identification of circumstance, internal state, and behavior is likely. Moreover, these systems can work complexly upon their environment to change it. Thus, as their knowledge of the range of comparative frameworks of choice, for example, democratic versus authoritarian, as well as the range of choices within particular types of frameworks, increases, changes may be expected in their pattern of choices.

COMPARATIVE METHOD

It is well known that our knowledge both of scientific "truths"—for example, Newtonian versus Einsteinian mechanics—and of the methodology of science increases with our scientific experience. In the same way, our knowledge of our nature, of our society, and of our human and social possibilities increases with our comparative knowledge about these. Just as most formulations of the mind/body problem misunderstand the character of human knowledge by trying to derive mental from physical behavior, other reductionist theories of knowledge are likely to be wrong (although this is not necessarily true in every particular case). Physics may set constraints within which biology operates, but important aspects of biology are not derivable from theories of mechanics or vice versa.

The world of physics, however, possesses one undeniable advantage over most other scientific arenas. Studies concerning its variables can be conducted, at least tentatively, as if there were no "contamination" from other sources. In the complex world of human behavior this is not true. Varieties of theoretical schema must be applied to human behavior, and this cannot be done in any simply deductive form. Complexity, ultrastability, and the contextual meaning of systems variables contribute to this result. (Even the multibody problem in physics requires an iterative procedure employing the two-body formula that produces an answer only for a particular case.) Explanation, therefore, either is only partial or the elements of explanation from different theoretical realms are linked together in particular explanations that do not permit singular deductive chains and that depend instead on consistencies between theoretical perspectives, partial relatednesses, judgment, and looser modes of analysis. The relevant realm is that of praxis. Thus, there is a partial quality about explanations of real historical events that is supplemented even by leaps of intuition.

Examples of cases where comparative knowledge is essential to understanding or explaining behavior are readily available. For instance, consider an old-style Chinese merchant who charges more per item to the customer who wishes to buy his entire supply because he must be compensated for his loss of face when other customers find his store unable to provide service. He responds differently from the merchant in a modern American community because of differences in the two systems. The south Italian villager discussed by Edward

Banfield[10] is amoral in his behavior with non-family members whereas the English villager generally observes moral standards. Westerners tend to help others during periods of natural catastrophe but older-style Japanese did not. Their behavior was not understandable unless one was familiar with the burden of obligation this would have placed upon a person who was helped and the strain this would have produced within the Japanese society.

Still other examples of the ways in which comparative knowledge assists us in understanding behavior are provided by studies of cultural differences within the same society. For instance, early sociological studies showed great differences between the behaviors of racial groups. Later investigators studied the effects of income level upon behavior and discovered that many of the differences attributed to race by the earlier studies disappeared when a more complex system of classification was employed.

These examples indicate the extent to which our generalizations about behavior are based upon observations limited either to particular groups or to particular classification systems. It is the extension of the frame of reference that permits us to place these behaviors within the framework of the constraints that produce them, to compare them systematically, and to derive conclusions from these comparisons. Such comparisons, in addition to impressing us with the range of human variability in behavior, also permit us to determine the factors that produce the differences and, in this sense, to understand human or social behavior far better. The differences no longer appear as reified absolutes.

Changed environmental or changed social conditions are likely to produce corresponding changes in behavior. All elements, including behavior, function together within a system. But the system cannot properly be understood only in its own terms. Only in the comparisons of systems with each other do we gain a fuller understanding of the functions being filled by different combinations of social and cultural practices. It is also within this framework that we are able to determine that some of the practices represent secondary-type gains in the same way as do certain types of individual behavior.

Examples of societal secondary gains include, for instance, putting female children out to die of exposure or eating aged parents. Anthropological studies have shown that in societies in which aged parents were eaten, the parents tended to accept these practices as good and even to insist upon them, just as in India the widow wife of a prince used to insist upon suttee (her fiery immolation on the bier of her husband). In the example of the infant children and the eating of the aged parents our inference that these societal values represent secondary gains is based upon evidence that such practices occur only under conditions of great poverty.

Most Westerners would assume that the older Japanese practice of refusing to aid the victim of a catastrophe also represented a secondary-type gain. However, this is far more difficult to demonstrate, for a conclusion with respect to this practice is not related to an environmental fact in the same simple way as in the earlier examples. Moreover, it may be the internal relationships of the elements of the system rather than an environmental condition that is essential to analysis.

The relationship between the human organism and the social and cultural environment is extremely complex. There is no reason to believe that a univocal and transitive order of values in macrosocial systems is possible even in principle, let alone in practice. Moreover, because the elements of a social system bear some relationship to each other—as, in the Japanese case, where the refusal to aid the victim of catastrophe was related to the extensive role of "obligation" in the Japanese system—even in those cases in which our judgment affirms that some social systems on the whole are better than others, particular practices in them that cannot be grafted onto foreign systems, may be more "in tune" with human nature than the corresponding practices of "better" systems.

It is obvious that to the extent such evaluations are

possible, they require an extensive knowledge of how the elements of social and cultural systems fit together and of how they respond to environmental conditions. Moreover, we must never forget that human beings are information-using systems and that their beliefs concerning these relationships are essential elements of the systems to be studied.

We may thrill to, and understand, the great Greek plays and biblical accounts, but our understanding of society and of human nature in general, as well as of its manifestations under particular conditions, is always subject not merely to advances in techniques within particular disciplines but also to increases in our knowledge of human possibility as these are revealed by choices under novel conditions. Neither man nor society is a book to be read at one sitting. We may not yet understand the depth to which either may plunge or the heights to which either may rise.

SOME IMPORTANT CONCLUSIONS

Because this chapter is relevant to those that follow, I wish to emphasize several of its implications that will play a major role in my analysis. The prior discussion, for instance, deals with comparisons of social or political systems. The underlying hypothesis is that differences in the structure and functioning of systems can be related to differences in their environments and histories. Note, however, that one consequence of the absence of covering laws for different types of systems of the same genus in the social sciences is that the terms or definitions that are employed have major differences in implications in different types of systems. As Lewis Morgan discovered, for instance, the biological and the social "mother" are not identical; and the meaning of the social "mother" may differ from one social system to another.

This makes for an important problem in the social sciences that does not occur, at least to the same extent, in the physical sciences. The differences in the concept of mass in

Newtonian and Einsteinian physics, for instance, are differences in theoretical terms; therefore, the relevance or "truth" of the respective concepts—at least with respect to physical mechanics—is determined by tests of the respective theories within the framework of physical praxis common to both theories in important observational areas. Einstein's theory has been validated and its covering laws have broad application. However, because of the absence of covering laws in the social sciences, there may be as many correct concepts of "state" or "mother" as types of systems under study. Thus, theory sketches apply only to distinct types of social systems. This conclusion, as we will show later, has major importance for the study of ethical systems.

Also, for reasons given earlier, systems of explanation are necessarily decoupled. This causes particular problems in the social sciences. Unlike the case in physics, where usually only a single central system of explanation applies to a property, different systems of explanation often apply to the same property in the more complex world of social science.

If, for instance, one had wanted to predict (or later to explain) how President John F. Kennedy would have behaved during the Cuban missile crisis, no single framework or explanation is likely to have been central. A strategist might have argued that he would likely act as he did if the United States had conventional and nuclear superiority. A student of international relations might have argued that he would act strongly if he were afraid that a failure to do so would produce some other crisis elsewhere—Berlin, for instance. A student of domestic politics might have argued that he would act strongly if he wished to win the election. But another student of domestic politics might have argued that he would be reluctant to admit his mistake before the election. And a student of psychology might have argued that he would back down to test the principle of unilateral concessions. (I have indicated rather than fully stated the major and minor premises of each model.)

The point is that no single central logic applies to the

relevant descriptors of his predicted behavior. Therefore, it is not possible to apply only one of them by estimating initial conditions and to assume that it provides an adequate explanation or prediction. The realm is that of praxis; and methods appropriate to that realm must be used in assessing a prediction or explanation. This has important implications for the study of ethics.

Similar problems arise in a different fashion at the macrolevel. Although usually only one central logic will apply at the macrolevel to the relevant property, its operation may be swamped by factors external to its operation. For instance, it would not be a defect of a political theory if its predictions concerning the operations of a political system were falsified by a natural catastrophe. With respect to behaviors relevant to the macrolevel, if we know that different systems of reference are relevant to a prediction in the circumstances, and that we cannot merely estimate parameters, we must use a method of analysis appropriate to the realm of praxis. The following two chapters will show that this is also the case with respect to ethical analysis, which, only in the simplest, most restricted, and least important cases, can be treated from a single framework of reference.

Implications for Ethics

The prior distinctions reinforce our conclusions based on systems analysis and Quine's essay that ethics primarily is an area of practice rather than of theory. Even with respect to macrosystems, the relationship of appropriate moral codes to other system characteristics will be dependent upon choices from among a variety of theory sketches (rather than actual theories) and upon the appropriate characterization of system elements. In the absence of covering laws prescribing measures for concepts that are independent of their use in particular systems, some elements of judgment will necessarily guide use. When we come to the microlevel, where the individual must estimate his identification with a system and the potential impact of his rule violation upon the system, the role of judgment will become much greater. As a consequence, the belief that a single set of moral rules is applicable to all systems or to all actions within a single system assumes a world quite different from the actual world. The mistakes we shall find in Toulmin and Rawls will not surprise us. And the reasons for the iterative rule proposed in chapter 2 will be clear.

The foregoing remarks are not intended to imply that judgment is absent from the physical sciences. The verbal predictions of theories, for instance, are not connected with perceived events in a one-to-one fashion. Judgmental links are required.[11] On occasion, no clear decision may be possible between alternative theories. And, of course, different theories are applied to different subject matters. Nonetheless, in the physical sciences, key terms usually are theoretically defined. There usually are independent means of measurement and these usually permit covering laws to be applied to different types of systems. Moreover, if the initial conditions are specified, there usually is a salient central logic for particular descriptors or events. These are major differences from the realm of ethics, which requires (1) different sets of rule behavior for different social systems; (2) considerable judgment in the choice of rules relevant to particular cases within systems; and (3) greater richness in articulation and content than occurs in most current philosophical discourse.

The foregoing remarks concerning the differences between science and ethics apply only to the extent to which specific theories can be employed deductively. The entire realm of science is a realm of praxis, for it is the consistency of explanations and observations within the field that determines, to the extent the structure of the field permits, the centrality of particular theories and/or classes of observations. Our task now is to apply these concepts to the field of ethics.

Chapter 2

The Good

PROLEGOMENA

Before we turn explicitly to the concept of the good that emerges from a systems approach, let us examine several alternative ways of approaching this problem. Major philosophical questions arise in the examination of problems of values. Are values factually determinable matters or are they merely statements about preferences? Most contemporary students of the matter would argue that values and facts are disparate in character. The argument that a conclusion containing the word "ought" cannot be derived from a descriptive premise expresses this view. This argument is correct in a narrow sense, but it begs the issue in the form in which it is offered. As it is the purpose of this chapter to put this argument to rest, I shall not anticipate the conclusions to be drawn.

There is an opposing position. Some writers argue that values are an inextricable aspect of the factual world and so deeply embedded in language that they cannot be eliminated. According to this view, the positivist position that treats values as preferences, as distinguished from facts, fundamentally distorts linguistic usage.

It is undoubtedly true that the ordinary language employs words carrying moral overtones. "Corruption," "decay," "cowardice," "pride," "arrogance," and so forth do carry moral meaning. A language that failed to do so would be awkward, difficult to use, and unresponsive to natural understanding.

Nonetheless, superficially at least, it might appear that we could construct a stipulated language that kept so-called factual and moral elements separate. For instance, corruption could be defined as loss of texture, change in odor, chemical dissolution, merging with the environment, or, in social terms, as acting contrary to law for private reasons.

Those opponents of a positivist approach to ethics who point to the ordinary language as evidence against its position are correct in doing so. However, the worth of that evidence depends upon the framework within which it functions. Short of a framework that establishes a factual basis for "ought" statements, indirect evidence of this kind has only limited probative value. Thus, the resolution of this question also must await the arguments of this chapter.

TOULMIN'S ANALYSIS OF THE CONTENDING POSITIONS

Historically there have been three major approaches to value questions: the objective, the subjective, and the imperative. The clearest analysis of the three traditional approaches is provided in Stephen Toulmin's *Reason in Ethics.*[1] For this reason we will follow his examination of them and then show the cul-de-sac into which his own conclusion leads him. We will then show what he overlooked and how this helps us to resolve the problems of the objective character of the good and of the character of ethical systems.

The Objective Approach

Types of Properties. In opposing the objective approach, Toulmin argues that when one talks of goodness or rightness in any properly ethical sense, he is not talking about any indirectly perceived property of an object. More than this, he argues, it distracts us from any properly ethical inquiry. According to Toulmin, G. E. Moore, for instance, improperly treats goodness as a directly perceived, although non-natural, property.[2]

Toulmin argues that this analogy is false. Properties such as color, he says, are directly perceived by the senses and are unanalyzable, by which he means that they cannot be verbally defined in terms of either simpler qualities or of any set of operations without mentioning the property itself. Toulmin calls such properties simple qualities. Another class of properties consists of those things that are perceived directly but that can be identified only after certain procedures. Thus, for instance, a polygon can be perceived at sight, but its incorporation into the class of polygons containing the same number of sides can be determined only after counting. Toulmin's third set of properties includes what he calls scientific qualities. Thus, if one says that the sun looks orange but is really yellow, one is talking about a remark made within the context of a scientific theory. By this Toulmin means that the sun radiates "such-and-such types of electromagnetic waves."

An Ambiguity. Foreshadowing a later discussion, let us note, because of its great relevance at this point, an ambiguity in Toulmin's argument. In his "scientific" sense, we do not really mean that the sun is yellow. We mean that it radiates the number of angstrom waves associated with the color yellow on earth. The actual color would be directly perceived. The regularity between physical wave structure and perception of specific colors is not encompassed in, or explained by, electromagnetic theory in physics, although the special branch of optics, in combination with physiological analysis, may cast significant light on it. If, on the other hand, we say that a dress is yellow but looks green, we may mean that if it were seen under ordinary conditions of lighting and without the intervention of blue glasses, it would be seen as yellow. In all these cases, then, the attribution of a property such as color implies a (potential or actual) perceiving organism as well as a perceivable object or event. The qualitative natural property, as such, lacks meaning apart from the possibility of such a receptor.

Scientific properties such as angstrom waves cannot be given meaning apart from the actual or potential existence both of a scientific apparatus and of a perceiving organism that can interpret the counters of the apparatus. The sentences of the scientific theory can be composed of stipulative language terms. However, as Quine has shown, analytic stipulation cannot be complete in principle. And, in practice, these sentences could not be understood without a natural knowledge of the scientific subject matter and of the laboratory equipment and circumstances as well as of the connection between protocol sentences and experimental results. Thus when Toulmin claims no deep epistemological significance for his classification, and asserts the irrelevance of epistemological sophistication, he is wrong. Nevertheless, let us go on with his argument.

Complex Properties.   Toulmin argues that there are such things as complex qualities that require procedures for determining their existence. For instance, we can tell whether something is square only after measuring it with a ruler. Or we can tell that the sun is sodium-orange only because we have a color card to compare it with.

Doubtful Cases.   Toulmin then distinguishes cases where it is doubtful whether or not what we are talking about is really a property of the object. He includes within this category judgments of taste, that is, of what is sweet and what is sour, and so forth. He says that this begins to shape concepts such as pleasantness, but that the distinctions between subjective properties such as pleasantness and objective properties such as redness are sufficiently great not to worry us.

Another Ambiguity.   Again, I must call the reader's attention to the fact that the distinction between redness and sweetness is related to the physiological system under discussion. One who is red/green color-blind will not perceive any distinctions between these two colors, although our laboratory equipment will register a difference in their angstrom wave emanations. There is a greater variability with respect to physiological taste; and this may depend in part upon the history or conditioning of the particular organism and in part upon variations in its actual physiological functioning. Wine tasters develop their skills as a consequence of training; but what they distinguish is really there for a trained palate. These distinctions may not exist, except potentially, for untrained or jaded palates, or not at all, for damaged palates. Nonetheless, let us not yet pursue the argument with Professor Toulmin. Let him continue to speak for himself.

How to Determine Simple Properties.   Toulmin then goes on to consider goodness as a possible simple quality. How, he asks, do we teach people correctly to use concepts concerning simple qualities? Suppose, he says, we are trying to teach a foreigner to do something and suggest that he uses a specifically named liquid. He does not understand the name, so we tell him to use the red liquid. If he does not understand the word red, we might point out a red rose or a red book or so forth. If he is still at a loss, we go through the same process again. If he fails to learn, we conclude that there is something wrong with him, and with reason, Toulmin says, for the normal means of communication will have broken down.

Suppose someone comes along and says that the liquid is

green. This Toulmin argues is not how we use language. If this is the only occasion on which we notice anything odd in his use of color words, we may conclude that it was a slip of the tongue. But if he calls everything that is red green, and never calls anything green except those things we call red, we will conclude that he is simply using a different language in which green means red and red means green; and we can understand him by making the appropriate translations. Simple qualities, Toulmin argues, are taught.

How to Determine Complex Properties. Complex qualities, Toulmin says, may at first appear considerably more elaborate, but all that is involved is one additional step. If one argues over the number of sides of a polygon, all one has to do is to count them. The only disagreements that can arise remain linguistic. Thus, with respect to directly perceived properties, the possible sources of disagreement can be attributed to the following exhaustive list: deception, organic defect, incorrect application of a routine, or linguistic differences in language, dialect, borderline usage, or verbal definition.

Is Goodness a Directly Perceived Property? Toulmin then goes on to argue that goodness is not a directly perceived property. Is the sentence "Meekness is good" similar to "Sugar is white?" Will the instances of meekness pointed out by someone convince one that meekness is good? If one doubts that meekness is good, the supporter of this position may argue that meekness is good in the same way that paying one's debts is good. But if one doubts the latter, he will then retreat to something so vague as fundamental moral intuitions, as G. E. Moore did, Toulmin says. Or he may argue that meekness makes for smoother personal relations than assertiveness or truculence. This, he might argue, is one of the criteria of goodness.

However, Toulmin says, there is no standard way for applying the criteria of goodness in the way that one can apply the criterion of numbers in determining the number of sides of a polyhedron. Thus, as with Moore, he will retreat to the argument that the good is unanalyzable and therefore a simple quality. However, if it is simple, the arbitrariness of an ostensive definition is puzzling. If it is complex, the absence of a definite routine for confirming its presence is a difficulty.

Toulmin argues that, apart from all linguistic matters, people's moral judgments might always agree if all the facts were known to them. This was the position taken by Hume. Yet, Toulmin says, this accentuates the differences between goodness and the qualities we have been discussing because no one thinks it necessary to make any such assumption when accounting for general agreement about ordinary simple qualities. And it is this crucial difference between values and ordinary properties on which Toulmin's argument rests.

The major difficulties of the objective position, Toulmin says, arise when ethical disagreements occur. What happens if someone says that meekness is bad? Does one argue that he is wrong or that we may be mistaken although we like meekness or that it depends upon circumstances or that he is notoriously insensitive over matters of ethics? Whichever choice one makes, Toulmin says, we will not argue that he does not understand plain English. Yet, if goodness were a property, this would be required.

It does not help to call goodness a non-natural property unless one has some grounds for the assertion, Toulmin says. Moreover, if we consider the context in which ethical concepts are used, treating them as properties (natural or non-natural) leads to paradoxical results. Suppose, Toulmin says, one discusses with a supporter of the objective doctrine a person known for his high moral kindness who always gives a reason for his good deeds such as taking care of the needs of others or the importance of fair dealing. Suppose he says that the only reason he does these deeds is because of his reasons and not because of any properties they possess. To be consistent, the exponent of the objective doctrine would have to argue that he may know what things are good and what it is to be good, but that he cannot know what goodness is.

Toulmin argues that this is absurd. A champion golfer may not possess the ability to explain how he makes good shots, but he surely knows how to do it. Yet, if goodness were a property, the moral man earlier mentioned would be missing knowledge of the one thing that really mattered, reflective knowledge of its goodness. "Rightness" is not a property, according to Toulmin, because something is right when there is a right reason for choosing it. When one asks whether an action is good, what he wants to know is whether there is a reason for choosing that course of action over another. "All that two people need (and all that they have) to contradict one another about in the case of ethical predicates are the *reasons* for doing this rather than that or the other."[3]

According to Toulmin the objective approach in effect says that reasons are not enough. Ethical predicates must correspond to ethical properties and knowledge of the good implies knowledge of good properties. Therefore, according to Toulmin, the objective doctrine is positively unhelpful, for it diverts our attention from ethical reasoning to purely imaginary properties of acts. We will postpone our discussion of the flaw in Toulmin's position until we have examined it in its entirety.

The Subjective Doctrine

Toulmin goes on to state that the subjective doctrine, which says that ethical attitudes depend upon feelings, also has a fatal weakness: that an approach based on attitudes "or whatever concept a new theory relies on in place of 'feelings' " cannot give a good account of reasons for ethical judgments or provide a standard for criticizing ethical reasoning. Indeed, Toulmin says, supporters of the subjective doctrine treat the difference between good and bad ethical reasoning as a matter of personal preference.

The Problem Facing Subjectivists. There is a problem, Toulmin says, with respect to subjective perspectives in defining a neutral standpoint. For instance, if someone asks whether a drink is refreshing, what is he asking? If the question refers to his own taste patterns, why should he ask anyone else? Yet, if the question refers to the reactions of other people, there is nothing neutral about it, according to Toulmin. Each may be affected differently by the drink. There is no contradiction if one says it is refreshing and the other says that it is not refreshing.

A Further Ambiguity. Yet, we must repeat what we stated with reference to Toulmin's examination of properties. It is not a contradiction for a color-blind person to say that something is green when somebody else says that it is red, provided that one keeps in mind the framework of reference. An object that gives off the number of angstrom waves associated by people with normal optic structures with the color red is seen as red under normal lighting conditions. But it may be seen as green by a person subject to red/green color blindness.

In the ordinary use of words we say that the object "is" red but that it "appears" green in the former case. However, this ordinary usage seems to imply some entirely independent quality in the external object from which the observation deviates. Let us distinguish this case from that of a piece of flying paper that looks like a dove. Although we cannot speak of a dove independently of contextual conditions and the observing system—a dove could not be perceived within the sun or by a creature with a perceptual span of a hundred years—the tests to which we could subject the perceived object to discover whether it is a dove or a piece of paper are largely, even if not entirely, independent of the variations in our testing procedures. The paper will lack a nervous system, wings, and so forth. Although it is true that color is invariant with angstrom waves, the confirmation of this invariance depends on the natural perception of color under stipulated contextual conditions and could not be made if these varied outside of control.

Whereas, in the case of the flying paper, closer observation of its finer features will show that it does not possess biological features and that it therefore cannot be a dove, observation of color difference is restricted entirely to that quality. The differences between the assertion of "is" and "appears" depend upon a stipulation of "in light radiated from a sun like Sol I under specified conditions of radiation and of observation" as a condition for "is." The former type of statement—"This is red"—is elliptical for the latter type of statement. A stipulated difference between "is" and "appears" that depends on a normal medium of observation is useful in the actual circumstances of human life, for under most conditions of lighting and observation there will not be much variance in the observed color. Whereas the paper may appear to be a dove at a distance, it is not visual observation of external appearances alone that determines that it is not. Our "natural" definition of a dove includes its having biological features. Our natural definition of color is not associated with angstrom waves numbers although it is a fact that, given our present knowledge of electromagnetic theory, optics, and normal human physiology, a relationship exists.

Given these latter facts, we may even use angstrom numbers to define colors "scientifically" according to a standard not dependent on human variations or lighting conditions. These latter "colors," however, are no longer natural colors; and this fact affects the meaning of observational reports. The association of the name of a color with an angstrom wave scale does not exhaust the meaning of the report, as we shall soon make clear. Toulmin misses this point because he implicitly assumes "earth-normal" physiology and thereby defines color blindness as a defect. Suppose, however, the existence of a race that refers to colors differently from us but with a range of colors as great as that possessed by normal humans. Toulmin would say that they merely use words differently. Suppose, however, that neurobiologists are able to perform operations that will make either humans or the other race give the reports of the opposite group. It will now be clear that the attribution of color is intimately and crucially linked to the character of the observing system and that the difference in reporting color is not merely a matter of linguistic usage but of biological structure. Indeed, someone on whom the operation is performed may believe that his hospital room has been repainted.

So far, we have proceeded as if intrasystem physiological changes merely transform the perception of one color into perception of another. In principle, however, the range of the perceiving instrument might extend into the ultraviolet or infrared spectrum. Its discriminations might be either finer or cruder than ours. They might overlap with ours in some more complex way, although perhaps correlated with angstrom wave emanations in such a way that we would have a second-order reference for "communicated" observations. Or its observations might be so different that they are incommunicable to us. (See appendix 1 for a discussion of communicability.) But all such observations, including the incommunicable, are objective if the entire "experimental" situation is specified.

It is clear that practically we do not require such a sophisticated account if we deal only with colors. However, because Toulmin tends to reify "objective quality" and "linguistic usage," this discussion will be essential to our discussion of the good.

Toulmin's Argument against Subjectivism Resumed. Suppose, Toulmin says, one asks two people which is the right course to follow and they offer incompatible answers. I cannot, he says, follow the advice of both, for they are exclusive. Yet, if the concept of rightness were subjective, both answers might be right at once. Thus, two ethical statements could contradict each other; and, especially to a man who has to choose, this appears ridiculous. Moreover, if one fully accepted the subjective position, there would be no point to taking the opinion of other people into account, for one's feelings are the only ultimate criterion.

Strong Points of the Subjective Doctrine. Toulmin says that the subjective doctrine has strong points, for it connects notions of value with satisfaction and appears to explain the fact that there is no logical necessity for two fully informed people to agree in their ethical evaluations. Yet the arbitrary character of subjective differences on ethical standards is pushed too far, according to Toulmin, in the subjective position. Although it is nonsense to believe that everyone will have identical tastes with respect to foods, delicacies, reading matter, and so forth, it may be false, but not nonsensical, to hope that someday people may agree on ethical standards.

As Toulmin points out, C. L. Stevenson in *Ethics and Language*[4] attempted to restore the subjective doctrine by distinguishing between attitudes and beliefs. Beliefs concern such things as questions about the nature of light-transmission or the voyages of Christopher Columbus. Attitudes involve opposition of purposes, aspirations, wants, and so on. Our judgments, according to Stevenson, have two components: one referring to matters of fact which can be verified and the other aimed at persuading our hearers to behave in some way or other. If there is a gap or disagreement in the latter, it can be closed by compromise.

As Toulmin properly states, what we need to know is which of the arguments are worthy of acceptance and which reasons are good reasons. If persuasion occurs purely as a matter of rhetoric or of compulsion, this hardly is a matter of ethics. It is a weakness of the subjective doctrine that, as in the case of Stevenson, it declares the linkage between ethical conclusions and factual reasons to be "devoid of interest."[5] When one argues that it is bad to kill Indians, one is not merely asserting a psychological matter, Toulmin says. One is stating that the argument for doing so is invalid and the reasons for doing so are bad. If ethics is a valid enterprise at all, then it necessarily involves reasons. People who claim to act ethically offer reasoned justifications for their behavior. Although their motivations and physiological dispositions may coincide with the action toward which reasons lead them, they do not claim that the reasons are validated by their feelings. Whenever men are faced by conflicting courses of action, they choose from among different sets of reasons for acting in different ways.

Toulmin's distinction between good and bad reasons is not entirely wrong. It is obviously irrelevant to keep a promise because the sky is blue. Even a subjectivist would agree that if a reason is given, it should be relevant. However, what does it mean to say, as he does, that killing Indians is wrong, and that the reasons for doing so are bad? If one believes that the only good Indian is a dead Indian, does Toulmin's conclusion follow? And if, further, his society wants the Indians' lands and believes that only the working of property conveys title, is this reason bad? And if this analysis increases the distress of Indians, perhaps it decreases that of settlers. However, if Toulmin agrees that these reasons are good within that system of reasons, then where does that leave Toulmin? It is this problem, as we shall see later, that invests his false analogy between choices from among geometries and from among ethical systems.

The Imperative Approach

The third approach discussed by Toulmin is the imperative approach. It has much in common with the modified subjective theory discussed by him. It also sidesteps the question as to what constitutes a good reason for an ethical judgment. The philosopher of the imperative approach, according to Toulmin, has too narrow a view of the uses of reasoning and assumes too readily that mathematics or logic or scientific verification is the only means of providing good reasons for any statement. Because these are not available to him, he dismisses all evaluative inferences or arguments from facts to values or duties as rationalization or rhetoric and regards the central problems of ethics as essentially nonsense. Yet his arguments run counter to common sense.

The imperative doctrine is designed to avoid the mistakes of the subjective and objective doctrines. According to the imperative doctrine, ethical concepts correspond to processes neither in the object nor in the mind of the speaker. Therefore the supporter of the imperative doctrine regards sentences stating ethical values as linguistically misleading. Ethical statements, according to this view, are really disguised commands or ejaculations. They express attitudes.

This position, Toulmin says, does respond to many of the facts of conduct. Many ethical remarks are made with the intention that hearers should act or reflect upon them. They surely do express the feelings of the people who make them. Such statements cannot possibly be logically incompatible with each other. If someone says that you told on me and that you are a nasty fellow for doing so, the facts may be in question but not the reproach in the tone of voice or the imperative that you should mind your business. We may hope that others will adopt the same moral attitudes toward facts that we do, but, as for instance, in the position taken by A. J. Ayer,[6] ethical judgments as such have no independent validity. Whereas the subjective doctrine identifies moral statements with attitudes of approval and disapproval, the imperative theory leaves them unexplained, offering no explanation of underlying attitudes.

Problems of the Imperative Position

Toulmin then goes on to distinguish between genuine imperatives and ethical statements. If an officer tells a soldier to stand at attention, that is a command. If the soldier refuses, he may be put on charge. However if the officer says that the soldier ought to be standing at attention, the soldier may do so only because of the implied threat.

Still, Toulmin says, it is not nonsense to ask whether that is really what ought to be done. If that question is asked, there may be an answer provided by the appropriate regulations. Moreover, there is an understandable difference between good and bad reasons. If a child asks why he should pick up after himself, it is a good reason to suggest that he thereby saves work for other people. It would make no sense to state that he should do so because the sky is blue. In the case of a true command, no reason applies.

Yet, although Toulmin does not push the case against the imperative theory this far, the command implies a threat and the threat constitutes a reason. Thus a command to stand at attention in one sense says that you ought to do so because you will be punished if you do not. This may have nothing (or much, depending on one's theory) to do with ethics, but it does have something to do with relevant reasons.

According to Toulmin, a critical weakness of the imperative doctrine is that it treats the fact that questions of truth often do not arise in ethical discourse as if this fact were logically entailed, as in the case of true exclamations and commands where such questions cannot arise. Although it is true that factual reasons do not by themselves justify ethical conclusions, for it is not merely the fact that a man beats his wife that makes him wicked, the ethical conclusion involves a condemnation.

At this point, Toulmin, in assessing this strength of the imperative approach, essentially is making use of the argument, earlier referred to, that normative conclusions cannot be derived from non-normative premises. The imperative theory avoids the naturalistic fallacy of identifying the value of an object with an ordinary property of it. However, according to Toulmin, it goes too far. It is under the tyranny of the idea that in order to be logically respectable, that is, to be capable of being true or false or reasoned about, a sentence must be made up of concepts referring to something about either the object or the subject. It rejects both forms of the dilemma and thereby concludes that ethical sentences are pseudostatements or pseudoconcepts. However, what it overlooks, according to Toulmin, is that people in ethical disagreement really do have something to contradict each other about, although it is neither physically nor psychologically concrete. It is their reasons for action that contradict each other.

TOULMIN'S SOLUTION

Toulmin has set the stage for his own analysis of moral reasoning. If, he says, one asks whether a practice is right, the only fact at issue is "whether the action in question belongs to a class of actions generally approved of in the speaker's community."[7] This is not merely a fact, he says. What makes this judgment ethical is the fact that it is used to harmonize people's actions. He uses the analogy about driving on the correct side of the road. If there is an accident, and the driver has been driving on the wrong side, he must produce a justification for the police. If, however, he was driving on the correct side, the only required explanation is that he was following the rule of the road. If, for instance, one argues that someone ought to return a borrowed book, it is sufficient to point out that he has promised to do so and that it is a social practice to carry out promises. Where two recognized claims conflict, Toulmin argues, one has to weigh, as well as he can, the risks of ignoring either. In this case, one does not claim that he had a moral obligation to choose the preferred course of action but rather that the consequences of the alternatives were taken into account.

Disagreements over Practices

What about the case, Toulmin asks, where the justice of a social practice is called into question? In this case, he says, the analogy is to whether a line is really straight. The astronomer who uses a non-Euclidian geometry with respect to light rays in outer space defines straightness in a particular way. Thus, certain lines are straight by definition and no further explanation can or need be offered. Toulmin argues that within the framework of a particular moral code one can ask whether individual actions are really right but not whether the standards of rightness are valid.

Toulmin then examines the case in which the criteria of straightness used in alternative geometric theories are different and analogizes this to whether it is right to have only one wife as in Christianity or up to four as in the Moslem religion. If, Toulmin says, one asks, not whether it is right for him to marry one wife or four, but whether Christian marriage or Muslim marriage is the better practice, the decision is personal. It may be reasoned about, but in the final analysis one must decide what to do. In this case, we can make a decision to remain within a Christian society or to move to the desert and live as an Arab tribesman. If, he says, one inquires whether a light ray going past the sun is really straight, in the sense of non-Euclidean theory, or deflected, as Euclidean geometry would imply, one must raise the question in a different way. One goes outside the framework of the particular scientific theory. Thus, although Toulmin does not explicitly say so, adherents of incompatible ethical systems are unable to reason with each other in relevant ethical terms if they are in conflict.

If one calls the justice of an ethical practice into question, Toulmin says, it is similar to asking whether Euclidean or non-Euclidean geometry is relevant to the investigation of the physical world. Alternatively, if one wishes to change a moral rule within a society, the question can arise only if there is a genuine alternative within the given society. In this form, the question refers to whether the change would have happier or unhappier consequences on the whole. If this question cannot be answered, then, morally speaking, arguments about change have value only as rhetoric. In essence, therefore, he appears to be saying that it is nonsense to characterize a practice—or a society—as bad if there is not a good way to produce change in it. This is quite different from recognizing that latter fact while also recognizing the iniquity or undesirability of the situation—a distinction Toulmin does not note.

There are only two questions that can be answered, Toulmin says: whether a proposed action is an instance of a rule of action or whether it is likely to produce the best results. Which of the two answers one seeks depends upon the case. Neither prescription is right in the abstract. If there is no conflict of rules, the rule is to be followed. If there is a conflict of rules, then it is important to avoid the most distress. Where alternative actions following different but conflicting rules produce equal distress, there is morally nothing to choose between them. This is because the notions of duty, of obligation, and of morality apply to situations in which the conduct of individuals within a community affects the fortunes of other individuals. Ethics has the function of minimizing the effects of such conflicts. To attempt to pursue the matter beyond this point is to fail to recognize the nature of limiting questions, according to Toulmin.[8]

Let us see if we can clarify the argument. Because goods are not objective, ethics is restricted to an analysis of reasons for behavior that existing societies accept. Of course, the reasons must be ethical. One lights a stove if one wants to boil water, but presumably this behavior is not considered moral. Let us ignore this problem for the moment, as well as the fact that the capability of a stove to boil water can be explained objectively, whereas presumably moral or ethical reasons are conventional "givens" in Toulmin's analysis.

What other forms of behavior seem somewhat similar to Toulmin's discussion of ethical behavior? Playing poker or chess also depends on a set of rules. One doesn't have to play either game. But, if one does, the rules circumscribe behavior. This must be somewhat close to Toulmin's reasoning, for it seems to explain his contention that if one does not like a society's rules, he should move to some other society that he prefers. Toulmin says that this choice is a purely personal one.

What of the card "sharp" who cheats at poker and is not caught? Presumably Toulmin would say that he gained money but was not really playing poker. Moreover, if our system of ethics forbids cheating, cheating at poker is bad from the standpoint of the game of ethics. However, what of the cheat in life: the man who pretends to be ethical but is not? He is not playing the game. Yet why should he move to another society? By what right does the majority enforce its "game" upon him? And why should he feel obliged to do so rather than to evade or cheat on the rules? The standard of the game cannot serve to answer this question, and Toulmin recognizes this fact when he states that one must go outside of the framework of the system for an answer.

The same problem arises with respect to changes in the rules. The National Football League establishes its rules for professional football. Presumably changes in the game are made to attract more "fans." In some games, changes may be made to permit a greater exercise of skill. Custom usually produces changes in systems of ethics, but on what basis do people accept or reject these changes? Toulmin is aware that rules of ethics do change from within and that sometimes one must choose from among conflicting rules. Toulmin attempts to solve this problem by establishing a reduction in conflict as both the subject matter of ethics and the criterion of choice with respect to changes in the rules.

Deeper Problems

Toulmin's conclusion follows from his premises only if reducing stress is an ethical premise, in which case one is not going out of the system at all. All that occurs in this case is that an ordering principle is applied to conflicting ethical principles within the framework of a single theory. If reducing stress is not a principle of ethics, then the reason for the choice is irrelevant from an ethical standpoint and any other principle may be chosen with equal validity. Alternatively, the principle of stress reduction really functions in Toulmin's system as an implicit definition of ethics. We shall soon see that Toulmin partly recognizes this, although it trivializes his discussion of the subject matter of ethics.

Reducing Conflict. Toulmin tells us that ethics is concerned with reducing conflict among individuals. As an empirical proposition, this no doubt has something to commend it. Does he mean to say, however, that we cannot inquire why individuals desire to reduce conflict among themselves? Presumably, someone might argue, because it is "good" to do so. Perhaps some sociological reasons might be offered to explain why reduction of stress is a good. For instance, societies in which conflict is not reduced below a certain minimum level probably will not be able to survive in competition with other societies. This might then be used to explain why societies reinforce the norm of conflict reduction (within limits) as a system norm. It has survival value. However, is survival the primary good? If so, ethical systems can be evaluated according to the extent to which they have survival value. Suppose totalitarian societies turned out to be the most efficient—fortunately, an apparently counterfactual assumption—would their system of values then become the best system of values? Alternatively, suppose we could reduce human distress by automating society and tranquilizing individuals. Would the ethical norms of this society be regarded as good? Either Toulmin introduces the reduction of stress as a purely arbitrary element in his system or he will encounter some variant of the prior problem.

Apart from the prior difficulties of justifying his choice of a criterion, Toulmin's solution is subject to an additional difficulty: the fact that the property he has chosen as a criterion is not adequately defined by the terms "injury" or "stress." An injury to an automobile is quite different from an injury to the system of judicial determination. And the difference does not lie merely in the fact that the latter injury is greater or that more people are affected.

The quality of human life also plays a role, and it does so in a very complex way. Although we do usually believe that an injury to one person is outweighed by the gains of many, our evaluation is not merely numerical. A variety of considerations besides numbers of people and extent of injury (even if, counterfactually, injuries were simply additive) come into active consideration. The bifurcation between an abstract set of moral rules and an abstract principle of adjudication when change is considered fails to do justice to moral reasoning—a subject to which we shall return later in the chapter.

The reader may recall the discussion of covering laws in chapter 1 for the light it sheds on efforts to establish a simple criterion for choice that applies uniformly to different types of homeostatic systems. Examined more closely, this aspect of Toulmin's doctrine is merely a variant of utilitarianism and it is as vacuous as utilitarian theory in general. It advises a social utility rule where the norms of the society are in conflict: choose a set of moral rules that avoids the greatest injury. It is difficult to see why this criterion could not be employed also for the criticism of a single norm if it is valid for deciding a conflict among norms; but even apart from that, Toulmin's criterion is vacuous because it does not specify what an injury is or how it is processed within a particular system. It is consistent with any set of ethical rules and preferences and is incapable of explaining any particular choice. Thus, Toulmin cannot use it for his stated purpose—to choose from among conflicting rules or to change the rules—for it has no meaning until social institutions, rules, and more particular preference orderings have been specified.

Toulmin's Analogical Error.   The recognition of limiting questions is legitimate and its application to ethical discussion is appealing. If one asks why the speed of light is a limiting constant in all physical systems, no answer can be given within the framework of relativity theory. It does not make any sense to ask why unless one can develop a new theory and derive the fundamental axioms of relativity theory from *its* fundamental axioms and propositions. Thus, for instance, relativity theory can be used to explain why Newtonian theory gives predictions that are substantially accurate within solar distances. The grounds for accepting relativity theory are relatively independent of the framework of explanation given by it. Either it provides a good account of reality or it does not. If some new theory provides a better account, then we will accept it as the correct account. In the same way, Toulmin would argue, I suppose, that the test of an ethical theory is whether it refers correctly to existing social practices. Thus, Muslim ethics apply to a Muslim society and Christian ethics to a Christian society. Although within either system, one may apply the rule of reducing distress when the rules for conduct conflict, the choice between systems is a purely personal one.

The Hottentot's Revenge.   To make the difficulty in Toulmin's argument clear, let us return to an argument that Toulmin used against the subjective approach. He said that an anthropologist may assert on the basis of his experience that adolescent Hottentots have an acute sense of moral obligation when sober but lose all moral scruples after drinking a pint of beer and do only those things that they are psychologically disposed to do. However, the anthropologist cannot mean that "when forced to make moral decisions, we all behave like drunk Hottentot adolescents—failing for some reason to tell rhetoric from reason, or to distinguish between those arguments which are really valid (and which we ought to accept) and those which appeal to us, but are specious."[9]

But what does it mean to talk of arguments that are really valid? In Toulmin's sense, it means to reason accurately from premises, in this case, ethical premises. Suppose the drunken Hottentot were to argue that his drunken behavior or that "smashing" other people are the appropriate norms and that sober states are undesirable restrictions on human nature? Obviously, Toulmin would not believe this, for he has a different view of ethics. Ethics, in his view, reduces conflict. But how can he argue against someone who argues that it is good to increase conflict and that norms that encourage this are the appropriate moral norms? He retreats to personal choice, a subjective position, or a norm of conflict reduction that is imposed either by an arbitrary, and vacuous, definition of ethics or by a subjective preference.

The problem is that moral rules are really subject to judgment—or at least that is the way we behave concerning them in many cases—in terms of their consequences for men, institutions, other values, and nature. Toulmin does bring this in when he speaks of reducing distress, but that is an arbitrary choice on his part. The poems of Hesiod deal with the anguish of Athenians during the transition from a tribal to a societal morality. This conflict of contending systems of morality is at the heart of *Antigone*. Moral reasoning inescapably involves a continuing interchange between rule-oriented behavior and a conception of the good as human beings learn under changing circumstances. It is a far more complex form of behavior than Toulmin understands.

Toulmin's Contribution and Its Achilles Heel

Toulmin appeared to rescue ethical philosophy from a position that equated moral values with ordinary preferences, as in a preference for chocolate over vanilla ice cream. He did this by relating ethical discourse to reasoned conduct. However, since his system of analysis requires that moral systems rest on personal choice, he has no genuine argument to offer against someone who chooses to believe in an entirely different system, except the arbitrary comment that the other system may possibly increase distress. He does not even have a ground for arguing against moral systems that exclude reasoned argument if that is the personal choice of others, except to attempt to exclude them by definition.

It does absolutely no good to say to someone that his behavior is wrong when it violates an ethical precept of a society if there is no argument against his response that he rejects the ethical premises of the system (other than the practical argument that he may be punished). Whereas it is possible to test the conflicting predictions of Newtonian and Einsteinian physics theories within the contemporary framework of physics, Toulmin's explanation offers no way in which such tests can be made for ethics. A physicist who employed Eculidean assumptions in his macrophysical theory would be in a difficult situation if he attempted to justify this choice by the fact that the geometry is used by a number of geometers who work closely together. The physicist is aware that physical theories require testing. He knows that it is nonsense to argue that Newtonian and Einsteinian theory cannot be tested comparatively because, for instance, the concepts of "mass" employed in the two theories are incommensurable. Moreover, their adequacy is adjudicated within the frame of reference of modern physics according to which a "sufficiency" of theoretical terms, other theories, measurements, test procedures, and so forth, are not at issue. Where this is not the case, as in some competing cosmological theories of contemporary astrophysics, matters may be "incommensurable," at least in the present state of knowledge.

The case of geometrical theory as a purely mathematical theory is quite different. The geometer is concerned primarily with the consistency and elegance of his purely mathematical system. Unless ethical theories are to be considered as systems of pure logic—and their lack of elegance and logical interest disqualifies them as fit objects of study in this sense—the most interesting questions concern their valid application. It does not justify a system of ethics to show that some people or some society adheres to it. That is a mere description of behavior. It shows that behavior is consistent with the premises of the system. It does not validate the system as an explanation of the behavior except in that almost vacuous sense in which the statement that the Euclidean geometer follows the postulates of Euclid explains his behavior. It does not explain why he chose to work in that field and it tells us nothing about the validity of this framework of geometry for any human enterprise other than the strictly logical one. If a member of a society of Euclidean geometers developed a non-Euclidean geometry, his associates could hardly argue that his choice of assumptions was false or even inappropriate. Even the argument that he should found a new society would be arbitrary, for he might argue that the proper classification of the group should now be as a society of geometers without further restriction. They might outvote him or exclude him by force. But this would have no relevance to mathematics.

To argue that we ought to follow a rule is convincing to someone who accepts the rule. It then explains his behavior to say that he accepts the rule and therefore follows it. However, the intermediate step of accepting the rule as valid is essential to the moral enterprise. When we challenge the goodness of the code of our society, we think that this is a meaningful action in other than a purely personal sense. This view may be true or false, but we cannot escape either a subjective or imperative view of ethics unless it contains some element of truth.

To go back to Toulmin's examples, he says that a particular promise ought to be kept because of a rule that promises should be kept. However, what we really mean when we say that a promise should be kept is that the act should conform with the rule because the rule ought to be followed in this case. We may hold this view either because the rule is regarded as good in itself or because it is part of a good set which would be injured in its absence and because we regard the case as an appropriate member of the set.

Note how this differs from Toulmin's example of the rules of the road. It is quite clear that we need rules of the road to avoid accidents. We really don't care if the rule involves driving on the left or driving on the right as long as we do it consistently. We will not lightly change whatever rule we have, unless we are a small country surrounded by larger countries using a different rule, for this involves considerable uncertainty during the period of change. No one would think that following the rule involves moral behavior, although not following the rule would be immoral if it is immoral to risk the life of other people. But it is the latter rule that is a moral rule, not the rule of the road.

When we deal with rules regarded as moral rules—for example, not risking the life of other people—we do not regard them as easily interchangeable or subject merely to convenience. Although their importance partly lies in their coherence with the entire set of rules, they also have independent value. Thus, there is a resistance to change that is based not upon expediency but upon a sense of moral "oughtness" that does not attend discussions of changing the rules of the road. This is the fundamental subject matter of ethical discussion and Toulmin's analysis fundamentally avoids it by terming it a "limiting question," in other words, a non-question.

The Apparent Plausibility of Toulmin's Position. The collapse of Toulmin's whole system of analysis would be more evident except for the fact that much of what he is saying accords with our ethical beliefs. It is quite true that we do reason about right actions; therefore, his argument about ethical reasons is deceptively appealing. Our willingness to accept the argument is evidence that moral reasoning is part of moral behavior just as the common language is evidence for a strong interrelationship between factual and moral elements. However, the evidence is no better than the framework within which explanation occurs, and this framework is fundamentally faulty in the Toulmin study.

We are not interested in ethical problems either out of curiosity, which Aristotle cites as the motivation for science, or because of the elegance of their presentation, the motivation of some mathematicians. Physics or mathematics would be more appealing subjects for those whose motivation is curiosity or elegance. As a practical matter we are interested in ethical behavior because we wish to know what right behavior is. If all that we can be told is that it is fundamentally a matter of our personal choice as to which moral system we accept, we can only tell a person who violates a rule of an ethical system that he has violated its logic; and the "ought" in moral statements would really mean even less than the assertion that one ought to add one to three if he wishes to obtain four. At least that result is quite specific, whereas, in the case of Toulmin's ethics, we can only tell someone to act according to the rule when he prefers to act otherwise because contrary behavior is unethical by arbitrary convention.

If our choice of moral systems is personal, there is no reason why we should not, if we wish, change our ethical systems daily, as we change our linen, except the purely expedient reason of avoiding failures of communication or of being reprimanded by Toulmin for behaving contrary to convention and therefore unethically. These hardly seem to be reasons that would induce anyone to run any personal risk in order to uphold a moral rule. Honor, decency, and integrity would become valueless as soon as they entailed personal risk.

Surely a mathematician when confronted with a crazed gunman would be willing to state that two plus three equals six if that would cause the gunman to refrain from violence. And, in this case, the mathematician at least would have the counterincentive of integrity: that two plus three really do not equal six is not dependent upon his wishes. In situations of risk, why should an individual live up to a conventional societal moral code, when all that is involved is "playing the game" according to the rules? And even if it can be shown—and that would be very difficult in most cases—that his failure to observe the rules will injure society, why should that be a convincing argument on Toulmin's grounds? As we have seen, Toulmin attempted to evade this result by appealing to the principle of the reduction of stress—a choice that is both arbitrary and vacuous. Yet in the absence of this defense, there is no reason to follow a conventional ethical rule contrary to one's interests—except the vague fear of being unethical, a fear relating to a view that ethics really "ought" to oblige one to follow rules. If Toulmin's analysis is correct, however, this fear has no genuine philosophical foundation. It therefore rests on poor reasoning, psychological rigidity, or a commitment to conventional behavior. None of these grounds can serve as an adequate foundation for moral theory. And, although psychological characteristics play a role in my account of ethics, they do not do so in any such simple, and purely extraneous, sense. Behavior resulting from conventional rigidities may appear to be ethical, but this is quite superficial.

The Character of Moral Reasoning

Every modern society will be found to have complex systems of ethical and legal norms. Religion, philosophy, culture, community, class, and ethnicity may be among the sources of the norms. And, as a consequence, there may be discordances and even conflicts among the norms to which individuals refer. Moreover, the choice of norms by individuals may be validated, at least in part, by their consequences, a point that Toulmin notes but that he does not properly appreciate. The proper analogy is not to a particular theory, such as Einsteinian relativity theory, but to the entire framework of scientific or legal knowledge: the area of praxis.

Toulmin assumes an ethical system sufficiently precise to permit the derivation of ethical conclusions in almost the way in which the geometer develops his theorems, although he does not insist that the rules will never be in conflict. This assumption is quite arbitrary and is not justified by any reasons related to his analysis. Moreover, from the propositional point of view, it fails to do justice to the way in which ethical reasoning occurs, just as conceptual jurisprudence failed to do justice to legal reasoning.

We begin our ethical reasoning with a rich universe in which a variety of things are regarded as good and a variety of reasons are acceptable for pursuing them. As problems arise that involve matters of ethics, we reach our judgments by examining the interrelationships between our evaluations of good ends—or goods—and good reasons. Sometimes we change our conception of the goodness of ends because they are too inconsistent with reasons that we accept as good. On other occasions, we change our conceptions concerning acceptable reasoning because the reasoning is now seen to produce consequences that we no longer regard as good.

For reasons asserted in the paragraph above, there is a rich interconnection between our conception of good consequences and good rules. The laws establishing British public housing for workers, for instance, stated that dwellings should be fit for the inhabitants. Before the First World War, it was not evidence of unfitness of dwellings for workers that rats ran through the houses. After the First World War, that was conclusive evidence of the unfitness of the housing. Before the Jacksonian revolution in the United States, it was considered proper in many states that only property holders vote. It was thought that only property holders had a sufficiently substantial interest in the commonwealth to vote responsibly. Thus such a rule was deemed appropriate to the pursuit of good government.

The abstract view of moral reasoning (and of consequences, such as reduced suffering) that Toulmin takes fails to appreciate the extent to which changed conditions produce changed conceptions of either appropriate rules or appropriate ends. But changed conditions are not among the only causes of changed views. Conditions may not change at all, but we may gain new information concerning the interrelationships of elements of a particular system. Such changed views may emerge not only from knowledge concerning the operations of our own system; they may emerge also from our comparative examination of different systems and the insights that derive from this.

Morris R. Cohen long ago made this point with respect to legal reasoning. Quine has since generalized the point with respect to scientific knowledge. It applies in the realm of ethics also. There is a rich interchange in the area of ethics between our conceptions of good reasons and good ends. It involves our view of men and of the institutional arrangements that permit a good and human life; and it does so in a rich contextual detail that is essential to the conclusions that we reach. A complex behavioral system is rich both in rules for relating to the world and in part-system desiderata.

Thus, most of ethics lies in the realm of praxis. Although we could develop ethical theories within which sets of moral rules are related to other system and environmental variables— much as the essential rules of my international systems are related to other system and environmental variables—the comparative analysis of ethical systems and the application of a system's rules in particular cases tend to be dominated by the particularities of the case.

We cannot understand moral reasoning properly except in terms of its relevance to moral goods. Therefore let me first explain what I characterize as a good and then discuss its objectivity.

CHARACTER OF THE GOOD

For something to be good, it must be valuable. Its goodness in a particular context will depend upon its properties in that context, the properties of the subject, and other relevant features of society, including perhaps the needs of others. Choice, or preference, except in pathological cases, as argued in chapter 1, will be oriented toward goals that are believed to be good. For reasons already offered, if it is possible to discover what is good, this will require complicated inferences. These may be revised as our knowledge improves.

The perception of the good, as in the case of any type of knowledge, will therefore depend upon criteria. These rarely can be explicit *ab initio*. As they are made explicit, they are subject to refinement as we learn more about the consequences of their application.

This process applies to science in general, for the initial confirmations of a non-normative kind in the early history of science required criteria. As we learned more about science, these were refined and differentiated according to the realm of scientific inquiry. This is a process that is still continuing. It helps us to distinguish better moral inquiries from those that are less good as our extensive modern knowledge of science permits us to distinguish better scientific inquiries from worse. This parallel and its implications for objectivity will be pursued in other sections of this chapter; to complete the parallel, the objectivity of the good must be shown.

A RETURN TO OBJECTIVITY

If the fundamental problems of ethics are to be solved, some variant of the objective doctrine is required. It should be obvious by now that I do not use the word "objective" as it is commonly used or make an absolute subject/object distinction. The earlier epistemological inquiry was designed to show the failure of ordinary usage to account for experience. Values, and other so-called facts, are part of the field of experience. Words, or their equivalents, treat elements of the field recursively, but always as part of the field, in ways that permit objectivity or, in Dewey's sense, public communicability. This second- or higher-order discourse, which takes place in internal as well as in external communication, and which proceeds by reasoned empirical inquiry, is what I mean by objectivity. I shall show that the status of values and of other so-called objective facts is similar in this sense of objectivity. I reserve the term "subjective" for those parts of the field of knowledge that cannot be communicated, at least in principle, in a publicly replicable manner (see appendix 1 for a further discussion of this subject). Other aspects of being that distinguish individuals from each other more properly should be called idiosyncratic.

The Nature of Objectivity

Toulmin, in discussing goodness as a property, correctly makes note of the fact that scientific laws speak not of objects but of properties of objects. However, the concept of objectivity in science is far broader: it assumes that different qualified scientists, working independently and using recognized techniques of scientific experimentation, would arrive at the same experimental results. Thus, when we say that Einsteinian relativity theory is objectively meaningful, we mean that we can specify procedures by which it can be validated and that these procedures are publicly communicable to other properly qualified people.

If, for instance, we state that a certain type of gasoline is a good energy source for a particular type of combustion engine, we may imply either a theoretical or a practical explanation. We may explore the chemical structure of the gasoline and the mechanical construction of the engine and then explain why the engine efficiently uses this energy source to produce substantial amounts of motive power. Alternatively we may mean only that we have tried the gasoline in the engine and that it works well. If we say that one type of gasoline is good and another bad in either a theoretical or practical sense, there is no property of "good" or "bad" that is independently determinable by examination of the gasoline without reference to its potential use in engines. Yet the terms "good" and "bad" fit appropriately within explanations that are objective, for we can explain why the chemical properties of a particular type of fuel make it work badly in a particular type of engine.

Another example of the variability of propertylike qualities concerns foods. Foods are nourishing. In excess, they may become poisonous. Some foods that are harmless taken separately are toxic taken in combination. If one says that these foods are bad or good, those assertions are meaningless unless there is a specification of the circumstances in which the attribution of badness or goodness is made. In any event, goodness or badness is neither a simple quality nor an ordinary complex quality. Yet, in context, we can specify what we mean by good or bad with sufficient precision to permit meaningful and objective communication.

We may find it somewhat more difficult to explain why President Nixon's opening toward China was a good diplomatic action. We cannot reconstruct the situation and try out alternative actions. We may not be able to agree on an interpretation of the motivations and behavior of other states and of their reactions to Nixon's overture to China. Yet, even though the experiment cannot be carried out in fact, it can be stated in a meaningful way. That is, we can state which alternatives we think the action opened up, which we think it foreclosed, and what the balance of desirable and undesirable characteristics happens to be. To call the action good or bad therefore, is meaningful.

I cite these cases not as analogies for the problem of values but as insights into the nature of objectivity. In neither case does immediate perception validate the statement. In neither case is there a definitive iterated procedure that does so. In the first case of the gasoline, however, we do get a complex result in the terms of the operation of the engine that may give us quite high confidence in the attribution we make. In the Nixon example, our confidence level is low, but the statement is meaningful. Neither case is as simple as "red" or as "regular polygon," the examples used by Toulmin, but both employ meaningful procedures. In both, we consciously do something that Toulmin omitted: we examine the organization of the systems for which the objects, for example, gasoline, are good and relate our conclusions to their working. And, as we saw earlier, Toulmin's example of "red" also requires such a procedure if it is to be meaningful, although our normal elliptical use of language obscures this requirement. To call an object "red" or "hard" reifies that quality and treats it abstractly, that is, as something that has an existence independent of the interactive process that produces it in all like cases. To expect that external objects, events, or consequences can be called good independently of an interactive process is to be guilty of a similar abstraction that unfortunately is practically universal in moral theory and that confuses the subject. To make the concept of "good" meaningful for ethics, we must return to an analysis of purposeful systems.

The reader will note that so far I have been discussing only goods of a particular kind. That is because so far I am concerned only to make the case that the concept of a good is objectively meaningful. And I can do this more clearly by starting with the simplest case. Later in this and particularly in the following chapter I shall make the case for more general kinds of goods and for justice as a good.

Transfinitely Stable Systems and Objectivity. If the automatic ultrastable pilot mentioned in chapter 1 had consciousness, it might perceive its purpose in life as the maintenance of the stability of the plane in which it was installed. In this case, the good is achieved simply and the system would be subject to no uncertainty except possibly with respect to means. There is a very close relationship between the good and the instrumental goal, the adjustment of the plane. If we turn to the case of the self-moving machine that refills its own gas tank and recharges its own battery, it might on some occasion have to choose between recharging its battery and refilling its tank. If the machine has no means of making this decision, although we could provide it with one, it would be unable to choose and thus to act.

If we turn to our transfinitely stable system, the situation becomes far more complex. We do not know that its internal code is completely stated. We do not know to what extent its identifications may involve ambiguities. It is goal-oriented. It has purpose. In pursuing its purposes, it may err in its cognition of the world. It may believe erroneously that someone has done something or that certain resources are available when this is not the case. It may err in its logic. It may err in estimating the consequences of its action. To the extent that its coding system is incomplete or not directly known by it, it may err in reporting its own desires. In principle, each one of these possible sources of error is subject to some form of objective test, although with respect to such things as what the individual actually prefers we may be restricted to low-confidence types of tests.

How the good will be pursued depends both upon the state of the goal-seeking system and of the environment. The self-moving machine attempts to fill its tank only when the tank approaches an empty state. If its internal reporting system becomes inaccurate, it might seek to fill the tank when it is already full or to refrain from attempting to fill it when it is nearly empty. Although errors in its operations would produce behavior that would seem to contradict our statement of its purposes, this is objectively explainable. In principle, we can analyze its behavior and infer its values by means of that analysis. We infer its good from the purposeful system's choice of goals.[10]

If we characterize the valuable as that which would be judged good in the presence of correct information, we can distinguish between what is valued and the valuable. If "ought" statements are taken out of the elliptical imperative form, "X ought to do g," they would appear as "X ought to do g because g has the consequence h, which is valuable for X," or as "X ought to do g because g has the consequence j which is valuable for Y, the good of whom is valuable for X." These are goods of a kind. What is good, however, as we shall show, will differ with the system to which reference is made and with the environment. Therefore, there will be criteria according to which these determinations are made. As these criteria are applied and developed in different contexts, we become aware of differences and similarities in different kinds of goods as well as of more central kinds of goods such as justice. These further discriminations lead to knowledge of more general kinds of goods, although their relationships and character will vary with system context. The fact that we start with knowledge of what is good and with criteria of application does not involve a vicious circularity. I shall show shortly that it corresponds to the situation in science.

The statement by a person as to what he values is evidence of what is valuable for him; but it is rebuttable evidence. Note that this type of system can produce objectively definable pathological behavior. Suppose a person is in an extremely unfavorable environment. He may have to forgo important needs. Since this is unpleasant, mechanisms of denial may operate. In addition, the denial mechanism may be reinforced by the subjective overvaluation of the lower-ranking goals. The person now may pursue intensely his secondary-goal system to the extent that he is unable to recognize favorable changes in the environment that would permit him to pursue more primary goals, that is, goals that he otherwise would have pursued.

I do not contend that these distinctions are easy to make in practice, although there is some psychiatric evidence for them. Nor do I contend that the actual psychological mechanisms operate in precisely the way I describe. What I do assert is that this discussion makes meaningful the distinction between the valuable and the valued and that it does so in an objectively meaningful way.

This speculative explanation sketch makes meaningful the proposition that with full information a person will value what is valuable to him in his environment. In other words, we are talking about a system with a set of dispositional behaviors. What is good for the system involves a relationship between environmental possibility and system needs. What is valued by the system depends upon its cognition of these relationships and is subject to possible pathological distortion.

The system we are talking about is the homeostatic type. This means that no set of equalities defined according to a covering law can be used in an explanation sketch of the system. Because the operations of the system depend upon information, its ability to cognize and thus to value the valuable depends in part upon what it believes. However, its beliefs are only rebuttable, but not conclusive, evidence for the valuable. Thus, predictions about this system or explanations of its behavior involve statements concerning the beliefs it will hold under certain types of conditions. However, the beliefs by themselves do not suffice to explain its value-oriented behavior. The belief that beliefs alone matter in the validation of propositions in the realm of morals gives rise to the subjective and imperative doctrines as well as to Toulmin's variation of the former.

In fact, information is merely an element within a larger system; and although the logical forms which the conscious mind uses in reasoning constitute an essential element of the system, no explanation of its behavior limited to this set alone is sufficient to explain that behavior. Thus, to view moral behavior as resulting from the implications of an ethical system that is composed only of rules and that is validated by a personal choice that has neither further explanation or justification, fails to account for moral behavior.

Let me now reframe my prior arguments about objectivity and apply them to this analysis. "This is yellow" and "This is a dove" are elliptical expressions. "This is yellow" stands for "This is seen as yellow by such and such an observational system in such and such types of filters, atmospheric or otherwise." Even this latter statement is only comparatively non-elliptical, for, in principle, an absolutely non-elliptical statement would contain an exhaustive, and potentially infinite, set of conditions.

Each statement of the type "This is yellow" or "This is a dove" implies something about an observer, an object or event external to the observer, and the context of observation. In the common language, commonsense distinctions are made between "is" and "appears." If we are incautious, these can lead to reifications that produce false conclusions.

There is an important distinction between "dove" and "yellow" with respect to the "is/appears" disjunction. Although a piece of flying paper at a distance may appear to be a dove, the tests that can be performed to confirm the distinction between "is" and "appears" are consistent with an extremely wide range of contextual circumstances and perceptual systems. The distinction between "is" and "appears" with respect to color, however, depends upon a conventional stipulation of a specific type of observational context.

Although, for reasons obvious to the conditions of life in the solar system, a different conventional standard would be absurd in practice, it is not absurd in principle. Moreover, although unlikely for evolutionary reasons, in principle the observational system might report differently when in different states, as it does with respect to tastes for foods. Differently evolved creatures might report differently. And these differences in reports would not be merely linguistic differences, for there would be a difference in experiences. In principle these differences in experience could be confirmed objectively by operations on the physiologies of the two species that transform one into the other and that then reverse the process. In this case, a statement that reported that "X is yellow" would not permit second-order agreement on the referent X without specification of the instrument (observational system) used in making the report.

With respect to the good, this aspect of a report is essential, for the report is meaningless except for the relationship between the observing system and the context in which the observation is made. Thus, just as "X is yellow" is not invariant for two beings with different observational systems, "X is good" is not invariant regardless of context and system state.

We can distinguish between "X is good" and "X appears good," for we can relate the distinction to the information possessed by the system in context. Moreover, this distinction is not merely a convenient convention, as in the specification of "in light with the characteristics of Sol I" for color. It refers to an actual difference that is relevant to the judgment just as "biological animal" does for the case of dove.

The conventional standard for color depends upon a specified, but causally unlinked, context of observation. Its choice is a matter of convenience only. What is "good" depends upon the characteristics of the human system. The more important the characteristic to which the choice is linked, the more stable the linkage tends to be. Metaphorically, important choices, including but not restricted to the criteria of choice, are central to value systems whereas such things as tastes for particular flavors of ice cream are peripheral. (The point made by Quine about the entire system of science applies importantly to the investigation of values.) Thus, once we have specified the system and the environment about which we are making a report about the good, the distinction between "is" and "appears" is a matter of fact and not merely of convenience or "naming." In this important sense, characterizations of goodness are "more" objective than, even if not as easily decidable as, the distinction between "is" and "appears" with respect to colors.

Unlike hallucinations—the features of which may be quite decidable but which, apart from possible external triggering, are determined almost entirely by transient and idiosyncratic states of the internal system—preferences imply more enduring relationships between the perceiving system and the environment. As the preferential aspect of this relationship is the key aspect, univocality of relationship between perception of good and the world is a strong condition that is unnecessary for the assertion of objectivity concerning the good. A weaker, non-univocal ordering in which some external states of the world are perceived as better or worse than others is compatible with objectivity. Judgments concerning this ordering will vary with information. For certain states of the world—for instance, the state of being a paraplegic—the perceiving system may disvalue additional information. My hypothesis is that these preferences are secondary and that, for instance, no one would choose paraplegia, except in preference to something worse, if it could be avoided. With this conception we begin to approach the test in principle— soon to be discussed—in which successive orderings of states of the system, states of the world, and information permit in principle a weak but objective (transfinite) ordering of good and bad, even though the procedures for determining this ordering are low-confidence procedures. Judgments concerning this ordering will depend on the state of the perceiving system and its information and these will establish a partial ordering for the system in its current state; for both its situation and its beliefs are relevant to its good and are subject to reconsideration only within the limits of its existential plasticity. Extensive comparative information and the capability for using it are likely only in relatively advanced societies. Thus good in the form of justice is potentially developmental.

The goals sought by men are not good independently of circumstances, whether specific or general. We start with knowledge of the good, knowledge that is refined with further information. The test in principle, which is discussed below, points to the possibility of a common universe of good: one in which all human beings would share similar preferences under similar conditions. This is hypothesis, however. Later I shall give reasons for believing it may be the case. If it is the case, then in principle we could use the test in principle to discover the criteria of good that would govern choice within any social system and those that would permit a weak ordering of social systems that would influence our preferences for some social systems over others and toward risk-oriented choices with respect to modifications of existing societies. However, as I shall reiterate in the section on the test in principle, these choices are made in the realm of praxis. They are not derivable from a theory, of the deductive covering law variety, that treats other aspects of the larger realm of knowledge as if they were "givens."

One other aspect of this matter, which is also discussed in appendix 1 and in chapter 1, is worth mentioning, for it affects the discussion of objectivity. Despite advances in epistemology, most of us, except in technical discussions, implicitly assume that objectivity involves a correspondence between an internal or subjective representation and an external or objective reality. The valid procedures of science appear to reinforce this conception, for we measure with rulers, weigh with scales, and perform mathematical operations according to rules that others can follow. Such procedures constitute what John Dewey called publicly communicable information. But the appearance is deceptive, for we really compare test conditions and results in one experiment with those in another, not with ideas in our psyche.

There is a second judgmental process that accompanies this one. If we cannot recognize a scale as such, or a color, we cannot communicate to others procedures they can follow or specify results they can read and compare with ours. The same holds for logical or mathematical operations, for these cannot be conveyed to those who are incapable of recognizing them.

However, this is not a purely *a priori* phenomenon. Although we necessarily begin with a field of knowledge, for otherwise we could not receive information, we adjust parts of that field as improved information indicates inconsistencies or lack of "fit" in the field. Thus we can develop non-Aristotelean forms of logic; we can refine our ability to perceive qualities; and we can learn that an indicator stands for something quite different from what it seemed to stand for. An even more complex and sophisticated process of judgment is involved in our interpretation of the entire realm of science as contrasted with a particular theoretical area. Primitive terms, the axioms of a theory, the apparatus and test conditions, and the set of definitions constitute the "givens" of a scientific experiment. The entire mélange, as well as all other knowledge, "floats" in a constantly readjusting equilibrium with respect to the realm of scientific knowledge. The status of values is similar. Because the copy theory of knowledge mistakes this process, the distinction between values and other types of "facts" to which it leads is also wrong.

There is no external "color" or "size" to which an internal representation of color or size corresponds. Nor are values subjective because they do not refer to corresponding external objects. Instead there is a differentiated field of knowledge that presents some events as internal to a self and others as external. And every hypothesis that serves as a potential explanation of either employs categories that presume an interaction between a self and its environment that produces the categories in terms of which an explanation is offered and that is confirmed or disconfirmed by contemporaneous or subsequent elements in the field of knowledge or experience. Chapter 1 has shown that values are produced by the interaction of a transfinitely stable personality with its environment. This showing was conducted according to the ordinary understanding of science. Hypotheses about the values that are produced by different states of information, different social conditions, and different environments are of the same kind. Our analysis of linguistic usage showed how imperative assertions are part of this process and how their ordinary use is elliptical, as is the case with respect to so-called ordinary factual statements. Thus, both types of explanation, as I have shown, can be made in publicly communicable, or objective, terms, at least in principle.

We continue with the parallel between values and other facts. If assertions concerning the valuable refer at least in part to processes internal to the person, so do psychological and physiological explanations. Even if the latter made no reference to factors outside the person—and this is counterfactual—they would differ from valuations only in terms of the categories or explanation and not in terms of location. Thus, location inside the self does not make an explanation subjective even according to the ordinary usage that still carries over from the earlier epistemology that presumed a dichotomy between a real external and objective world—at least in terms of primary categories such as space and time if not in terms of perceptual categories such as color—and an internal, subjective world of representations.

This process is circular only in the philosophically universal sense that we cannot account for any information or knowledge, except on the assumption that the perceiving system starts with information or knowledge. This applies to information concerning both so-called ordinary facts and values.

Learning involves negative feedback; and this necessitates that at least the initial state of information be adequate for the correction of other elements. Thus, beliefs about the valuable will be altered as more is learned about man and his environment.

Although this process may appear to resemble what Max Weber called *verstehen,* it is publicly communicable in Dewey's sense. And it applies both to the social and the physical sciences, contrary to what Weber thought; for, as Quine has shown, the consequences of experiments and the protocol sentences of scientific theories do not have a one-to-one correspondence. The string-of-marks theory is as faulty as Morris Cohen argued. There is a metalevel of discussion in which language is used recursively, and in publicly communicable terms, in which we talk about social and physical experiments. At this metalevel, the self and its beliefs are also re-presented in experience and with the same status as theories, social alters, environments, and laboratory equipment. This is the sense in which, in terms of John Dewey's "public communicability," we call them objective, for we talk about them in an "object" language. In this sense, values and other facts have a similar ontological status. And we can communicate concerning them only to those capable of comprehending their meaning (see appendix 1).

Some failures in the application of scientific methods in the realm of human affairs stem not from the correctly perceived "intentionality" of much of human action but from the failure to appreciate the differences between mechanical and homeostatic systems. Thus, the application of terms and measurements to different types of social systems, as if their meaning were the same regardless of context, produces the error of overabstraction.

Whereas theoretically defined terms in physical science, such as energy, have a generally applicable meaning in a wide variety of texts—and whereas statements of equality or inequality are valid generally—terms such as "father" or units of such factors as "gross national product" are different in important ways when applied to different types of social systems.

However, it is a mistake to believe that either "holistic" or *verstehen* approaches to knowledge correct this error, for part of the "meaning" of terms and of measurements is inferred from differences in their employment in different types of systems and different milieus. The meaning, even within a particular system, of "father," for instance, is amplified both by analysis in context and by comparison across different types of systems. And judgments concerning measures of national product are also illuminated by such considerations.

The error of overabstraction also characterizes some philosophies of science that reify the general concept of "measurement," for "measuring," as distinguished from the measurement of particular theoretically defined terms, does not have identical meaning in different physical science spheres. This is the sense in which we learn "what science is from what scientists do," provided that the phrase is not taken literally, in which case we could not distinguish good science from bad science. It is the expansion of scientific activity into different realms that enlightens our understanding of science by revealing similarities and differences.

The failure to distinguish between a scientific theory and the realm of knowledge within which it is interpreted leads to the mistake in which the characteristics of theory are attributed to the entire realm of scientific knowledge. Thus, the requirement for a set of initial axioms—a requirement that does apply to a theory—is falsely attributed to the entire body of knowledge. However, the latter is a realm of praxis rather than of theory; and its elements reinforce each other in a loose equilibrium, in which considerations of consistency, economy, and so on determine which elements are tentatively held constant and which are tentatively varied.

Fundamental axioms have been altered—for example, no action at a distance—when inconsistent with an economical theory. Observations are disbelieved—for example, the statistical evidence for telepathy—in the absence of a theory consistent with theories of physics that will explain them.

Standards of evaluation are changed—the distinction between warm and cold—when confronted with theoretical requirements for a concept such as temperature. Even more revolutionary changes in the most "solid" aspects of scientific belief will change if the "loose" equilibrium of the realm of knowledge (praxis) requires this.

A similar process occurs in the realm of values; and that is why the comparative test in principle—rather than the effort to discover a single system of moral rules that is general for all systems and environments—is the correct approach. The latter mistake replicates the overabstraction found in some mistaken philosophies of science and social science theories.

Thus, the world of values, and of the valuable, is a world susceptible to scientific analysis, provided that the latter concept is properly understood. Objectivity, in the only sense in which it is meaningful, is possible in that realm also; and circularity, at least in a methodological vicious sense, is avoided.

Therefore, we recapitulate the position: the report of a person concerning values, if honest, constitutes the valued. It is evidence concerning the valuable but is not an independent criterion for it. A judgment concerning the valuable requires further information about the state of the evaluator including, but not restricted to, its state of information and its environment. This test is a low-confidence test but meaningful. The test in principle, soon to be described, shows how an extension of this procedure potentially permits a weakly-ordered valuation of social systems.

Good and Evil as System-related.   Modern utility theory is not genuinely adequate to the concepts of good and bad. It presents us with a set of preference orderings. Although we may place pluses and minuses before the utile numbers we use, it would make no difference in the operations of this system were we to establish the base of the scale at zero. If we maintain a systems reference, however, the "good" may be conceived of as consisting of those things that improve the state of the (social or personality) system and the "bad" as consisting of those things that worsen it.[11] Good practices could then be thought of as those practices that reinforce the retention of specific goods and bad practices as those entailing bad consequences. Moral goods would somehow be more central to the "web" of good things and would include considerations of justice. Evils could be defined as those bad things that injure the more central characteristics of a system. For instance, if we view man not as a featherless biped but as a rational animal, then it would be evil to keep him in a drugged state. If man's nature requires the expression of love and dependence, then it would be evil to produce a sanitized social system that outlawed sentiment.

This returns us to the speculative problem that we discussed earlier. What is the nature or the character of the particular type of system we are talking about? How do we make this type of speculation meaningful? If we look only at the practices of mankind, we can discover every extreme. The ovens of Buchenwald and the spires of Chartres are both manifestations of human nature under certain conditions. The competitiveness of the Kwakiutl and the cooperativeness of the Hopi are also manifestations of human nature. Chivalry and barbarism coexist as potentialities in man. Do these extremely different manifestations depend merely on environmental conditions, in which case man's behavior is purely relative to the circumstances in which he finds himself? Or can we restore the meaningful character of speculation about human nature?

It is quite true that the alternatives that present themselves to individuals are related to the environments in which they find themselves. It is the rare washerwoman in a weak country who envisages the personal conquest of power over a neighboring country. We are no more able to build utopias from the whole cloth than we are able suddenly to start speaking in a strange language. Our understanding about our own human possibilities is grounded in our interaction with our social alters in contemporary society. Our understanding of right and wrong is grounded in our individual socialization. Our acceptance or rejection of such standards, regardless of the reasons therefor, is precisely that: an acceptance, rejection, or modification of a particular code. We can learn about our potentiality only from experience, including our interaction with our actual environments.

The Test in Principle.   Reason, abstraction, and generalization require a clay which, despite its manipulability, has definite characteristics. But it is not true that we are merely a prisoner of empirical experience. Systems theoretic models may provide us with a concept of the inherent autonomy of self-regulating systems of the type we are talking about. Our knowledge of ethnology and physiology may cause us to reflect upon certain emotive and social characteristics of human nature, however speculative these may be. Our knowledge of history confronts us with alternative arrangements of human affairs. A systematic study of these may relate them to specific environmental conditions, the state of human knowledge, and the alternatives that could be visualized at those times by members of those systems. Our exercise of empathetic imagination can illuminate the situations of other individuals in particular types of roles in other social systems. In principle, this entire sequence of potential choice can be elucidated by the test in principle I stated in the introductory essay of *Macropolitics:*

> Consider a situation in which a man would be able to relive his past in thought. He could be confronted with each of the branching points of his major life decisions and allowed subjectively to live the alternative lives. If individual choices could be tested in this fashion, social and political and moral choices could be tested in analogous fashion by confrontations with different

patterns of social, political, and moral organization under different environmental constraints.

Presumably this would confront men with choices that are meaningful. Thus, where the material environments of the social and political systems were presented as "givens," the individual would observe the consequences of different positionings and different circumstances within the systems. He could observe which roles he would prefer if he could choose his roles and how much he would like or dislike the system if roles were chosen for him. Within his own life patterning, he could compare choices over those things where he in fact had the freedom to choose differently. Within these constraints, his conceptions of the good depend upon the limitations of institutional life and environment. In the second form of testing, he could vary institutional life and material environment, again in two ways. He could compare systems as to which he would prefer if he could choose his role and which he would prefer if his role were assigned to him. On the basis of a more limited freedom, he could compare differences in the existing institutional structures with respect to his past decision points, where he had had some freedom to effect changes in them.

After experiencing these alternatives, the individual would return to his actual situation. He would then have to choose in the present on the basis of the limited alternatives available to him. He now has a standard against which to judge his practicable choices; if he has interdependent utilities, it will be too uncomfortable for him not to make some effort to move the system closer to alternatives that are practicable, not too deprivational for him, and better for others as well. Presumably he will not confuse himself about the harm he does to others because of his needs under existing constraints.

If we are dissatisfied with the concept of a standard for values that is asserted to be meaningful but that is very far from even a practicable test, we might propose the following kinds of quasi-tests. Children could be raised under controlled conditions and then compared in aspects of their functioning. Alternatively, if the future provides methods whereby memories either may be erased or impressed upon the mind, it would be possible to run experiments in which separate memory tracks could be impressed simultaneously and compared on an A, B basis. Since the order might not be entirely transitive, discarded sequences might be re-compared with seemingly dominant patterns.

If these suggestions seem too fantastic, we could consider the more limited kinds of comparisons that we in fact make when we talk about propositions of this kind. These do not have the fullness of comparison suggested above and they suffer from the fact common to all scientific work that we reach conclusions by treating our test procedures as if they were exhaustive. None the less we can and do make at least limited comparisons and occasionally we even decide against our own social system on this basis, as many Germans did during the time of Nazi Germany. The degree of confidence to be placed in such localized comparisons is limited, for we do not fully know upon what conditions the system consequences are dependent. However, our ability to relate positions to life and social experiences is itself a solvent and does produce a broader set of comparisons. In any event, our conception of the nature of man as an evaluating system is meaningful, the conception of limits to plasticity and costs for wrong choices is meaningful, and therefore at a minimum the concept of local comparisons is meaningful.[12]

In addition to the tests considered in *Macropolitics,* we might also seek empathetic insight into those with different psychological propensities, and enter it also into our judgments.

There is one other form of empirical testing that in principle sheds light on our problem. Individuals confronted with evidence that would militate against particular practices that are to their benefit in existing social and environmental circumstances presumably would be forced into pathological processing of information because of their need to avoid empathetic knowledge of the harm they are doing to individuals whose needs or rights they would otherwise be forced to recognize. We are rarely confronted with desperate choices of this kind because the process of socialization produces both the expectation that certain reward structures are justified and inattention to the deprivations they entail. As a consequence, individuals do not have to divert their attention from the deprivations of others; they are on the whole not confronted by them. However, where such information is presented to the individual, presumably it would generate information-processing pathologies and these would give rise to cognizable physiological disturbances.

This suggestion is offered hesitantly, for I fully recognize the immense difficulty of attempting to validate a particular explanation of an informational disturbance of this kind. Moreover, in social systems that are sufficiently pathological, it would be the empathetic individual who recognizes injustice who might manifest the most disturbance. However, although the empathetic individual would suffer in most actual situations because of his greater sensitivity to information, in principle we could show that it is his cognition of, or at least his belief concerning, the ways in which current conditions deprive other individuals that produces the pathology. Presumably by forcing others to confront data of this kind, we could also produce similar pathologies in them.

Thus, we have essentially two different types of test in principle that make the concept of objectivity meaningful. Full information, of course, is not possible. We cannot have full information about the physical world. Someday we may learn that our presumed laws of nature are poorly stated and that this is a consequence of our incomplete perception of the conditions under which they function. Comparative knowledge, however, at least widens our perception of the range of human possibility and permits the formulation of a more extended reconstruction of the range of human possibility. Our ability to perceive this problem broadly depends upon the range of comparative experience available to us. The primitive man of 5000 B.C. could not have conceived of modern technological society. If we were able to go back in a time machine, to teach such a primitive man English, and to present him with a book stressing the problems of the modern age, we would merely bewilder him. He would not understand our science or our customs.

Let me be more specific about how this comparative evaluation might proceed and what it has in common with scientific method. My examples for this purpose will be the most obvious I can find, for the complexity of man and of society, as well as their complicated interlinkages, make it very difficult to acquire even low-confidence information about the values represented by "resting states" of man under different circumstances. If we examine any society and its norms, we discover complex interlinkages between any single norm and the set of norms as well as with institutional features of the society and environmental conditions. In those societies in which children are abandoned, or in the smaller number in which aged parents are eaten, for instance, institutions and other norms reinforce these customs. And, in the case of the society in which aged parents are eaten, the latter verbally reaffirm the norm even though they are to be sacrificed. Suppose, however, that we discover that such customs occur only in societies in which food is, or historically has been, insufficient for the entire group. We might then hypothesize that this factor, rather than any inherent worth, is the producer of the particular norm. In principle a member of this society who becomes familiar with social anthropology might come to the same conclusion and become an advocate of increased food production to ameliorate conditions and, eventually, to produce a better society with changed values.

Information, therefore, and not merely the existing set of norms is used in arriving at this conclusion. And, although we cannot imagine any particular norm evaluation that is entirely divorced from the existing set of norms, a series of comparative judgments over time might completely change the normative and institutional structure of a society. Of course, this is what does happen anyway as societies adjust to changed conditions. Usually, however, these normative changes occur in response to particular environmental changes without regard to the comparative experience of mankind and, therefore, without an enlightened comparative perspective on relationships among elements that might change our judgments concerning how the adjustments should occur.

The information we bring to bear upon this process is not restricted to comparative knowledge of social institutions. Comparative knowledge of economics, increased knowledge of human physiology and psychology, and indeed all of human knowledge comes to bear upon judgments as to what are good outcomes and good normative rules.

Let us see what this process has in common with science. Physics assumed the "truth" of Newtonian laws until neo-Euclidean geometry, the Michelson-Morley experiment on the speed of light, and the Lorentz equations permitted the development of the special theory of relativity. Only with modern equipment did we learn of the "strange" behavior of elements under conditions of superconductivity. These, of course, are high- rather than low-confidence conclusions, and range- or subject-limited generalizations rather than generalizations drawing upon all the fields of knowledge. Yet the comparative aspect is genuinely analogous. Our beliefs as to the laws of nature are not necessarily the same as the laws of nature just as our beliefs about values are not the same as the valuable. Improvements in knowledge concerning behavior under changed assumptions or parameter conditions give new insights into presumed laws of nature or presumed valuables. The individual aspects of knowledge going into value judgments—knowledge of man, of society, of economics, and so forth—are analogous, except that usually they warrant only low-confidence conclusions.

The global judgments we reach that take all these factors into account are analogous, as we have earlier stated, to science as a corporate body rather than to any particular theory. In this respect, knowledge, whether of science or of the valuable, exists as a field that is constantly readjusted to changes rather than as a single deductive system, whether normative or non-normative. Thus value judgments are not deduced from normative rules, from factual elements, or from assessments of good outcomes. Rather, these coexist in a loose "balance" in arriving at a value judgment.

One consequence of this is that the normative rules for a particular social system coalesce in a way that is relevant for that system rather than deducible from some overarching normative system. The relationship is not deductive or thoroughly systematic. And, because our judgments concerning values are often low-confidence judgments, they come closer to what the ancients called opinion than to science. The use of the test in principle in specifying these weakly ordered normative systems is a potentiality of the transfinitely stable character of the human system.

The transfinite process is one of discovery—fundamentally of discovery of what it is to be human as this is illuminated by the test in principle. If being human involves being moral—as I believe it does—then transstability is the process by means of which men, in their learning of their humanity, become human and learn how to build a society fit for humans. In this sense, being human involves subjection as well as freedom: subjection to moral rules and considerations for others; and freedom to express one's humanity. Because this transstable process takes place in the realm of praxis, these conceptions develop through comparative understanding of how human behavior, social institutions, culture, science, and so forth, are linked in alternative possible or real worlds, each of which is characterized by a world view. Thus, a developed conception of humanity is not derived from, or reducible to, any specific theoretical or propositional foundation. It is textured and enriched by the entire web of social existence and deepened by comparative understanding of alternative possibilities. Unlike classical philosophy, however, the standards for this process are objective in Dewey's sense of public communicability and in Peirce's sense of the pragmaticist test.

The Test in Principle and Objectivity. We can now tie up the loose ends in the discussion of objectivity. The fact that a partly color-blind person cannot distinguish some colors or shades does not mean that he can distinguish none. And these distinctions are objective in the sense previously described. To the extent that his optic system functions, his judgments will coincide with the perceptions of a normal person. In turn, the normal person cannot make other distinctions made by laboratory equipment.

The fact that two societies may be distinguishable in many characteristics, even including characterizations of the good, need not mean that they are distinguishable on a scale of moral goodness. Although we do not mean this technically, a reader may think of an indifference curve for different quantities of the same goods or for different quantities of different goods. In principle, we would argue that these are therefore in some sense substitutable. Presumably, we could find some second-order criteria in terms of which we would argue that their value is similar. These societies, then, would occupy a similar place in a scale of preferences that is weakly ordered. However, there is still an ordering, if only qualitative, according to which differences in moral standing are discernible. Thus, a weak ordering can be consistent with objectivity.

Let us now distinguish what objectivity means in terms of the test in principle. I repeat that I am not asserting that we have in fact carried out a test in principle. The moral order is probably only weakly ordered. Individuals, in any system, will have a weakly ordered preference for roles in that system. This preference order will depend upon information and environmental conditions. Within any system, individuals will have a weakly ordered preference for the individual values that characterize the system's cultural norms. These preferences will depend upon information and conditions. Individuals will have a weakly ordered set of preferences for alterations in any system. These will depend on information and conditions. Individuals will have a weakly ordered set of preferences for other types of systems. These preferences will depend on information and conditions. Individuals will have a weakly ordered set of preferences for alternative environmental conditions. These will depend on roles, systems, and information. The complete set of weak orderings will establish a weakly ordered hierarchy of preferences. It may be invariant.

However, we can carry the weak ordering one step farther and it will remain consistent with objectivity. Let us assume that under conditions of the test in principle, some agree that some societies are among the worst and some are among the best but that they differ in other comparative evaluations. We would call the latter personal or idiosyncratic and the former second-order objective aspects of the problem. The fact that not all aspects of moral orderings were subject to even second-order evaluations—second order because of possible conflicts in moral choices under real-world conditions—would not erase the existence of those aspects that are subject to either first- or second-order rankings.

Let me now state how second-order criteria are used to determine an invariant order for changes within systems or for transitions between them. The second-order criteria for choice will be determined by step functions. By this I mean that any significant alteration in conditions or systems will trigger a new constellation or ordering of values. The possibility of such change will bring to consciousness the possibility of such a new ordering as a guide to decision. Because the order is weak, some alternatives may not be morally distinguishable, although the relationship of values in each will be different. Because first-order choices are related to actual choice conditions, the potentially best set (or sets) of values do not govern moral choices, except possibly as a minor qualifier so as not unnecessarily to foreclose it as a future possibility. Nor is this required for objectivity, because we have an invariant guide for relevant transition states in terms of moral equivalents. Although reasons can be offered for the choice of transition values—for example, as there is no longer a shortage of resources, the functional values associated with shortages are inappropriate—the area is one of praxis and judgment. Hence, no unique theory will permit derivation of uniquely appropriate reasons.

Objectivity and Human Nature. These preference orderings represent dispositions of humans under different conditions. By human nature, I mean the dispositional ordering established by the ordered hierarchy outlined in the previous section.

One other possibility may be mentioned. Hereditary physiological differences may produce temperament differences that in turn produce differences in what is valuable. This is consistent with objectivity, for we can produce an invariant moral hierarchy for each physiological type. As this ordering becomes weaker, however, the identification of the different types will weaken. It may become so tenuous that no common moral universe will exist for them. This will produce a variant of the frame-of-reference problem discussed in chapter 3.

One variant of the test in principle may be applicable even in this case—a variant in which individuals compare the preferences for moral rules that they would have, depending upon their hereditary physiologies and upon their preferences for physiological types. This might permit recognition of a "best" type or, at least, of "better" types. Almost surely this would be the case for those whose "crippling" is obvious, as in the case of those who have undeveloped physical parts or brain damage. Although existential identifications would still produce conflict over moral principles, common recognition of "best" or "better" would serve as a modifying agent that restores some common moral ground.

Human Nature and Alienation. The test in principle permits an individual to detach himself from his "accidental" setting in making judgments, but it is sufficiently contextual to permit meaningful moral judgments in deciding upon political activity in seeking change. Thus, he does not have to attach himself blindly or unreasonably to any social class or "motor" of history. His judgmental process remains rational. Although he is detached from blind adherence, a framework is established that permits a reasoned and ordered attachment to causes and thus to an avoidance of alienation.

CONCLUSIONS

In this chapter I have attempted to sketch an explanation of the objective character of knowledge concerning the good. This is related directly to the characteristics of the type of purposeful system that makes the conception of the "good" meaningful. In the absence of speculation concerning the nature of the system, few constraints are placed upon the character of what may or may not be good. Nothing in the nature of this discussion requires that goods be compatible with each other in terms of the individual person, of larger societies, or of the society of nations. There is no requirement that justice be a good.

To the extent that our knowledge of our selves and of societal possibilities is limited by the range of our experience, our beliefs about the good have a necessary historicity. However, just as knowledge in general can be self-corrective, knowledge of the good can be self-corrective. We may never advance to an ultimate state of true knowledge, any more than we can ever be sure what are the true laws of nature. But, through historical comparisons, we may rise above the particularities of immediate historical circumstance.

There are many ways in which our evaluation of other contemporary and of former societies may be limited both because of inadequacies of information and because of inadequacies of empathy. However, my earlier statement that the man of 5000 B.C. would have been incapable of understanding modern technological society is not inconsistent with the assertion that modern man is capable of recognizing the human being who participated in previous societies. We can read the Bible and the Greek plays with some genuine understanding. We can comprehend, even if we cannot fully feel, the conflict that confronted Antigone.

In the absence of non-Euclidean geometry, the Michelson-Morley experiments, and the Lorentz equations, Newton was unable to conceive of relativity theory. Yet the modern physicist can fully understand Newtonian physics. However, I do not claim that we can fully understand other societies in the same sense in which the modern physicist can fully understand Newtonian physics. The experiences that alone provide this kind of full understanding are not vicariously possible in the same sense in which the physicist can fully understand the mathematics and mechanics employed by Newton.

The materials on the basis of which the preconscious judgment can recognize "fits" is thus more essential to the understanding of social and moral differences and less accessible to knowledge than are rules that can be formally stated. This necessarily reduces to some extent the validity of our ordered comparisons in making generalizations about values under different environmental and social conditions.

Moreover, we cannot know for certain that irreversible

change has not occurred because of particular turning points in group experience. Just as some individuals may be so damaged by their experience that they can never again become "whole," it is possible that the entire community of mankind has undergone changes of a kind that, although they do not invalidate the test in principle as a praxical device, make it inapplicable even in attenuated form in practice. If this is true, we could never learn this, for we would have lost the capacity to make the comparisons according to which this judgment is possible. We would then be in the position of a brain-damaged child who would never be capable of learning mathematics.

If this seems a paradox, it is an inevitable paradox of human knowledge. Thus, at most we claim that if we have not been damaged in this respect, the test in principle will be applicable by us and our understanding of the human enterprise will grow and be enriched by the development of human experience for so long as it continues.

Chapter 3

The Just

JUSTICE AS A SUBJECT

Much of the difficulty in the discussion of justice results from a failure adequately to distinguish between the just and the good. This has a number of consequences, for it may lead to a supposition that justice is an overriding good: a conclusion that, as we shall see, is inadequate to the complexity and ambiguity of the human situation. If we are prepared to believe that there is always a just solution to problems, which people should therefore accept, the moral dilemmas that confront us are reduced to insignificance. It is the identification of "justice" with a univocal and transitive order of obligations that is the source of difficulty.

The existence of a concept—in this case, justice—does not imply an objective referent for its employment any more than the name "unicorn" implies the existence of that mythical entity. Moreover, even if justice does refer to something real that men need, it may be no more an overriding need than that for a form of transportation. It may be that societies require some rules as a foundation for socially acceptable conduct and that in our communications with each other as members of that society we are required, as Paul Kecskemeti has pointed out, to phrase our demands upon each other in these terms.[1]

If true, even this modest proposition would not be entirely without significance, for it would establish justice as at least a secondary requirement of human existence. However, in this form it need not set limits on the moral behavior of individuals, although it may set limits on the moral claims they publicly can make of each other.

Our problem, therefore, is twofold. We need to inquire into the limitations on the character of the things that can be called just and we need to inquire into the role of justice as it relates to the good.

Whether or not justice is a good, its characteristics must conform to some constraints to remain consistent with linguistic usage. Whether this usage is entirely consistent is questionable. However, even gross inconsistencies in usage would be consistent with boundaries that place certain types of usage outside its range. For instance, "to make sure that no man receives his due" would be recognized as clearly inconsistent with a standard of justice. Whether we can appropriately define what a man's "due" is, whether, for instance, it is related to need, to ability, to performance, to position in society, or to inheritance, the concept assumes a regulative principle within which the justification of particular distributions is made. The concept of giving everyone his due involves both the "due" that is to be given and the means by which the distribution is to be made. The former is substantive and the latter is procedural.

Procedures and Substance

A just procedure will not necessarily produce a just substantive result. The rules of baseball, for instance, are designed to allow the better team to win. Each team plays an equal number of games against every other team. Each game is played under standard procedures and according to a schedule that has been determined in advance by methods regarded generally as fair. Particular games, however, are sometimes determined by accident. A ball may strike a pebble and produce a winning run. A pitcher may have so much marital trouble on a particular day that he pitches below his form. Rains may cause so many games to be postponed in particular areas that particular teams have trouble with their pitching rotation.

The assumption is that these accidental circumstances will cancel each other out, but we know that this is often not the case. In some years, sportswriters might agree that the team that won the pennant was not the best team. Substantive justice, therefore, would call for replacing the pennant winner with the best team. Procedural justice demands that we abide by the consequences of fair procedures. The procedures determine an "objective" verdict, whereas evaluations of team excellence are subject to possible biases among sportswriters. Thus, we usually stay with the procedurally determined results. If the procedures consistently produce results judged to be unjust, we change the procedures rather than the particular results. Yet, on occasion, a procedural result may be so substantively unjust that we ignore the procedure. We may argue about particular illustrations of this fact—as in the cases during the Great Depression of the 1930s when farm foreclosures according to law were frustrated by popular action (more illustrations will be given later in this chapter and in chapter 4)—but each of us will be able to find some limiting case where achieving a substantive good appears justified to us even at the price of damage to procedures. (Revolution is always a case in point, for it occurs only when some prefer the substantive result to the sanctity of due process.)

Problems of Restriction

Usage permits inconsistent determination of both procedural and substantive justice; and it includes the standard
of Thrasymachus in *The Republic,* according to which justice
is the interest of the stronger. To rule out justice as inconsistent with the argument of Thrasymachus by definition, as
Rawls does, is illegitimate. That decision requires a standard
or criterion for values. The dialogue of *The Republic* is not
merely definitional; it examines the implications of usage and
compares rules and substantive results within a field. In this
sense, it treats the subject of justice as Quine's concept of
scientific pragmatism treats the subject of science.

In investigating the subject of justice several lines of
inquiry are suggested. Is there a procedure for choosing from
among competing principles of substantive or procedural
justice? Are there procedures for identifying correct conduct
in cases of conflict between procedural and substantive rules
of justice? To what extent are choices among alternative
procedures dependent upon a conception of the good? And
to what extent is justice a good?

RAWLS'S NON-ONTOLOGICAL THEORY

The most ambitious contemporary effort to develop a
comprehensive and well-ordered theory of justice, without
major resort to a conception of the good, is that by John
Rawls in *A Theory of Justice.* Rawls states that his aim is to
present a conception of justice that "generalizes and carries
to a higher level of abstraction the familiar theory of the
social contract as found . . . in Locke, Rousseau, and Kant."[2]

The problem that leads Rawls to his proposed solution
likely stems both from a belief that values are not objective
and from the inadequacy of deriving a theory of obligation
from a moral or ethical framework that merely represents the

custom of a community, as in Toulmin's position. Moreover, the utilitarian arguments that Toulmin grafts onto his theory, as we have seen, are recognized by Rawls as unsatisfactory. Although in the absence of a prior moral or legal system there would seem to be no reason for a contract to be morally or legally binding, Rawls attempts to show that, properly understood, obligation does occur. In part, this conclusion is produced by an implicit definition of morality—that one cannot demand from others what one would not accept in their place. In this sense, the conclusion is in part begged by the definition, for unless morality is a good or men are moral, the argument would not follow. Indeed, because Rawls's arguments for his rules are instrumental rather than primarily moral, the difficulty might seem to be even greater, as I believe it is. However, his theory of justice is an extremely sophisticated effort to avoid this difficulty.

Although the analysis that follows will reveal the defects of Rawls's treatment of justice in their specific and particular aspects, the reader should keep in mind our earlier general conclusion: any attempt to state a unique set of principles or rules that would actually apply to different types of homeostatic systems would be vacuous for the reaons given in chapter 1. Rawls's ethical prescriptions do have restricted content. However, as we shall see, he has selected them illegitimately from a set that also contains their contradictories. In any event, they are irrelevant. The reader will see that there are several reasons for this. Rawls's heuristic analysis is so vague that major differences between competing models are blurred. In game theory, for instance, there is no general solution for the non-zero-sum game; and, to the extent that any game models serve as useful metaphors for ethical choice, every real society provides important instances of alternative appropriate models for which different types of solutions are appropriate.

Furthermore, the conclusions we derive from a model—indeed its capacity to serve as a metaphor—depend to a considerable extent on the numbers in the payoff boxes and on other assumptions concerning information, communication, and so forth. In more practical and relevant terms, moral "goods" and moral rules are judged on the basis of other aspects of our knowledge concerning man, society, and nature. The discussions of praxis, judgment, and realms of knowledge in chapters 1 and 2 and in appendix 2 apply specifically here. Moral decisions can be derived neither from catalogs or hierarchies of good things nor from sets of moral rules considered independently. We shall see in particular in this chapter how this complex "balance"—rather than a mere application of moral rules within the context of social science knowledge—is essential to moral conclusions.

The prior arguments in principle rule out Rawls's derivation of general rules. The extensive discussion of the defects of Rawls's methodology that follows has several additional purposes. It demonstrates that the prior general principles really do exclude Rawls's general solution and that no ingenious alteration of his argument will permit the derivation of any rules as universally applicable. The detailed critique reveals the intimate dependence of moral principles upon factual assumptions and frameworks of choice. Furthermore, by showing that crucial variations in the former are produced by variations in the latter, I demonstrate that no single set of rules can possibly apply regardless of differences in social and environmental settings—even apart from the ambiguities involved in such terms as freedom and possible conflicts among different kinds of freedoms. Finally, I shall show how the test in principle does permit the choice of different moral principles in different settings and of preferences among settings and that this knowledge is based upon comparative social knowledge (rather than a veil of ignorance) and analysis of the systemic (transfinite stability) character of man and of his dispositional behavior. Thus the possibility of discovering an optimal set of rules for an optimal social setting as proposed in earlier books of mine is reaffirmed—but by a methodology fundamentally different from that of Rawls. The earlier discussions of praxis and appendix 3 show why such an optimal set could not be strictly hierarchical.

The Hypothetical Contract

Rawls's version of the contract doctrine is not based upon a belief that such a contract ever was made. It assumes instead a hypothetical contract that governs the principles of justice for the basic structure of society and that would be entered into by "free and rational persons concerned to further their own interests" and making their decisions from an original state of equality. Rawls understands this purely hypothetical contract to be characterized by certain essential conditions that constitute this original state of equality, among which are that no one knows his place in society, his class position or social status, his fortune in the distribution of natural assets and abilities, his intelligence, strength, and the like. Rawls assumes also that the parties "do not know their conceptions of the good or their special psychological propensities."[3] (We shall soon see that no conclusions at all can be derived on the basis of Rawls's assumptions unless some additional assumptions are made, including one about a propensity toward risk.)

The Veil of Ignorance

The principles of justice are "chosen behind a veil of ignorance." For this reason, according to Rawls, no one is at an advantage or disadvantage in deciding upon principles as a result of natural chance or the contingency of his particular circumstances. All are similarly situated and no one is able to design principles to favor his particular conditions. Perfect symmetry exists with respect to the relations of everyone to each other person. In this sense, he says that the initial situation is "fair between individuals as moral persons, that is, as rational beings with their own ends and capable of a sense of justice." Although Rawls agrees that justice is not fairness, justice requires fairness; and the initial situation, according to Rawls, is therefore fair.

In addition to personal ignorance, the veil of ignorance assumes that those who choose do not know the particular circumstances of their own society, its economic or political situation, or the level of civilization and culture it has been able to achieve.[4] Nor do they have any information about which generation they belong to. These restrictions, Rawls says, are necessary because questions of social justice arise "between generations as well as within them, for example, the question of the appropriate rate of capital saving and of the conservation of natural resources."

Another feature of fairness[5] is that the parties are rational and mutually disinterested. This does not imply that they are egoists, according to Rawls, or that they are interested only in wealth, prestige, and domination, but rather that they do not take "an interest in one another's interests." They presume that their spiritual aims may be opposed. Rationality is defined by Rawls in the narrow sense of economic theory, that is, of taking "the most effective means to a given end." It is important, he says, to avoid introducing any controversial ethical elements into a theory of justice.

The Principles of Justice in Rawls

Rawls articulates two principles of justice as the core of his system. "First: each person is to have an equal right to the most extensive basic liberty compatible with a similar liberty for others. Second: social and economic inequalities are to be arranged so that they are both (a) reasonably expected to be to everyone's advantage, and (b) attached to positions and offices open to all."[6] The ambiguities in these formulations are later given greater refinement by Rawls. The basic liberties include political liberty together with freedom of speech and assembly, liberty of conscience and of thought, freedom of the person with a right to personal property, and other elements defined by the rule of law. The second principle applies to the distribution of income and wealth and the organization of the institutions of authority. Values are to be equally distributed except where inequality is to everyone's advantage.

However, the formulation of the rules excludes giving up liberty for economic advantage.[7] Offices and careers must be open to everyone. Although it might be possible to improve everyone's situation by certain restrictions of access, this is forbidden on principle. "It expresses the condition that if some places were not open on a fair basis to all, those kept out would be right in feeling unjustly treated"[8] even though they benefited from the greater productivity of those who were allowed to hold them.

The "difference principle" allows the preference ordering of the least favored person in the community to be given substantial consideration. In general this principle "holds that in order to treat all persons equally, to provide genuine equality of opportunity, society must give more attention to those with fewer native assets and to those born to less favorable social positions."[9] Nonetheless, according to Rawls, the difference principle is not an overriding principle. It is to be weighed against the principle to improve the average standard of life or to advance the common good. Thus it does not require society to "even out handicaps, but only to allocate resources so as to improve the long-term expectation of the least favored."

The general conception of justice as fairness states that an unequal division of primary social goods should occur only if an unequal division would be to everyone's advantage. There are no restrictions on exchanges of goods other than that which restricts the exchange of liberty for economic advantage. Particular liberties are to be restricted only in the long-term service of liberty, according to Rawls. Slavery, for instance, can be justified only in preference to the killing of prisoners.

In the latter portions of his book, Rawls states that the greater the extent to which the material problems of society are solved, the less relevant it would become to trade off particular liberties for economic or other advantages. [10] However, Rawls is no longer talking about the basis of the original position and thus it would not be fair to tax him with taking specific social conditions into account.

Rawls does not claim that his arguments are derived with logical precision. He recognizes that the chain of argument is incomplete. However, he clearly regards it as compelling, as more than plausible. Therefore it is important to inspect the character of the reasoning leading to the two principles of justice to see whether it possesses even that limited rigor that Rawls claims for it.

JUSTIFICATION OF RULES

Critique of Derivation

Rawls's derivation of his rules for justice depends upon his assumption of a veil of ignorance—a device he generalizes from game and bargaining theories. [11] In bargaining theories in which one's "accidental" position on an axis provides an outcome favorable to him, a rule for determining where the bargain should occur is called fair if an arbitrator regards it as the rule that each player would prefer if he did not know in advance on which axis of the matrix he would be placed. One metaphor for this is the pie-cutting example in which the person who cuts the pie must accept the piece left by the other person. Thus Rawls's heuristic devices and his emphasis on fairness owe much to the most recent work in the areas of game and bargaining theory. Correspondingly, much of the acclaim his work has received stems from his apparent integration of ethical theory with game and bargaining theory; for the bargaining theorists who have done most to develop the concept of fairness have been careful to distinguish it from ethical theory.

Rawls's use of game and bargaining metaphors has one additional virtue. Theories in these areas reach the present limit of rigor with respect to the generation of solutions. However, game theory is incompatible with Rawls's endeavor, for, analogous with the principle that no general theory applies to all kinds of systems, different types of game models apply to different types of game situations.

Moreover, no general solution exists for the non-zero-sum game. No universal criterion of rationality applies generally. The character of a matrix is ultimately dependent on the preferences expressed by the utile numbers in the payoff boxes. And no social system can be adequately represented by a zero-sum game. These facts should have suggested insuperable difficulties for Rawls's mode of endeavor. I shall demonstrate that this is so even with respect to its application to an individual social system, let alone to society generally.

It can be seen from the foregoing that Rawls attempts to develop a formal theory of justice that is not dependent upon differences in social systems. Let us examine, however, an easier case for the successful application of Rawls's methodology: a society so simple that a single game or bargaining model would constitute a genuinely formal analog for it. Would it be possible to derive a univocal and transitive set of moral rules for that society independently of other factual variations?[12] If this is not possible, the method fails *a fortiori.*

I shall now show in detail that Rawls's assumptions and

procedures cannot perform this function and that they are consistent with contradictory moral or ethical rules. To do this I shall first show how Rawls attempts to derive his rules heuristically. Rawls advises us to consider his "two principles [of justice] as the maximin solution for the problem of social justice." This analogy rests on the fact that the two principles are those a person "would choose for the design of a society in which his enemy is to assign him his place." According to the maximin rule alternatives are ranked by the worst possible outcomes. One chooses the alternative that guarantees the least bad of the worst outcomes for any course. Consider figure 1, the matrix Rawls provides.[13] Rawls points out that d_3 is the maximin (or minimax) solution because it guarantees that 5 is the worst that can happen to one, whereas the worst possible outcome for d_1 or d_2 is even worse. Although the diagram used by Rawls seems to imply a game against nature, minimax is justified as a sole, but not indubitable, criterion for choice by the attempt to find a rule for action in a zero-sum context in which one's opponents have completely opposed interests and are completely and perfectly informed and rational. Now, no social situation is ever fully zero-sum (even poker is doubtfully zero-sum in terms of utiles) and the other assumptions are counterfactual. Although there is nothing wrong with an appropriately chosen

Circumstances

		c_1	c_2	c_3
Decisions	d_1	– 7	8	12
	d_2	– 8	7	14
	d_3	5	6	8

Figure 1

counterfactual example, no reasons are offered to justify the particular example. However, let us overlook this difficulty for the moment and treat the example seriously. We may learn something from examining it, for minimax is one of a number of alternative principles that may be used in games against nature.

For the purpose of examination, let us change the numbers in box d_2/c_3 somewhat, as in figure 2. The minimax solution would still call for d_3, although the reader might begin to entertain doubts about the principle, and these likely would increase with the size of the utile number in that particular payoff box. Let us therefore consider an alternative principle.

The minimax regret principle states that a player should consider what his payoff should be for any row strategy compared with his payoff if he had correctly guessed nature's strategy. For instance, if one knows that nature will choose c_3, then d_2 is clearly called for. Thus, if he chooses d_3, and nature is in c_3 position, he loses 6 utile points in the matrix used by Rawls and 22 in the matrix in figure 2. The minimax regret matrix derived from figure 2 is presented as figure 3; the minimax regret matrix for Rawls's diagram (figure 1) is presented in figure 4; both are on the following page.

In figure 3, one chooses d_2 because it guarantees -13 as the least bad of the worse outcomes. In figure 4, one chooses

Circumstances

		c_1	c_2	c_3
	d_1	-7	8	12
Decisions	d_2	-8	7	30
	d_3	5	6	8

Figure 2

d_1 for the same reason. A third alternative is to use the Laplace principle and consider the states of nature equiprobable. One then chooses the strategy with the highest expected value. A fourth principle would depend on Bayesian subjective utilities. Whether one would prefer minimax, minimax regret, or a Bayesian solution depends upon personality and perhaps life conditions. Styles with respect to such principles of choice change from age to age. The Renaissance produced many personalities who believed in Fortuna. Most of these would have chosen minimax regret. Thus, leaving psychological propensities out of account makes it impossible to derive a rule, although Rawls has implicitly assumed a conservative psychology.

Circumstances

	c_1	c_2	c_3
d_1	-12	0	-18
d_2	-13	-1	0
d_3	0	-2	-22

Decisions

Figure 3

Circumstances

	c_1	c_2	c_3
d_1	-12	0	-2
d_2	-13	-1	0
d_3	0	-2	-6

Decisions

Figure 4

We need not examine in detail the fact that different game
or bargaining models generate different solution sets. Let us,
however, choose the heuristic device employed by Rawls that
provides the strongest argument for the necessity of moral
rules in society, the prisoners' dilemma.[14] The prisoners'
dilemma is a well-known case in which individual rationality
produces collective irrationality. Consider figure 5, in which
each player must make his choice without knowledge of the
other player's choice. Because of the dominance of the T
strategies—and dominance is the strongest criterion of rationality known to decision theory—a jointly undesirable outcome is achieved. If the players could be presented with a
choice between mutual use of the NT strategies or mutual use
of the T strategies, they would clearly prefer the former. In
this case, if the players were offered in addition the freedom
to follow T or NT independently, it would look unattractive
to them. Neither would expect the other player to mistake
his interest in so clear an example (unless he had very
convincing contextual information to the contrary). Moreover, the potential gain from one's own choice of T is large.
Therefore, it is rational to follow the T strategy because this
decision cannot affect the other player's independent
choice.[15] Consequently, the players would reject what
appears to be an expansion of their choices.

	T	NT
T	1,1	10,0
NT	0,10	9,9

Figure 5

The choice between promising mutually to follow T or NT in figure 5 is counterfactual and not compelling morally. However, the players might wish that they were able to bind themselves to the NT strategies; that is, they might wish they were part of a moral or, alternatively, a disciplined community. But in the restricted example, this wish is worthless for the reasons Harsanyi has shown (see note 15), and therefore they prefer the T strategies.

Rawls also ignores the fact that the particular figures in the matrix of the prisoners' dilemma were chosen to emphasize a situation in which individual rationality produces an extremely undesirable joint outcome. Other numbers can be placed in the boxes without changing the case from that of a prisoners' dilemma. In figure 6 the players may not prefer the cooperative solution.

Consider figure 6. Each might now prefer a third alternative in which the intelligent, wise, or sensitive (the reader should choose his own adjective) will rely upon sentiment, lack of intelligence, or lack of discrimination in others. In short, in a society characterized by such a matrix, some might be opposed in principle to moral rules, although not necessarily opposed to others' believing in them. Even in the pie-cutting case, where it might seem obvious that no one would choose any rule other than equal division, one might

	T	NT
T	5,5	9,3
NT	3,9	6,6

Figure 6

prefer otherwise if he thought that by cleverness he might convince the other player that the smaller piece was more desirable. We cannot determine a rule in the absence both of a specific determination of the type of decision matrix and of the specific numbers in the payoff boxes.

To treat the cooperative solution like a moral rule is somewhat like a situation in which a man is asked to choose between ham and beef and then expected to ignore chicken, even though he prefers it to either, because he chose beef over ham. Decision theorists have long taught us to ignore irrelevant alternatives; now Rawls instructs us to ignore relevant alternatives.

General Reasons for Failure of Rawl's Methodology

In the first place, no general game model exists. Even John von Neumann was unable to find a general solution for non-zero-sum situations. Alternative models are available that more or less resemble different real-world situations. The early enthusiasm with respect to the application of game models to the world (even poker, which as a zero-sum game has a general and precise solution in principle, is zero-sum only on the often counterfactual assumption that dollars are linear with utiles) has faded for these reasons and because of the difficulty of establishing the appropriateness of particular models.

Moreover, the criteria for rationality that are used in game theory cannot be divorced from the context of use. Dominance is the strongest known criterion. Minimax applies to zero-sum games only; and, although a very strong criterion, it is not as unassailable as dominance. Weaker solutions exist for other types of games. It is doubtful that rationality can be given a sufficiently restrictive meaning for there to be a rational solution—regardless of the strength of the criteria—for all choice models.

Solutions for bargaining games are sometimes called "fair" rather than rational because they are presumed to coincide with what an arbiter—or a player who did not know his position on the axis—would choose under certain specific game and utility assumptions. To the extent that such a distinction permits an arbiter to distinguish between "fair" and "unfair" rules, that result is obtained because of the detailed specification of the bargaining model. Moreover, the meaning of "fairness"—like the meaning of rationality—is confined to the stipulated type of case and with respect to the stipulated contextual conditions. Whether similar rules apply to symmetric and asymmetric bargaining games is subject to dispute. However, even if we took the strictly minority position that a Nash-type solution would provide a unique solution for the asymmetric game—a position I believe to be wrong[16]—not every decision context is properly represented by a bargaining game. The various game models have individual solutions, some strong and some quite weak and subject to dispute.[17] Thus the mathematicians can speak of solutions only with respect to particular types of conflict situations (our analogy would be social systems).

These models do abstract from particular contexts. They can be, and have been, abstracted from preknowledge of role [axis] positions. However, as we have shown, whether or not one likes the solution rule is not independent of the numbers in the payoff boxes and of assumptions concerning the rationality of the other players. If one does not like the implications of a solution rule for a particular model, given the numbers in the payoff boxes, and if he believes his "opponent" is likely to find the solution rule, he may exercise his capacity to change the real world to make it resemble this model less.[18] Models cannot be used to generate rule preferences that are independent of context. Hence, their attempted use in this manner, even if only heuristic, is fallacious, even apart from the fact that alternative models are available.

Minimax and Ethics. The situation is even worse from the standpoint of the core of Rawls's argument. Even if we grant him the minimax rule, it carries with it the implication of a conservative or fearful mentality in a framework of ignorance. This is quite different from a conception of fairness, let alone of justice. The rule is fair only in the limited sense that conservative or fearful persons in a state of ignorance would choose it. They would not likely choose to be in such a state of ignorance and much of our effort in actual life is designed to avoid being forced to choose in a state of ignorance. Thus, as we shall see, few would regard their choices within a veil of ignorance as compelling moral reasons for a moral rule of choice in more favorable circumstances.

The Role of the Factual. We have seen that even at the abstract level of analysis that characterizes game and bargaining theory we require more specificity concerning matrix structure, game conditions, and payoff numbers than Rawls provides. In the absence of that much specificity, Rawls's assumptions do not exclude contradictory moral prescriptions although his incompleteness of analysis obscures this fact. Let us now examine the role of the more concretely factual, for this examination will enrich my critique of the irrelevance of Rawls's rules for some actual and possible social systems and of its inability to represent the actual character of moral decisions.

Let us turn from game matrices to more concrete or qualitative considerations to make this clear. Some people would be willing to run the risk that someone else might become a member of an aristocracy if personal fortune and circumstance did not favor them in order to retain the opportunity to become a member of an aristocracy if good fortune provided them with this opportunity. It may be the case, although it is not clear that it is so in every society, that most people are fearful and conservative, in which case most would prefer minimax to minimax regret. Clearly, however, one principle is as neutral as the other and the advocate of either has no moral claim against an advocate of the other.

If one believes in natural excellence, then one might believe the excellent should rule and that those who are inferior should consent to be ruled. Many more people might accept this argument than Rawls imagines. Freedom may be a good (and, in any event, according to Rawls we cannot know what the good is behind the veil), but it is not desired by all. It is a heavy burden to some and some regard democracy as a poor form of government.

It is far from clear how much political or economic opportunity people really do desire. We have much information concerning the extent to which individuals refuse promotion in industry. Responsibility frightens many people. There is reason to believe that contemporary social and economic mobility produce great personal unhappiness that would not freely be chosen by many.

When people were locked into rigid social structures, bound by fixed class distinctions, they had an excuse for their inferior positions. That was the way society or nature ordained it. When they have freedom, their failure becomes a personal failure. Thus, apart from the fact that those preferring high risks may opt for a chance at dictatorship or aristocracy, those who prefer low risks in a state of ignorance might opt for social and political systems that restrict opportunity. We are not talking about the verbal formulations contemporary Americans are taught in school and that they repeat as if by rote. We are more concerned here with the actual pattern of their behavior. For these reasons, the characteristics that Rawls wishes to exclude in arriving at ethical judgments may be far more relevant than he believes. Let us now examine some of these cases.

Intelligence and the Original State.   In the original position, Rawls assumes enough intelligence to carry through the reasoning that is needed to understand his theory of justice.

He then assumes, however, that the rules to be developed apply only to human beings, for only human beings can engage in moral activity. He does recognize, although he does not discuss, obligations toward animals; but he states that these are of a different order.

Insofar as moral activity involves self-reflexively thoughtful mutual engagements, Rawls is correct by definition. However, in this case his recognition of obligations toward animals is left hanging in midair, for their source cannot lie in the contractual obligations he assumes in the original state.

Rawls again has been arbitrary in the assumptions he makes, except in the sense that they serve the conclusions he desires to reach. One could as easily assume reasoning creatures in the original state who could not know whether or not they would be reborn with intelligence. In principle they could be reborn either as morons or as animals, if we are to take the original state seriously.

If we accept the latter thesis, the obligations toward animals or morons might be either more or less extensive than Rawls assumes. If people feared they might be reborn as morons or animals, some might wish for circumstances of extreme obligation to protect them from arbitrary adversity. Others, who operated either on minimax regret or the risk principle, might be quite willing to run the risk of extremely poor treatment.

Accidents and the Original State.   Rawls regards beauty, strength, and intelligence as accidents of birth and therefore as improper grounds for human advantage. As one did not acquire these assets by his own efforts, he has no right to exploit them. This seems a rather one-sided view. Many intelligent people do not use their intelligence and it is not clear that intelligence and strength have much worth in the absence of use, although they cannot be used if not potential in the person. Thus, it might be argued by some that their utilization of their capacities justifies their success.

Moreover, although it is an accident in one sense that we are men rather than animals, it is not an accident in another sense, for we could be no other than the product of the sperm cell and ovum that produced us. But this is true regardless of whether the comparison is made with another individual or with an animal.

Moreover, Rawls argues later in his book that our obligations toward our family are stronger than toward others. He does not regard them as possibly less strong under some circumstances; but this is by fiat. He has not examined cases. Should a mother turn in to the police a child who has engaged in theft? We do not expect this of a mother but we do expect this of strangers. Yet "son of" is an accident in terms of being human; and, indeed, it can be so regarded in hypothetical discourse: the children of the guardians in *The Republic*. What is accidental depends on a prior choice of a frame of reference, that is, of identification. This is factual, not logical.

Rawls is familiar with the breakdown of the Kantian ethic. He no doubt is aware of the reasons that led the neo-Kantian Stammler [19] to develop his theory of concentric circles of obligation. It is, of course, legitimate to adjust theories to account for facts—but not in that case where the adjustment is antithetical to the character of the theory, as it is in this case. The veil is lifted, and those adjustments made that accord with our contemporary ethic. But the reference to the development of moral ties within the family does not really function within a theory that employs a veil of ignorance and that eschews "accidental" qualities. Moreover, if this concession is made, we have no grounds for excluding any other type of contextual discrimination that determines the framework of identification, for example, genus, sex, age, reproductive condition or proclivity, and so forth. In any event, to eliminate from moral consideration those characteristics Rawls calls "accidental" is to eliminate what makes us particular individuals and establishes our sense of identity.

Rawls's theory fails to cope with the factual problem of the "identification" of men with other men, with institutions, or with aspects of nature that establishes part of the frame of reference within which moral rules apply.

Problems with the Difference Principle. Rawls argues that inequalities are justified if they improve the condition of the worst off. I doubt that he would claim great originality for this idea, although most actual claims are for a redistribution of wealth. Rawls's originality lies in wedding his rule to the principle of Pareto Optimality,[20] thus providing it with scientific credibility. The point of Pareto Optimality is that in a convex bargaining space any bargain within the space can be improved for one of the players without worsening it for the others by choosing an appropriate path to the Pareto Optimal line bounding the space. What Rawls has failed to note is that some contests may be over where on the line—a line so broad that it includes one of the bargainers' getting everything and the other nothing—the bargain should take place. He has also failed to note that the model applies primarily to situations that are quite simple. His examples indicate that he believes incorrectly that dollars are linear with utiles and representative for all important outcomes.

In the real world, choices in complex situations often—indeed almost invariably—involve damage to some men. Most major, and much minor, legislation involves a redistribution, and not merely in terms of dollars. Fair employment practices produce rules that change the distribution of job opportunities. Tax law changes always have a damaging impact upon some businesses and they have consequent damaging impacts upon careers and self-images that can never, in actual practice, be fully compensated for, if at all. The loss of freedom in the sense of political self-determination may seem a small price to impoverished peasants and yet in some cases it may be possible to bring them to a reasonable minimal level of subsistance only by damaging the freedom of others.

We fall into all the difficulties of utilitarian theories if we look at Rawls's rule closely. If we accept redistribution as inevitable, how great a tax can be imposed on the better off to provide how small an improvement for how many of the worst off? If we assume counterfactually that we can avoid all deprivations, Rawls might on some assumptions be in difficulty. How great an improvement—or, more important, what kind of improvement—can be foreclosed to the better off to achieve how small an improvement for how many of the worse off? Even if we restrict our consideration to monetary income—the most favorable consideration for Rawls—it seems obvious that for a sufficiently small worsening of position for the worst off (e.g., five cents a year), most would be unwilling to foreclose some sufficiently great improvement to the better off (e.g., $5,000 a year), although egalitarians might argue this latter point, particularly if we specified "noticeable differences." Rawls, however, is not a simple egalitarian. And what is noticeable to one person may not be to another.

Problems with Rawls's Argument for Tolerance.   Rawls argues for religious tolerance on the ground that no one can know in advance whether his religion will succeed or not. Thus, from the veil of ignorance he can protect his religious position only by recognizing the right of each person equally "to decide what his religious obligations are." No one can "give this right up to another person or institutional authority."[21]

This passage demonstrates only that Rawls does not take religion seriously. Even if we accept the somewhat academic argument that individuals do not know what their religion is behind the veil of ignorance, if they have a conception of religion implying exclusivity and great faith, they might think it of supreme importance that the true religion, whichever one it is, have an opportunity to establish itself as the religion of the state. Thus, it is quite conceivable that one could opt for a position of intolerance from behind the veil of ignorance.

However, the position taken by Rawls is even weaker than this. Suppose for the moment we grant him the veil of ignorance and make it so thick that those who choose the principles of justice have no conception of what a religious person means when he asserts that there is one true religion. Conceivably we would now be able to establish the rule of tolerance with respect to religion from behind the veil of ignorance.

However, if we remove the veil, suppose that the individuals belonging to a particular church now discover an opportunity to impose it as a state religion and really believe that this desire is a manifestation of God's will. One now argues to them that they must recognize this position as unjust because they would have opted for toleration behind a veil of ignorance that excluded knowledge of "true" religion. In my opinion, "unconvincing" would be far too mild an expression to apply to their view of this argument concerning justice. What they would regard as unjust would be the convention by means of which they were hypothetically forced to choose behind a veil of ignorance without access to knowledge concerning the truth of religion.

There are other grounds also to reject Rawls's conclusion. To those who fear confusion and disorder or excessive individualism the loss of the liberty of conscience might be a small price to pay. So liberty of conscience is not the only principle that can be acknowledged in the original position. Of course, Rawls may argue that if loss of liberty is a good, he has stipulated that this good also cannot be known behind a veil of ignorance and that representative men can will only their freedom to pursue any goal they wish in the real world. However, if this is what he means, it hardly seems an effective argument for not giving liberty up. Indeed, if men have no knowledge of what is good, they have no basis on which to choose any rules prior to becoming aware of real-world conditions; and this defeats the argument for the veil of ignorance. If they know at least what their preferences may be, then these may include loss of freedom. And, as we shall see, if they do not know into which society they may be born, they can hardly know what they might prefer.

Problems with the Argument against Secondary Prudence. Rawls contends that, although his rules do not require self-sacrifice, they do override the demands of law and custom and of social rules generally. They also override considerations of prudence and self-interest, for in drawing up the conception of right the parties have already taken their interests into account. Personal prudence, Rawls says, thus has been given its appropriate weight in the final scheme and cannot be taken into account again in actual circumstances. Would this argument convince anyone who accepted one or more of my earlier arguments? I think not. Again, the argument would be that no reasonable person would have made these arrangements if he had properly taken the uncertainties into account.

It is interesting to note in this respect that personal service contracts in American industry almost invariably are renegotiated when they become highly disadvantageous. This results partly from the fact that the respective bargaining strengths of the parties have changed—an element related to force—and partly from the increased popularity of performers—an element related to chance. Rawls might regard this as unjust; and it is in his terms. But this practice may reflect the reasonable point of view that such elements are related to existential justice and that no one should be required to make too great a sacrifice in terms of the expectations not of representative, but of historical, men.

In this respect, another provision of law seems apt. Contracts are not binding on underage individuals without the approval of a court. This has less to do with reasoning ability—for in terms of abstract reasoning many young people are much better equipped than are their elders—than with their lack of experience, that is, of an ability to relate choice to existential contingency, or of an effective knowledge of risk or self-management. This reinforces the earlier argument that the only relevant choice in a state of ignorance would be the choice of freedom to choose an appropriate rule once we become aware of real world conditions. This, however, makes the choice behind the veil of ignorance worthless.

Practical Reasons for Accepting the Rules. Rawls is aware that some reasons of secondary prudence argue against his rules. He regards secondary prudence as illegitimate. I have shown that it is not. He argues that secondary prudence often reinforces his two rules. I shall show that this is unlikely.

Rawls contends, for instance, that one might favor a high-risk situation for oneself but not for one's kin.[22] However, the argument does not hold; otherwise no circus stuntman would ever train his son to be a stuntman. Rawls's case is based on something short of the general principles of psychology.

Rawls also provides a practical argument for keeping the rules: those whose liberty is worth less because they achieve less would not likely do better if a different system were followed.[23] This does not follow at all. They have proof that they do poorly in this society. They might do better in others (and, at least, many would suffer less envy). Werner Sombart noted the success of soldiers in the age of chivalry and the success of merchants in the nineteenth century. It is well known that certain types do better in different types of society. Rawls is again far too abstract.

Alternative Rules Compatible with the Veil. The rules proposed by Rawls may be generated behind a veil of ignorance on grounds antithetical to those he chose and opposed on the grounds he uses. Nothing in his framework of argument makes one result more germane than the other.

Consider a world in which behind a veil of ignorance, except for general principles of social science establishing the superiority of aristocracy, individuals decide on the question of just rules. Now consider the case of fearful individuals who are aware that they cannot know whether they will be intelligent or unintelligent, among the leaders or the led. And they are fearful of the personal deprivations that will be entailed if they are among the led. Therefore, out of fear, they argue for the two general principles that Rawls proposes despite the empirical evidence that this will be to the general disadvantage of society. This is primary prudence, which Rawls does allow.

Conversely, under Rawls's assumptions, many might regard his rules as desirable for the able but as dangerous for those who are inferior—that they will provide economic opportunity at the expense of proof that one is inferior if one fails to succeed under conditions of equal opportunity. Hence, as they cannot know in advance whether or not they will have ability, they prefer certainty of status and opt for aristocracy under the minimax principle. Here we have reversed the entire line of argument and there is still no means of making a choice.

The Reflective Equilibrium.   The major device in Rawls that might relieve the prior difficulty, if it were developed in a manner similar to the iterative test in principle, lies in his conception of a reflective equilibrium in which there is a mutual adjustment of principles and considered judgments. However, Rawls's sketchy account of the reflective equilibrium rules that possibility out, for it is consistent with his concern for a fully general set of rules.

According to Rawls, one can start with a set of weak conditions and see whether they will "yield a significant set of principles." If not, one looks for other conditions that are reasonable and that match "our considered convictions of justice." But, he argues, if there are discrepancies, we can either change the account of the initial situation or revise our conclusions.[24] He assumes that eventually it will be possible to produce an account of the initial situation "that both expresses reasonable conditions and yields principles which match our considered judgments duly pruned and adjusted."

Yet except for a few heuristic game models, some simple assumptions concerning self-respect, and an account of the economic market in modern capitalism, Rawls does not even relate social science to the derivation of his principles, let alone show us how to adjust the principles to other assumptions. We have already seen that social science consists of different disciplines and that their conclusions, except at a truistic level, do not produce generalizations that are universally applicable. Rawls assumes that he does not face this problem. Yet in a book of more than five hundred pages, he does not provide a clue as to what the adjustment of principles means.

In short, the principle of reflective equilibrium makes a modest concession to the obvious objection that empirical propositions are not certain. It does not function within his analysis. Thus, even with his concession to a "reflective equilibrium," Rawls's system remains neo-Kantian in the sense that the rules, finally discovered, are independent of context and applied to all social systems.

Rawls does make minor modifications of his conclusions at various points by removing aspects of the veil of ignorance, as in deciding that some restrictions on liberty may be countenanced where economic scarcity exists. These, however, function in an ad hoc fashion in his system. They are employed to cope with well-known difficulties, for instance, the fact that modern constitutional democracy would not have worked in ancient societies. This is not a new observation (Hegel referred to property as a prerequisite for liberty), although it is far from clear that economic deprivations alone account for non-democratic choices either in older or in more contemporary societies. Although the veil of ignorance is conveniently lifted for a small number of inconvenient but well-known complications, from the standpoint of principle we cannot know when and for what purpose to lift the veil. The contextual richness within which freedom, love, and other important values acquire important meanings is not part of Rawls's system of analysis.

The possibility that values may fit into systematic patterns—that the meaning of various elements of the pattern cannot be comprehended in the absence of knowledge of the relationships—is foreign to the analysis. His ad hoc method of occasionally lifting the veil of ignorance could never lead to a comprehension, for instance, of the meaning of Bushido to a Japanese warrior. Form has triumphed over substance and it has done so in a manner that desiccates each.

A Reconsideration of the Critique.   Perhaps, the reader may feel, I have imposed false alternatives upon Rawls. Surely, Rawls is aware that no rule can be derived by a representative man from introspection of his own psychology if he is not allowed some psychological propensity. Rawls fails to note this point specifically only because it is so obvious. What Rawls really is saying is that the representative man derives a rule for decisions from knowledge of the motivation of real people according to the general principles of psychology, but without consideration of any "special" respect in which he may differ from the norm. Moreover, Rawls does use the qualifier "special" when specifying ignorance of psychological propensities. Unfortunately, this does not remove any of the problems we have discussed and it introduces new, and even more difficult, problems.

We must first ask how we determine the psychological propensity of a representative man. Rawls tells us that we cannot know into which society we will be born: whether as a Hun during Attila's reign or as a burgher in late-nineteenth-century Amsterdam or as a member of some future society of which we know nothing. How can we generate anything from this?

Let us stretch a point, however, and assume that we can determine what a normal or representative man is. Why should the representative man behind a veil of ignorance choose Rawls's rules? To do so, he must have a preference for the majority or a fear that he will be in the minority. And, if so, and if he decides minimax is the rule, we are in effect telling Attila that he is unjust because if he had chosen behind a veil of ignorance and if he had decided that representative men were fearful or conservative and if he had decided to choose on the basis of "representative" or "normal" preferences, he would have decided not to become Attila, although in his society Attila is the norm and he is Attila. We could reverse the argument for the burgher of Amsterdam. Thus, the choice is based either on fear or on conservatism, which hardly seems morally compelling; or it is based on probability grounds, again a morally unconvincing reason, or on a preference for the majority, a choice we will soon examine.

Should we tell Attila or the burgher that he fails to understand his moral obligations and that he should opt from the standpoint of all men, past, present, and future? How can we make such a concept meaningful?

Let us assume that we have some way of measuring the concept "all men." Even granting this impossible phrase, what is representative? Would there be a "modal" man? On the basis of what kind of statistical theory, system of classifications, and so forth, would that judgment be made? And even if we assume counterfactually that we can overcome this difficulty, are we not merely asserting that it is advantageous to make this choice because the probability of a good choice is somewhat better than in the case of other choices? Yet, is this not merely a variant of rule utilitarianism? However, Rawls said that his theory was designed to avoid the pitfalls of utilitarianism by formulating rules that are independent of such considerations. Thus, on this view of the derivation of the two principles of justice, his use of a representative-man concept either results in a patent absurdity concerning moral obligation or it reimposes a utilitarian calculation.

Yet if Rawls accepts this last alternative, his problem is even greater than in the ordinary utilitarian calculus. Whether a utilitarian decides on the basis of the greatest good of the greatest number or some other utilitarian principle, he has *only* the (insuperable) difficulty of determining the numbers, finding a scale according to which he can add the utilities of different people, and finding some method of establishing the result as morally binding on those who get hurt. However, according to Rawls, one does not know in which society he is to be born. Does he decide again for the entire community of mankind past, present, and future? What would this mean?

Even if we ignore these difficulties, given this interpretation of Rawls, he is still not out of the woods. His utilitarian derivation is now dependent on the general principles of social science. And these do not permit unique general deductions. A belief that most people will be fearful might lead our representative man to choose aristocracy to avoid the personal insecurities of a free society or democracy to maximize opportunity. This choice again requires knowledge of his psychological propensities, which are thus reintroduced at a secondary level. However—and even more important—psychological propensities do not exist in the abstract. The psychologies and motivations of individuals are related to the specific features and conditions of particular societies.

In chapter 1, in my discussion of homeostatic systems and of how explanations concerning them differed from the general covering laws applicable in mechanical physics, I explained why general equilibrial formulations in the social sciences are vacuous. Rawls's insistence on non-existent general principles of social science—for, even if they *were* possible in theory, they do not exist in fact—leaves his representative man "up a tree." It ignores the extent to which psychology functions within social and political contexts. He is proceeding as if one aspect of a complex system of human and social interrelationships can be considered in abstraction from all the others that give it context and meaning. In the last analysis, Rawls's own conclusions merely reproduce the preferences of an intellectual, middle-class American of the mid-twentieth century. This should not surprise us.

Psychological Propensity and Choice. An even deeper problem besets Rawls's approach than any we have yet discussed. Rawls evades some of the problems of utility theory by a discussion of indifference analysis. This approach, which uses paired comparisons and which, in this respect, bears some minor resemblances to my test in principle, depends upon the "givenness" of the commodities that are paired in the ordinary illustrations of the technique. This is not a problem for a consumer in a market. The price is established for him and he need choose only that single pairing of different commodities that provides the preferred outcome. Rawls is on firm ground when he uses this device to determine proportional satisfaction of his two principles. He does not seem to note, however, that the numbers in the payoff boxes of his heuristic examples are utiles, that they presume attitudes toward risk, and that, in this respect, they make meaningless Rawls's condition behind the veil of ignorance that special psychological propensities be ignored. The von Neumann utility axioms generate these numbers specifically through risk comparisons. The indifference analysis of uncertain choices also implies psychological propensity. Most of our real choices are of this kind, for, outside of buying commodities in the market, we make decisions under conditions of uncertainty, as when we decide to invest in a business, pursue a career, or court a woman. The minimax principle lacks meaning except in this context.

This way of conceiving the problem was not arbitrarily chosen by von Neumann. The preposterous conclusions of the St. Petersburg paradox [25] could be avoided only by some solution similar to that of his utility axioms. An even simpler example will demonstrate this point aptly. Consider three gambles. Each involves a fair coin toss. In the first, the stakes are plus or minus $1. In the second, the stakes are plus or minus $500. In the third, the stakes are plus or minus $5,000. The statistical value of each game is the same: $0. Yet it is easy to see that the disposition to play each game will not be the same regardless of this fact. Preferences are not linear with dollars, let alone with the non-fungible goods that constitute the most important payoffs of real-world choices.

The argument extends further. Choice is impossible without considerations of psychology and context. Choice consists of motivated behavior. And, unless we know both the preferences governing choice and the framework of contextual alternatives within which choice becomes operative, we have no way to generate a decision. The abstraction from knowledge of position on the axis works in the Nash bargain[26] because the principle of choice generates a solution in a precisely specified context. Because this is the case, we can consider how we would choose if we were on either axis; and only because this is so can we isolate particular preferences for a rule from that particular aspect of location on an axis. When the theorist of bargaining calls this "fair," this is all that he means. That this preference may not be independent of other cultural characteristics is not important because "fairness" has a strictly limited meaning. Moreover, if we can show, as we probably can, that different psychological propensities do not permit a univocal rule,[27] a univocal solution no longer exists and the concept of fairness becomes quite ambiguous even in this limited context.

Relevance and Applicability to Other Societies

It is now easy to show that Rawls's set of ethical rules is not relevant to many past societies and perhaps to some future societies. Therefore, we will not labor the point.

Imagine someone arguing to Caesar Augustus that he should institute democratic practices because he would have willed them in an original condition, or haranguing his soldiers with the notion that they should overthrow the emperor because his rule is incompatible with Rawls's first rule.

Moreover, what do we mean by freedom? Freedom to vote? Freedom to speak? Freedom to use property any way one chooses? Freedom to despoil nature? Freedom from bureaucracy? Freedom from risk? Freedom to run risks?

Because Rawls treats freedom as a pure abstraction, he fails to see the extent to which freedom can be defined only in terms of constraints and the extent to which choices are required among different kinds and degrees of freedom under similar and different conditions. He does not see how our conceptions both of what freedom is and of the desirability of different types of freedom depend on our views of human nature and its possibilities and of societal constraints and available alternatives. Because real political situations require choices—sometimes at the margin and sometimes centrally— among different types of freedom and between individual freedoms and other social values important to human beings, Rawls's criteria are largely irrelevant to the actual subject matter of politics.

The issues facing a society in which the choice is between a centralized monarchy and a decentralized feudalism in both of which there is not enough food or shelter for all cannot be related to Rawls's set of rules. Even where freedom in some sense is an issue, how do his rules permit choices between intellectual, moral, and physical freedoms? What if maintenance of intellectual freedom requires large-scale police surveillance and restrictions on human movement to prevent an intolerant party from acquiring rule? If the population problem is as bad as some believe—counterfactually, in my opinion—and if mandatory control measures became necessary, how would these relate to our conception of freedom and how would Rawls's set of rules guide choice?

Rawls's principles provide no reasonable guidelines to questions concerning justice in non-democratic systems and do so for democratic systems only in an illusory fashion. They ignore the extent to which considerations of justice require a rich field of factual and moral assumptions and an intricate pattern of relationships if conclusions are to be determined. A variety of possible principles are relevant and the degree of their relevance depends on the actual conditions of choice, including the availability of alternatives. The idea that a transitive ordering of a closed set of moral rules can illuminate the real problems of justice in real societies is as faulty as that of conceptual jurisprudence. The attempt to apply conceptual jurisprudence to actual court decisions quickly became absurd, as would the attempt to apply conceptual justice to the real problems of ethics.

Ethics as a Praxical Field.   Finally, we shall see, as the previous section has already indicated, that Rawls's use of a closed moral system mistakes the character of ethical inquiry, which is primarily that of a realm of praxis. Although it is possible in principle to construct ethical theories in which sets of ethical rules are in equilibrium with other system variables and system boundary conditions—much as the essential rules function in the various international systems of *System and Process in International Politics*—the rules of particular social systems and subsystems may give rise to inconsistent prescriptions even if the specified boundary conditions for each system hold. In such cases, individuals have to decide which system of ethical prescriptions will be given priority, as, for instance, in the case of a man who must choose between nation and religion or nation and ethnic group. The key variable is identification in these cases. And, of course, the boundary or environmental conditions may differ from those specified for rule equilibrium. Systems of formal ethics that make deductions from rules central to ethics are as inadequate for the investigation of matters of ethics as were systems of conceptual jurisprudence for the analysis of legal reasoning.

I am not arguing either that rules or sets of rules are irrelevant to moral decisions or that questions of transitivity, generality, publicity, or universality are never relevant, particularly if their appropriate range of application is taken into account. Rawls's treatment of these desiderata, however, is far too general and abstract. To show this, let us consider some examples of cases in which the formal constraints he places on principles of right[28] would produce results inconsistent with justice. (Appendix 3 offers additional reasons to doubt that values can be placed in a hierarchy.)

First, he says, the principles should be general. That is, it should be possible to formulate them without the use of proper names or rigged definite descriptions. The predicates employed in their statement should express general properties and relations. The principles must be universal in their application. They must apply to all by virtue of their being moral persons. Thus, Rawls assumes that each person can understand these principles and use them in his deliberation. A principle is ruled out if it would be self-defeating were everyone to act upon it.

The difference between generality and universality, according to Rawls, lies in the following fact. Egoism in the form of a first-person dictatorship satisfies universality but not generality. Everyone could act in accordance with the principle, but the use of the personal pronoun violates the first condition. General principles, on the other hand, may not be universal. They may be formulated to hold for a restricted class of individuals, for instance, those who have some special biological or social characteristics.

The third principle that Rawls asserts is that of publicity. Those who make decisions behind the veil of ignorance act to choose principles for a public conception of justice. They therefore assume that everyone will know as much about these principles as if they were reached by an explicit agreement. Rawls points out that this principle differs from that of universality, as it is possible that everyone might act on a principle without this being widely known or explicitly recognized.

The fourth requirement expressed by Rawls is that of imposing an ordering on conflicting claims. This ordering should be complete and transitive. The fifth condition is that of formality. The parties to a dispute are to assess the system of principles as "the final court of appeal in practical reasoning."[29]

It is easy to see that the scheme devised by Rawls is not required by a terminological explication of "justice" but is required by one particular conception of justice: that in which every case of choice involving values finds a unique and definitive solution within the framework of a closed moral system. It is a fact that to date no one has ever been able to devise such a scheme of justice or of any other endeavor, including that of law. Every complex choice system of which we are aware requires reference to more than a single framework of explanation to solve questions of choice. The conceptual theory of jurisprudence, as noted in chapter 2, has broken down on this ground. Game theory, which operated in that mathematical realm in which demonstration is therefore easiest, provides us with a general solution only for the zero-sum case: a case that is of little or no interest in social or political matters. Moreover, even in zero-sum games against nature there is no formal ground for choosing between the minimax and minimax regret principle, a fact with which we have already tested some of Rawls's propositions.[30] Finally, the realm of praxis, for reasons offered in chapter 1, fundamentally excludes such solutions.

Self-defeating Arguments and the Conditions.   We have already considered a number of ways in which the conclusions of Rawls fail to follow from his premises. Let us now relate these to his discussion of fundamental principles. Rawls argues that a principle must not be self-defeating if all act upon it and that obligations only extend to those who reciprocate them. (This conclusion can be derived more elegantly from Bertrand Russell's theory of types.) This would justify lying to liars or robbing robbers. It is quite true that most people would agree that they do not owe obligations to those who do not observe them in return (although this does not always hold for children, parents, spouses, or others who are loved or revered, even if unrelated). But it does not follow from pure logic that we should be truthful toward those who are truthful toward us; and a violation of that rule might be justified by reference to the attributes of others. For instance, it might be believed that moral rules are required for the "stupid masses" but not for the "elite." That is not self-defeating if the intelligent can distinguish between explicit and implicit rules and the stupid cannot. But lying to liars may be self-defeating, for we then may lose the ability to discriminate between honest men and liars. Whether this is so or not depends on conditions in particular places at particular times. It cannot be derived from a set of *a priori* rules.

On the other hand, Rawls argues that it is irrational to be bound by extorted promises.[31] Yet in many prison outbreaks, when hostages are held by prisoners, promises extorted by threat are kept and are expected to be kept. There are quite understandable reasons for this, including the good faith of public officials, the possibility that the hostages might be killed if past experience justified the expectation that promises would not be kept, and so forth. This again illustrates that many statements that Rawls offers as truths are quite contingent and cannot be investigated without a far wider range of considerations than he is willing to take into account.

Stipulated Examples. Let us now consider some stipulated examples. Let us apply the principle of the reciprocal extension of rights to the case of a scientist who invents a doomsday machine that anyone could build for fifty dollars.

This scientist wishes to publish his results for purely scientific reasons. He does not want anyone to build such a machine; he declares that no one would be so immoral as to set one off; and he recognizes the rights of all to engage in self-expression. Therefore the ground Rawls earlier chose, that we can restrict the rights of those, and only of those, who do not reciprocally recognize ours, does not apply; and, if we wish to keep the principle, we are driven back to the empirical proposition that the scientist is objectively denying the rights of others to self-expression (dead men cannot express themselves) regardless of his intentions or of the moral rules he claims to be following. This involves a remarkable modification of Rawls's position, for we no longer have a clear ground for the extension reciprocally of rights by representative men, independently of the facts of particular cases.

Moreover, we do not need this extreme example to make the point. Suppose the device is not a doomsday machine but is only sufficiently deadly to blow up a hundred square miles, and suppose that any child can build it. We might reconsider the first amendment in such a case.

Let us consider another example. We have a democratic system of government in the United States and we have adopted rules for fair elections. Suppose we know that a particular candidate for office who is very charismatic and even well-intentioned will engage in actions as president that will precipitate a major international war or that will lead to the destruction of the democratic system unintentionally. For the moment, we will ignore the fact that such matters are quite uncertain and that those who believe that they know them with certainty and that their activities are likely directly and substantially to preclude them are more likely than not to be paranoidal or megalomaniacal. We are choosing a stipulated example in which we indeed possess this information. Would we be justified in engaging in dishonest electoral practices to prevent this consequence? Rawls's restriction against secondary prudence—that is, prudence based on the particular case rather than that prudence employed behind the veil of ignorance in choosing principles—would preclude this.

Let us take a third example. There is a war going on. The war is just. The service regulations meet standards of justice. The regulations state that as of a certain age soldiers are eligible for discharge. A soldier, recently wounded, and who has been wounded in combat on five previous occasions, returns to a reception facility where regulations call for his returning to his combat unit. He is within thirty days of being eligible for discharge. Is it just to apply the regulations in an even-handed manner? Or might justice be better served by losing his records for thirty days?

If rules are violated in this fashion, it is important to deny that these violations have occurred. Otherwise, there would be a direct confrontation with the formal rules, something the system could not easily stand; for if it admitted the justice of doing this, it would not be able to limit properly the occasions on which the rule is violated. Indeed, if violations are discovered and if they can be proved, punishment may be appropriate (although it may be mitigated by consideration of the circumstances), not because the "crime" produces a specific evil, but because formal exculpation would limit too much the ability of the larger system to prevent self-serving applications of behavior that is desirable only in exceptional cases. In chapter 4, this will be relevant to our discussion of cases in which some may be genuinely obliged to engage in acts, such as civil disobedience, that others are obliged to punish.

In our next example, it is important to recognize that most complex systems can function only if their rules are violated. For instance, during the 1972 Italian mail "strike" (more accurately, slowdown), postmen "followed the book" and virtually no mail was delivered in Rome for two months.

Although every system requires some degree of hypocrisy or perhaps even of dishonesty, it is important for the maintenance of systems that the occasions on which these are resorted to not be self-serving; for self-serving use of lies or hypocrisy will almost surely create too great a discrepancy between ideals and behavior. The great difficulty is that the occasions on which breaches of rules are required are situational and cannot clearly be defined by any set of rules or controlled by review boards. Therefore, the stability of moral systems depends in large part upon the capability of social systems under existential circumstances to maintain motivations that limit practices that are required but that in principle should not occur. These obviously are cases for the exercise of judgment, as that concept is used in chapter 2.

Thus, in circumstances in which important goods can be pursued only in violation of important rules, hypocrisy or lying protects the appearance of the system—unless we assume that all citizens are philosophers and are thoroughly informed as to circumstances—and in its absence cynicism concerning the rules might undermine the system. Of course, too great a discrepancy between actual behavior and the moral rules of the system also will produce cynicism, so that every system of empirical justice may become unstable under unfavorable circumstances.

If moral agency has an ontological element, as I argue that it has, moral behavior will involve the actual character of the personality system, the person's conception of himself and of other persons, the actual character of the various social systems within which activity occurs, beliefs concerning the ways in which social systems operate, and the interrelationships among these elements. This, in part, shows the incompleteness or the unreasonableness of Kantian and neo-Kantian rules, for the protection of appearances is an important agency for perpetuating moral behavior. Thus, we have called into question publicity, universality, generality, and finality as categorically correct criteria. Only transitivity remains.

Transitivity and Its Problems.   The assumption by Rawls of transitivity of preferences is one much used in the literature on individual decision making. It is an unproved assumption even for individual decision making, although it is necessary if a hierarchical ordering for preferences is to be made. Its justification lies in the fact that the behavioral manifestations of preference either establish such an ordering—in which case by definition we call them rational—or they manifest inconsistency, in which case we call them irrational. We do not examine the extent to which consistent behavior requires a suppression of particular types of motivation within the individual; nor do we inquire into what pathologies of information processing or exaltation of secondary gains may or may not be required to produce "rational" behavior. (Appendix 3 calls into question the patent character of a value hierarchy that is independent of circumstances.)

At least the particular individual has a distinct identity. Although the boundaries of that identity in certain respects may be drawn according to conventional standards, the fact that individual identities distinguish particular individuals from each other is beyond question.

Rawls, however, takes the bold, but unjustified, step of assuming value transitivity for the entire collectivity of mankind on the basis of individual decisions. The ring of identity is drawn around all of mankind without distinction, although Rawls later introduces particular distinctions in ad hoc fashion.

Thus Rawls begs the issue of how extended the group is. Should it include all whose claims are in conflict or only those whose claims are in conflict within agreed bounds for decision? In effect it assumes that there cannot be such a thing as irreconcilable claims none of which is illegitimate or wars in which no party is in the wrong. That needs to be proved and not assumed. Later in this chapter, during the discussion of objectivity, we shall see that the assumption of a common first-order frame of reference is unjustified in many circumstances.

Even apart from the problem of disparate frames of reference, Rawls is forced to cope with the problem of transitivity by a major assumption, that of a representative man. This is reminiscent of Hegel's contention that the imposition of a criminal penalty required assent from the criminal's conscience, which was rendered in surrogate form by a jury. It is also reminiscent of Alfred Marshall's representative firm.

Rawls's use of Marshall's concept, however, is illicit. Marshall's representative firm was representative only for a particular type of economy and on the basis of particular motivational assumptions. Neoclassical economic theory assumed a linear relationship between dollars and utiles. Although this assumption was counterfactual, it did permit a useful theoretical analysis of a "pure" market economy. Even so, later analysis showed that the same rules did not apply to "imperfect" markets. The assumption of linearity of dollars and utiles failed to hold for the older-style traditional Chinese merchant. Thus, even in economics the attempt to find a single set of rules for the market breaks down and the overall orientation is misleading for certain types of nonmarket economies.

Whatever problems utilitarianism may have encountered in attempting to generate rules for social welfare, it at least faithfully copied the techniques of economic theory for individual decisions. And thus, as in economics, there was a basis for a distinction between theory and practical application, if not for a single set of universal, transitive rules. Even within utilitarian economic theory, "representative" men would be "representative" only for particular models of activity. When Rawls steps out of this framework, "representative" loses all meaning.

It has been argued, for instance, that if General Motors wished to maximize its profits, it would cut its price to take greater advantage of economies of scale. This, it has been argued, would drive Ford and Chrysler out of business. However, if this happened, the federal government would step in and it is this fact, it is alleged, which dissuades General Motors. Whether or not the argument is correct, as a stipulated example it shows that an analysis of General Motor's activities in the real world must move out of the representative firm context. It is not valid to use a representative concept in moral theory except perhaps within the framework of a best set of rules for a particular institution at a particular time. And even here, we would not be able to prove *a priori* that individuals holding roles in that institution should follow the rule in particular cases, for that involves us in a question of praxis that immediately raises questions concerning human obligations to different institutions at the same time and the problem of identification.

Were the Jews justified in asserting their right to a homeland in Palestine or were the Arabs right in resisting that goal? Which was the superior right: that attributable to former possession of the homeland, the absence of any alternative, and the need created by remarkable circumstances or that resulting from then-current, but not exclusive, possession?

A basic problem here is that even in disciplines where an ordered set of rules exists, the problem of applying it to varying circumstances cannot be solved by the set of rules. Principles of physics are used in designing atomic reactors, but the design of such reactors cannot be derived from a set of physical rules. Physics and chemistry set constraints on the design and construction of airplanes and bridges, but these designs cannot be derived from the relevant physical theories. In part, this result follows from the complexity of the engineering process.

In human affairs, and especially in moral matters, our explanations of, and our prescriptions concerning, actual behavior require evidence from a large number of explanatory realms, for instance, those of economics, psychology, politics, and anthropology. This requires a different form of reasoning—that of praxis—from that involved in examining the logical structure of an abstract theoretical system.

Neo-Kantianism and Tensions between Rules. The neo-Kantian framework is inadequate to an understanding of the tension between moral rules, between different goods, and between the good and the just. When Hegel spoke of existential absolutes as relative absolutes, he was pointing to the character of the problem that is involved. Every rule has inherent limits, some of which are produced by the tension between the good and the just. Rules, however, function only within sets of rules and these have equilibria depending upon the contextual conditions in which they become manifest.

Our extensive demonstration of the failure of Kantian and neo-Kantian approaches to ethics has had a purpose. The point that general formal systems cannot account for ethical behavior was made adequately by our analysis of Rawls's use of game and bargaining methods. We have been concerned, however, to show the rich interdependence of values with what are usually considered ordinary facts. We have attempted to show that slight variations in our conception of human and societal possibilities will have major, and highly unexpected, consequences for our preferences concerning social rules. That is why we examined the reversibility of the conclusions that Rawls reaches.

Are family ties important in devising moral rules? How can we answer this unless we know what kind of man would emerge in a world in which they were not and how, in turn, this would influence the form and substance of various social institutions and groupings? Is nationalism obsolete? Does this not depend on the means for bringing about changes and the consequences, not merely of the changes, but of the attempts to produce them?

Obviously our beliefs concerning these depend upon the conditions of the world in which we live. These beliefs do not exist in a vacuum. And this is true in the world of ordinary science—including beliefs about what constitutes proof as well as which hypotheses have been proved—as well as in the world of values. Physicists reject the idea of mental telepathy because, in the current state of physical theory, the energy required for transmission cannot be accounted for. Sufficiently large changes in the evidence supporting telepathy might produce a search for physical theories consistent with it. If these were found, a major rearrangement in our perception of the realm of knowledge would occur. Several major, although perhaps less radical, rearrangements were produced by the theoretical innovations of Galileo, Newton, Einstein, and Heisenberg.

Many major rearrangements have occurred in value systems. Usually, these are triggered by social or economic changes that force major readjustments of important institutions. Sometimes changes in knowledge help produce them; sometimes mistakenly so, as in the case of the inferences from relativity, quantum mechanics, and Freudian theory that many have made about the nature of man.

The point to keep in mind is that "facts" do not exist in a vacuum. The determination of what a fact is depends on the field of knowledge. Yet publicly communicable, or objective, knowledge is available. Elements of the field can be, and are, "disproved"; and when the weight of evidence becomes sufficiently great, the field is rearranged.

In the same way, the factual judgments to which values are related are subject to publicly communicable test: the characteristics of men; the relationships of these characteristics to social institutions; the consequences of these institutions for the character of men; our technological ability to produce change; important changes in circumstances and information. All of these are subject to publicly communicable knowledge.

Conclusions concerning all cannot be fitted into or derived from a single theory. But reasons can be offered for the consistency of the field. Thus, it might be shown that certain social changes are inconsistent with certain valuable consequences or that these consequences are not really valuable in the new circumstances. The test in principle and comparative knowledge permit ordered choices concerning preferences that relate them to the interactions of a transstable human nature with actual existential circumstances rather than to a mere subjective adjustment on the basis of immediate possibility.

Values are inherent in the nature of man and his relationships with other men and with society. Statements concerning them are objective because they are publicly communicable in principle within the wider framework we have discussed. They are not merely random or orderless subjective reactions to a valueless factual external world. Neither the world of values nor the world of so-called ordinary fact consists of representations of either an external or an internal corresponding reality. Both exist within an experiential field in which explanations refer to relations between a person and an environment. In both cases, truncated aspects of the field are subject to relatively high-confidence testing. In both cases, the entire field is subject to partial rearrangement and is not testable as a whole. However, publicly communicable statements can be made about consistency and "goodness" of fit. Both are realms of praxis.

Because covering laws and their derived mechanical equilibria abound in physics, its statements are of a higher order of confidence than statements in the realm of values. Otherwise, the parallel is genuine.

In the realm of values, the rules appropriate to particular societies or to their subsystems constitute a parallel to the laws of physical theory. Whether change is desirable depends on the fit between these rules and the values of other institutions and on how these various sets of values meet human needs and accord with human nature in historical circumstances. Judgments concerning these relationships constitute the praxical field of values. And they are as publicly communicable—although lower-confidence in character—as statements within the realm of physical science.

Linguistic Meaning and Justice.   Statements concerning values or rules for justice employ words that function within sentences that are meaningful to the user. However, these meanings are neither primarily conventional or arbitrary nor natural in any universalistic sense. "Man," for instance, did not mean the same thing to the aborigine that it does to us. Its meaning is not independent of the range of knowledge available to us, including our identifications. In turn, these are related to other social, political, economic, and ecological conditions.

Meanings depend upon the leverage that choices among meanings give us in relating our actions to consequences, including but not restricted to the scientific, in the circumstances of particular epochs. We never start *de novo* in this process. Our "testing" of alternatives usually proceeds in a piecemeal fashion until major reconstructions are required because of discordance within the universe of concepts and the realm of praxis.

Whether the meanings of "man," for instance, will remain so close that we might perhaps designate different uses as family relationships, as Wittgenstein does, or whether they will become so distant that the various uses of the name have in common only some biological characteristics, depends on the entire range of knowledge (praxis). Conceivably, in some future society, non-organic thinking beings might be thought of as men, say for citizenship purposes; and we might then distinguish between subclassifications of men who are animals and men who are non-animal. In this case, the relationship between the aboriginal concept—which specified the biological characteristics of the species but which perhaps might not have included theoretical thought—and the future concept might be only historical. For similar reasons, justice and ethics also require a treatment that is not restricted to universalistic meanings for language, even in the loose sense of "family" relationships. This is even more important in considering the rules or principles of justice than in considering the meaning of the term itself.

However, before we focus more specifically on how ethical inquiry should proceed, we must consider briefly other alternatives to Rawls's position and we must reconsider the problem of objectivity, including in particular the important distinction between first- and second-order objectivity.

Alternative Solutions

Alan Gewirth applies the concept of moral agency to the justification of moral principles.[32] Gewirth argues that the egalitarian results in Rawls's work depend upon the original position (as a matter of fact, we have shown that they cannot be derived properly from the original position). However, he says, it is impossible to remove from the consideration of rational decision makers certain factors including actual empirical inequalities and dissimilarities which obtain among men and which, together with their self-interest, would influence them to make inegalitarian choices. As he argues, the stipulations by which Rawls avoids inegalitarian results lack independent rational justification: men are not equal in power or ability nor so lacking in empirical reason as to be ignorant of their particular qualities.

Gewirth argues that the difficulties of Rawls's argument and of those positions based upon the argument of universality are avoided by an argument related to agency. Agents' acts are voluntary acts, Gewirth says. They are made for a purpose considered good. Hence, "every agent necessarily claims, at least implicitly, that he has a right to participate voluntarily and purposively in transactions in which he is involved."[33] These two rights must be accorded to others or he contradicts himself. The right to participate voluntarily entails a correlative obligation on the agent's part not to coerce other agents, to frustrate their purposes, or in basic respects to harm them. The general principle is "Apply to your recipient the same categorial features of action that you apply to yourself."

This argument avoids some of the difficulties entailed by Rawls's argument, but it is also too abstract. The claim, which Gewirth says is implied, may be intended only as a deception. In this case, the agent sees himself as an agent engaged in voluntary action but does not in fact claim that no one has a right to frustrate his objectives or to harm him. Claims concerning reciprocal agency, which even may be overt and not merely implied, may be intended as deceptions. In this case, the agent's actual position is that each shall use his voluntary agency to acquire as much control over others as he can. If he succeeds, apart from the areas in which he is aided by good fortune, he has succeeded because he has exercised his agency better than have others.

The positions of both Rawls and Gewirth imply the primacy of second-order agent symmetry in moral analysis and a universal value system. This begs the question of moral behavior in either case; for agency may be either complexly related to other values or merely instrumental in implementing them. In either of these cases group membership, social role, other characteristics, or the consequences of particular decisions may determine the appropriate behavior of moral actors toward each other. This is the case in many actual societies. The empirical investigation of the requirements of moral behavior is evaded by excessively abstract definitional solutions.

J. C. C. Smart attempted to state an act-utilitarian standard as a guide to moral behavior.[34] If an almanac asserts a rule of navigation (based on probabilities) for a particular area of the ocean, the captain, according to Smart, should forget the rule if he has more particular and better information. Smart then argues that as long as people are altruistic, the social good will be produced by an act-utilitarian standard. Apart from the other difficulties of utilitarianism, it was possible to show that the *reductio ad absurdum* by which Smart attempted to prove this conclusion did not work. For instance, in a water-short community the size of New York City, even altruistic, utilitarian residents would take showers rather than baths, if they preferred them, because the deprivation to others would be unnoticeable and the gain to themselves significant. Yet if each had similar preferences and acted this way, there would be an acute water shortage. However, this was not a *reductio*, as Smart thought, but a prisoners' dilemma. Therefore, Smart retreated to a single and highly abstract neo-Kantian but utilitarian rule—that each should act as he would have others act in the same circumstances.

There is no doubt that this solution avoids the prisoners' dilemma. However, such abstract rules entail many difficulties. Hobbes noted one, that the rule would become self-serving. Individuals tend to see their own interests in near-sighted form. In situations in which diffuse affective relationships are central, Smart's neo-Kantian rule would be injurious to the personality, which is responsive to particularistic concerns, and to its sense of identity, if applied in the continually calculating manner he recommends. Consider, for instance, how quickly a marriage would become self-destructive if each partner continually assessed the advantages of divorce. At best, however, Smart's neo-Kantian rule is merely truistic, for it leaves the solution entirely undetermined except for the constraint of universality. And it denigrates existing rules—which do at least provide useful guides to behavior—without providing any useful method for criticizing them.

Although Smart avoids the selfishness tautology into which some analysts fall, the problems of his solution shed light on the difficulty of overly abstract rules. Some have argued that all actions are essentially selfish because each does what he prefers to do in particular situations. This assertion is really an implicit equation of selfishness with motivated behavior. It fails to distinguish between actions that help and those that injure others and between motivations that take the interests of others into account, even if they are contrary to one's own interests narrowly considered, and those that do not.

The form of neo-Kantian but utilitarian rule to which Smart retreated is essentially a definition of rational behavior; and it obscures more than it clarifies. Sometimes economists make similar but individualistic assumptions in attempts to show that behavior in traditional societies really accords with economic theory because individuals do not desire the goods they would buy with a second (cash) crop and therefore act in accordance with economic assumptions when they fail to grow it. This argument confuses economic theory with a definition of rationality.

It is by such an evasion that some economists are able to assert that the market maximizes preferences. An individual who wants to keep up with the Joneses may have to buy a car each year, given his preferences in a competitive market; but he might prefer governmental regulations that forbade yearly model changes. Each form of the economy permits some preferences to be expressed and excludes the expression of others. The test in principle provides an iterative procedure that permits a weak ordering of different systems. Truistic rules obscure the fact that choices among systems may be the most significant choices and that the rules to be followed depend in part upon such prior choices or upon the historical fact that particular institutions exist and can be transformed only in certain ways and not others.

These aspects of human choice in social and environmental circumstances exclude an ethics based on a single set of principles. Principles, the consequences of implementing them, and environmental circumstances coexist in a loose equilibrium, as Quine has shown to be the parallel case with respect to science. Our conclusions concerning an appropriate set of ethical principles—or at least of their relative rankings or relationships—will differ with the circumstances of each type of society. A definition of rational behavior is only one possible element in a theory or assessment. Without the other elements of social structure and environmental constraints, we have neither an economic nor an ethical theory or assessment. All that rationality in an instrumental sense requires is that individuals act according to their preferences, whether these be individualistic or social, universalistic or particularistic, and so forth. If this is then compounded with another rule to do the maximum good for the greatest number, it does become propositional, but impossible to apply to any complex case and detached from any relevant understanding of ethical choices because we still do not know what is good and why it is.

The failure properly to appreciate this point has led to an argument between Kenneth Arrow, John C. Harsanyi, and John Rawls.[35] The basic position of Harsanyi and Arrow is that where utilitarianism differs from the maximin rule, which they regard as the justification for Rawls's rules of justice, the former is to be preferred. Rawls correctly responds that his first two rules of justice have nothing to do with utility maximization—he would have been even more accurate had he argued that his use of the maximin rule is only illustrative and heuristic—and that utility averaging is applicable in his system only when the first two rules of the system are in at least partial conflict in particular applications. Rawls then disputes a particular example of Harsanyi's involving the allocation of scarce medical manpower by asserting that his principles apply only to macro- and not to microsituations. Harsanyi regards this defense as inapt on the ground that moral principles should apply universally and that his example could be extended to the macrolevel in any event.

In the first place, in analyzing this dispute, it is important to remember that utility theory and utilitarianism are not the same thing. Utilitarianism is an ethical doctrine designed to regulate individual choice with respect to individual and social consequences. In addition to other problems, utilitarianism entails problems of generalizing from individual preferences to social outcomes—problems that are produced by difficulties with respect to interpersonal comparisons and the formulation of a satisfactory social utility function.

Utility theory, regardless of the utility axioms from which one starts, is a theory that establishes a transitive ordering of preferences for outcomes. In the case of the von Neumann utility axioms, this is done by means of paired comparisons of payoffs under circumstances of risk. That a higher utility number is always to be preferred to a lower is a logical entailment of the utility axioms, although the common belief that the utility numbers assigned to outcomes will not shift with the circumstances of game matrices is not logically entailed.

However, in games against other individuals or against nature in which one does not know the probability with which a strategy will be chosen either by other players or by nature, simple utility maximization cannot be used as a decision rule. The maximin criterion is preferred in a zero-sum game as a rational rule because of its specific characteristics, including, among others, the guarantee of a minimum expected utility. If one chooses a strategy other than that determined by the maximin criterion, there is no guaranteed expected minimum or maximum utility. Thus the choice of the maximin rule is not based upon a paired comparison of expected utilities for payoffs.

One may regard the preference for maximin in a given type of situation (or in general) as a utility preference. But it is a different type of preference from the paired comparisons produced by the von Neumann axioms. Moreover, apart from our earlier demonstration of the need for moral rules, there can be preferences for moral rules. Consider, for instance, a professor who is grading the barely passable examination of a student who is disrupting the entire university. In a pure paired comparison he may prefer to fail the student. If he takes into account the moral or ethical rules that many teachers believe apply to their profession, he will not.

The central difficulty of utility theory as a guide to ethical theory is that it is vacuous. Where preferences are determined by moral rules—as in many cases they both are and need to be if desired outcomes are to be obtained—the application of utility theory masks the problem of determining what moral rules are appropriate. Utility theory is an empty procedural theory that tells us to produce the preferred result, not a substantive theory. There is always something outside the theory and this "something" is often more important than the formal rules for aggregating results. Thus, to critique Rawls from the standpoint of utility theory is to mistake the problem of analysis—the justification of his decision (moral) rules—as we explored it during our critique of Rawls.

An appropriate critique of ethical theory will inquire into what is good and why it is. Such an inquiry will establish that appropriate ethical rules are related to the characteristics of social systems and to the conditions in which these social systems are embedded. It is precisely this conclusion to which our analysis of homeostatic systems and praxis in chapter 1 leads. Any attempt to formulate a set of global rules for ethics or social science will be either truistic or actually tautological. Appropriate rules of behavior or sets of moral principles covary with the other elements of social systems and environments.

Justice and Objectivity

Objectivity and Frame of Reference. In chapter 2 we noted that statements with respect to colors, for instance, always had an implied system reference, even though the usual elliptical statements did not specify this. We then showed how statements concerning the good were also elliptical. The system reference of each type of statement provides the frame of reference from which we can develop the concept of objectivity pragmatistically.

Josiah Royce pointed out that we normally observe the stars as stationary and the planets as moving. However, a creature with a span of perception of 10,000 years would observe the stars as moving and the planets as stationary circles of light. We ordinarily think of our bodies as solid. Yet from the standpoint of an incoming gamma particle our bodies are porous.

Although such simple statements as "This body is solid" and "This body is porous" might appear to be contradictory when referring to the same object, the apparent contradiction disappears as soon as the appropriate contextual constraints are observed. A second-order language could be constructed in which the significance of the apparently contradictory statements could be related to the type of system for which the statements had referential import. These statements are objective. (Yet it must be noted—and this is ontologically important—that a creature with a span of perception of 10,000 years would have difficulty in empathetically understanding human beings and vice versa. Their existential dissimilarities would reduce to an infinitesimal probability the likelihood of their communication with each other within the terms of some second-order language.)

This pragmaticistic use of concepts also helps to resolve the old debate over relativism and absolutism. Change and permanence are no more characteristics or properties of "things in themselves" than are colors. Just as color requires a perceiving system to become meaningful, change requires an "unchanged" reference system. The atoms of a ruler are in constant motion, but the ruler is "unchanged" with respect to measurements that are not atomic. If, as communication theory tells us, structure is a more slowly changing function, both structure and function are essential correlatives for meaning. Change is always relative to something that is unchanged, although that unchanging something may be changing relatively to something else. There is no single external standard from which everything else is measured.

In principle we can always establish a second-order meaning for correlary terms from some frame of reference. In practice, the experiments that we can devise may restrict the scope of "objectivity," as in quantum mechanics where speed and location cannot be made simultaneously meaningful.

Justice and Relativity. Both second- and first-order objectivity in values are relevant to a conception of justice. To illustrate the difference between the two concepts, let us employ the clock "paradox" of Einsteinian relativity theory. According to this theory, an observer on each of two systems moving with respect to the other will observe time on the other system as going more slowly. Common sense tells us that it is contradictory to believe that time in each system can be moving more slowly with respect to time in the other system. Yet, because of the relativity of motion with respect to independent inertial systems, an observer in each observes time on the other to be moving more slowly. Each observer, if he is familiar with relativity theory, will recognize that his opposite number on the other system is reaching conclusions that mirror his and will understand why he does so from his frame of reference. Thus, we have a second-order system within which objective and non-contradictory statements are made concerning what the two observers observe. On the other hand, the "truths" of the two observers on different inertial systems lack a common point of reference that permits first-order determinateness concerning the two systems.

If, on the other hand, a twin enters a spaceship, flies out into space, and returns, biological measurements will establish that he is younger than the twin who remained on earth. In this case, however, the twin who went into space needed to accelerate to leave the gravitational pull of the earth and to return to it. The fact of acceleration was observable by physical instrumentation and measurable. The system that accelerates is known to move with respect to another system and, therefore, the former Einsteinian constraint does not apply. The twin who goes into space expects to be younger than the twin who remains on earth. Common measurements made by both predict and confirm this fact. The apparent paradox arises only with respect to systems that are on independent inertial paths. The observers who share a common universe also share a common framework of first-order objective, physical truth.

The reader is already familiar with my argument that values are generated as the consequence of the interactions of transfinitely stable persons with other persons in real environments. The analogy with Einsteinian relativity, although partial, is genuine. Time-space coordinates in Einsteinian theory give rise to measurements only from the standpoint of the interactive observer. This produces the disjunction between the conclusions of observers on different inertial systems, although each conclusion is objectively given by each observer's framework of reference and each observer will know what conclusions the other will reach. Placement in an inertial system is a historical fact.

Similarly the existential identifications of the valuing person with other individuals, groups, or organizations constitute the focus for establishing a first-order framework of justice.

According to the test in principle, all individuals with similar information will share a common hierarchy of social systems and their norms. Each, therefore, as in the case of observers on different inertial systems, will understand how each will attempt to optimize in similar circumstances. Many, however, will have different identificational standpoints and thus will disagree as to whose success is preferable or which of alternative, but equally applicable, principles should be applied to the particular case.

If two independently inertial systems somehow coalesce into a single inertial system, first-order as well as second-order objective statements thereafter would become possible for the observers. Our account of justice implies that this is what occurs as the extension of identification among individuals and among systems produces a common frame of reference within which common first- as well as second-order statements have validity. However, existential circumstances may break this bond for particular individuals within systems or may attenuate it to the point of extreme ambivalence with respect to the requirements of just behavior.

To understand this problem better, let us examine briefly the differences and similarities between the use of relative frames of reference in Einsteinian physics and the use of a similar concept in ethics. The space traveler can be in one and only one inertial system at a time. Individuals may identify with themselves, with other individuals, or with one or more social systems. Whether any solution is possible in a given set of circumstances that produces "good" results from all frameworks of reference is a factual matter. Even if this is possible, it will still be necessary in most cases to compromise the good from one or more standpoints. If it is not possible, the strength of the individual's identifications will determine which framework of reference will be sacrificed.

Measures for frameworks of identification, even though of low confidence, are possible, much as a psychologist may determine whether or not a person is projecting. However, these determinations are made by weighing evidence from a variety of areas; and terms are used, the meanings of which are at least partly determined by the contexts in which they are employed. The meanings and measurements are not determined by an overriding theory employing terms for which universal measures are available as in the case of physics. This thrusts the problem into the area of praxis. Further, the fact that "solutions" involve adjustments among frames of reference, rather than derivation from a unique perspective, emphasizes criteria of consistency and adjustment, key elements of the arena of praxis. This is still within the ambit of science—for the selection of axioms and definitions within theory is determined in part by the "praxis" framework of science, including consistency with other theories and propositional information—and hence of objectivity, at least in John Dewey's sense of public communicability. The understanding of this partly explains the error in attempting to reduce ethics to a theory with a universal set of rules that governs all situations and all individuals.

Justice and First-Order Agreement. The discussion thus far demonstrates the existence of second-order objectivity. Whether first-order objectivity exists is the question that is crucial to the concept of justice. The thrust of my argument in this chapter, as distinguished from that made by John Rawls, is that justice is related to values generated by human nature in actual circumstances. Therefore, metaphorically speaking, different societies, or even some individuals within a given society, may be on different "inertial paths." This is rarely entirely true, for, where contact or communication is sufficient to produce a perception of the problem of justice, there are usually some shared interests, including at least a partial shared interest in justice. On the other hand, there is rarely an entirely shared first-order framework of justice. Therein lies the omnipresent potential for tragedy.

The Relative and the Absolute. The moral absolutist argues that what is good in a society does not depend upon the features of that society or of its environment. Thus, what is morally required will depend either on an absolute hierarchy of goods or, à la Rawls, on an absolute hierarchy of rules. It is this characteristic, as we show in this chapter, that makes Rawls's principles irrelevant to most societies. Although I do not discuss absolutistic positions concerning the good, it will be easy for the reader to see that the same argument holds.

The relativist, à la Toulmin, will agree that different rules apply to different societies; but he will argue that if one lives in a society, he should accept its rules. Although many reforms can be carried out within a society's rules—and practically none will be possible that ignores them—this forsakes the leavening that comes from the judgment that some societies are better than others either for given environments or, even more compellingly, in environments that are preferred because they are better.

Thus the absolutist reifies moral and social orders—as mechanists once reified time and space—as absolutes; and the ordinary relativist—as opposed to the Einsteinian relativist—

identifies them with social and cultural boundary conditions. The latter is as theoretically inadequate as treating time-zone specifications independently and without any relationship to choices in other areas or to the relative relationships of sun and earth. In both cases—that of the absolutist and that of the ordinary relativist—values are detached from their pragmaticist significance.

Let us now use these distinctions to clarify the character of moral rules as "absolute" or "relative." We have claimed no more than a likely weak ordering of societies: that is, that some are clearly better than others and that some are worse. Even within societies some moral rules might well have been otherwise without any discernible gain or loss in general, although particular formulations may be costly to particular individuals in particular cases. Why then should a moral rule be observed in these costly cases?

This problem will be discussed from a somewhat different perspective in the section of chapter 5 of *Alienation and Identification* entitled "The Dysfunction of 'True' Autonomy." Philosophically, I recognize that these values are relative to particular conditions and that other rules—that perhaps are preferable to some individuals—would have been as good or better under the same conditions. However, to the extent that my argument holds that man—at least potentially— is moral in character, the social existence of a particular rule establishes its priority over alternative rules that are comparable in their effects. This priority is important to the sense of identity and the character structure of moral men. Therefore, to treat the "accidental," or "relative," qualities of moral rules as preeminent is to attack the moral cement of society and to injure gravely the interest the moral man has in the welfare of society. This is why a philosopher will recognize the imperative force of actual moral rules whereas a sophist will recognize only their "relativity." And that is why a set of normative rules that is not specifically related to a specific society will lack relevance in the formulation of moral judgments within that society.

Moreover, even in a society that is not the best, a philosopher will recognize that it may not be possible to substitute or even to work for the best. Therefore, depending upon conditions, he may regard even the norms of an unenlightened society as binding, particularly with respect to the publicly visible aspects of performance. However, existential circumstances may shatter the identification of the individual with the group. Or there may be no real identification between one group and another.

We have shown that the distinction between first- and second-order moral references is meaningful. Moreover, first-order references in principle are developmental. If they are factually potential in human being, wise men will recognize their interest in them. Therefore, the essential question for an examination of the subject of justice is: Are first-order moral references genuinely potential in human being and, if so, what are their implications?

JUSTICE

Justice as Might

We have already noted that no *a priori* consideration rules out the possibility that the good may be idiosyncratically personal and that justice may be merely instrumental. In such a case whether or not one would prefer a system of liberty would depend upon its advantages over alternative systems. Even if a libertarian system were established, the instrumental character of justice would be consistent with overthrowing this system if doing so was advantageous for the leaders of the coup. Even those who were disadvantaged by this change, if they were philosophically aware, would acknowledge that they would have done the same thing under the same circumstances. Thus, they might perceive the change as bad for themselves but not unjust.

Alternatively, if the system is dictatorial, conspirators who would prefer dictatorship in principle if they were the dictators—and if the mass of people are not philosophically aware—might lead a democratic rebellion against the actual dictators on purely instrumental grounds.

Rawls attempts to rule out this possibility by claiming that justice cannot be based on force. But all this means is that justice in the strong sense used by Rawls is not applicable to this asocial people. There still will be necessary rules of minimum cooperation within the dictatorship and these will establish some form of justice and fairness that applies to this particular kind of system. The dictatorship itself, if not just, is certainly not unfair, for everyone else would have done the same thing as the dictator. Moreover, if it is not just, it is surely not unjust. To call it unjust implies that some legitimate expectations were frustrated. And perhaps it is even just in a weak form of Rawls's usage. Although it is true that if each could not start at an advantage, each would prefer to start in a position that was not at a disadvantage. Each nonetheless would attempt to use the facilities available to him to establish control. Thus, even in Rawls's contractual sense, each has agreed implicitly to the outcome.

On the other hand, whether we call the outcome just or unjust, it does not morally bind anyone; for it is a fact of this system that except for the dictator each will seek to cause a change in the dictatorship and, if possible, to acquire the position himself. His failure to do so will be based only upon fear that the attempt might worsen his actual circumstances. To this extent, it then may be fair to say that conflicts within the system are in part decidable only by force. The weakness of the system of justice in this set of circumstances arises not from a failure to apply Rawls's form of reasoning, for it has been applied, but rather from the nature of the people we are talking about. Rawls attempts to rule this case out by his definition of justice; he leaves out of account—or at least does not take sufficiently into account—the relationship between ontology and justice.

Justice and Human Nature

In principle, we could conceive of a system with purposive, self-regulating characteristics that was incapable of moral behavior. This system would recognize that in a society with a large number of members moral "rules of the road" are required for generally optimal results; but its members would not feel obliged to follow them.

We cannot prove on the basis of current scientific knowledge that man is a moral being. However, in addition to making the concept of the valued and the valuable meaningful, we can speculate about those aspects of the human personality that might make moral behavior an inherent requirement of human being. The reader can then decide for himself whether the insights upon which this speculation rests accord with his assessment of the evidence.

In the first place, the evolutionary history of man probably has produced at least some bonding sentiments that are important to the personality and that, although more clearly tied to intimate relations than to social ones, are not expendable. It is possible that bonding applies not merely to kinship but to more extended social relationships as well and that this is a consequence of evolution. If so, these relationships would be intrinsic goods for human individuals. If we believe this to be the case, it would change the conception of the rules we believe to be applicable. But this by itself would not be sufficient to rule out aristocratic systems; for aristocratic systems would be consistent with the belief that everyone should desire government by the best. Moreover, biological differences between the members of a species—and therefore in their needs—may be as great or greater than those between species. Hence, to expect that moral rules that ignore such possible differences are adequate is to mistake the character of the moral problem and of the moral differentiations and identifications that are relevant to its elucidation.

In the second place, the fact that societies require at least some moral rules probably results in the evolutionary success of those organisms most disposed to value such rules as intrinsic needs. In the third place, much of moral behavior occurs at a conscious level and requires a conception of the self. The conception of the self arises through interrelationships with other individuals and membership in a social system. It seems unlikely that the degree of philosophic detachment required for a purely instrumental approach to others would be consistent with the sense of identity as it develops during social interchanges or that it would produce anything except dysfunctional or pathological information-regulating mechanisms. In addition, there is some evidence, although perhaps not too substantial, that so-called socio-pathic or psychopathic types of individuals fail to develop certain types of connective tissues in the frontal lobes of their cortex. In the fifth place, self-reflexive thought operates at high levels of generality that tend to push beyond individual distinctions toward more general characteristics. Although this, in turn, can probably become a pathological process, it militates against an extreme individualism as anything other than a pathological response. It may be that no single one of the reasons offered suffices to account for the moral character of human beings but that several in combination—for instance, the (expansible) sense of identity and generalized thought—might. I do not wish to push this reasoning further, for it is admittedly speculative.

Conceivably we might view autonomy as a central characteristic of human beings. In this case evolutionary bonding and certain characteristics of reasoning might incline us toward more democratic systems on the basis of principle rather than on the basis of pure instrumentality. But this is too abstract, as is the discussion by Rawls, for we might in principle recognize this and still opt for less democratic forms. However, if we noted that we tended to do this when resources were scarce or when the external world was hostile, and if democratic forms of government seemed inefficient in managing external relations, we might then provide an explanation for a preference that would establish more democratic procedures as a desirable goal in more favorable circumstances.

I do not wish to push this any further, for the reasoning is intended only to illustrate how on the basis of comparative historical information we may develop conceptions concerning political values that are related to our understanding of human nature and of social, economic, and political possibility. The existential elements of the problem are interrelated in a far more complex manner than any of my illustrations imply; and an adequate account of this matter would carry us beyond the confines of the simple point I wish to make. However, the companion book, *Alienation and Identification,* is intended to illustrate how the requirements of the personality generate a need for moral rules and how these are linked through the sense of identity to specific social relationships.

One other point, however, needs to be made here. Although we may be able to show that democratic systems, at least in optimal circumstances, accord best with human nature, conclusions regarding politics cannot be deduced from human nature alone; they are judgmental and include other factors as well. For reasons explained in chapter 1, social requirements cannot be reduced to individual motivation. The elements of social and political organization require study in their own terms. The requirements for a bridge cannot be derived from the study of materials, although different materials may require different architectural adaptations and vice versa. Both moral rules and political organizations require examination from a variety of perspectives among which are their impact on human personality and their macrosocial consequences. These may produce inconsistencies and problems of "fit." And one of the great problems in ethical thought lies in the temptation to legislate for one perspective entirely from the framework of another.

The Test in Principle

The test in principle avoids the prior difficulty by taking contexts into account. It thus permits the generation of rules appropriate to these contexts. Because of its iterative procedures, it then permits a comparison of contexts. In principle, therefore, we can produce a weak-ordered evaluational standard for alternative potential social and political systems that is common to all men as are the Einsteinian relativity equations for observers on different inertial systems. Moreover, just as the Einsteinian relativity equations are consistent with mirror-imaged estimations of movement by the different observers, the common set of social and political evaluations is consistent with conflicting existential judgments concerning paths to them or conflicting interests in progress to them.

Although it is nonsense to argue that the rise of absolute monarchs increased human freedom—except in a long run that no one then could foresee and the longer-term results of which we cannot yet judge—absolute monarchy was a relevant and arguable preference in that historical context. The test in principle permits in principle the justification of that choice in that context, its rejection in others, and forms of analysis that can serve as longer-run "utopian" corrections.

The test in principle distinguishes between the systems involved, thus keeping system references clear; it relates the concepts of justice and of good to the environmental constraints within which propositions concerning them have meaning; it permits comparison and evaluation; and it permits us to state preferences for different types of environments. It permits the systematic relating of psychic needs to social system and environmental constraints.

The "fit" between the psyches of individuals and the operations of a particular social system may be illustrated by Edward Banfield's example of moral behavior in an amoral society.[36] Social cooperation was so foreign to the society he

studied that it would have been positively harmful to particular individuals and their families for them to have observed moral rules in the larger society because there was no
easy way for them to break through the massive strength of
social practices. Consider, however, the case of an individual
with a strong, almost puritanical moral conscience who is
forced to live in such a society. This society might create so
much conflict for him as a consequence of forcing him to
choose between enormous personal deprivation and maintenance of his sense of identity and integrity as a human
being, given the limited plasticity of the adult human psyche,
that mental pathology provides his only "solution."

These examples help us to distinguish between several
important cases concerning judgments that are limited to
particular societies. The individual sees his empirical circumstances, including the physical and social environment, as
parametric "givens" on the whole. If he is reflective, he will
then have a perception of what is good for him in this
system; of the social rules required in general to maintain
these goods, that is, of the just in this society; and of the
institutions and practices required to maintain these rules,
that is, of the good for society. More than this, he will reflect
upon the differences between the different types of social
systems in which he participates. (In the next chapter, the
distinction between the national and the international system
will be discussed with respect to its consequences for the
kinds of rules that are respectively functional.)

Other Tests

There is a more direct form of analysis that is applied to
the psychic system of individuals. An analysis of this is
attempted in *Alienation and Identification.* Other potential
types of objective tests were adumbrated in chapter 2. Let us
reconsider the case of the individual in Edward Banfield's

amoral south Italian town. This individual is not amoral in general. He has a strong sense of obligation to family and those closely related to him. Moreover, he has a conception of the external society that justifies his behavior. Ignorance of this is why so many observers are startled to find that some Mafia members perceive themselves as good individuals. If, however, we can show that there is some inevitable loss of identity in such situations, some loss of authenticity, and so forth, we again will have an evaluational standard.

It may turn out to be the case that no possible combination of environmental and social circumstances permits avoidance of all deprivations with respect to the characteristics we consider in *Alienation and Identification.* Different personality systems may respond to different environments. There is no requirement in principle—indeed, in principle, it is extremely unlikely—that all sets of requirements can be maintained at the highest possible level. However, in principle we could recognize the costs to a personality system of any "solution," provided comparative knowledge enables us to attain sufficient objectivity to identify them. Comparative analysis of different social systems might then permit us to make judgments as to which combinations of systems and rules permitted fuller expressions of the "whole" person. These would be revealed by actual existential choices in circumstances of greater knowledge.

There is, however, as we pointed out earlier, no logical requirement either that justice be an important good or that relatively irreversible changes in the characteristics of man be postulated as non-existent. We know that particular individuals become so bound to their circumstances that they lose their capacity to perceive alternative modes of life as genuine alternatives. Whether the history of the human race has produced system constraints that irreversibly limit our capability to perceive particular types of alternatives or whether different national experiences have done this for the populations of different nations is a question that we have not resolved. However, we have provided a method for investigating it.

Justice as Becoming

Neo-Kantianism, despite the attempt by Rawls to wed economic productivity to his theory, attempts a type of generality that is independent of contextual constraints. The attempt by Rawls to graft the findings of social science onto his theory also fails for this reason, for the findings of social science are never as general as in the covering laws of physics, where independent measures are available. Comparative analysis is essential.

Rawls's difficulty in part rests on a misunderstanding of the function of general rules. He believes that general rules can decide particular cases.[37] Justice Oliver Wendell Holmes was more correct when he said that general principles do not decide particular cases. More often, the legal problem is to decide which of alternative and contradictory rules is to be applied. More primitive conceptions of law are better adapted to empirical distinctions but they lose the power of modern law which is obtained by inattention to particulars. It is the combination of the power, but partial inapplicability, of general rules, and of incompleteness in the bonding together of different moral frames of reference, that gives rise to moral dilemmas—dilemmas that Rawls attempts to legislate out of existence.

The Good and the Just. The system of justice is a very loose system. Even in comparatively primitive social systems, their highly specific norms do not exactly fit individual cases, although in many of these cases the discrepancy may not be, of major importance. The more complex the social system is, the more general the normative structure is and the looser the fit between norm and case.

Even with respect to formal rule systems, there may be more than one rule applicable to a particular case. Law and morality may conflict, as may moral obligations to different institutions, such as state, family, church, and humanity. Rule observance and those acts required to maintain the institutions that sustain the rules (the good for the system) may also conflict in a wide variety of circumstances, as some of our earlier examples indicate. The public rules and the unstated ones may also conflict. There may be a societal need to break the rules and a public need to condemn the rule breaker that in turn conflicts with the moral rule to reward each according to his due.

The great power of the system of justice in modern society—a power that is lodged in its generality—insures conflict among rules in their application to cases and requires a "balancing" of considerations in the determination of particular cases. The system of justice, therefore, defies precise specification. The very attempt to achieve such precision will defeat justice. Thus, it would be unjust to formulate rules, made in ignorance of actual circumstances, that deprive men of their actual goods and social roles merely because these were gained within the framework of rules that are abstractly unjust, whether according to a framework as general as that of Rawls or even according to one more closely related to the circumstances of particular societies and codes of value.

So far we have been attempting to establish that there is a genuine, although complex, relationship between the nature of human beings, social systems, environmental conditions, and systems of justice. The good is intimately linked to the just; however, it is not identical with it.

The worthy innocent who has been convicted according to fair procedures has been done an injury, an evil, despite the justice of the rule. Whether he is obliged to accept the evil in preference to injury to the rule is a difficult question. In the words of Hillel: "If I am not for myself, who will be? If I am not for others, what am I?" The next chapter will discourse further on inconsistencies between procedural and sub-stantive justice.

Rawls attempts to burke this point by insisting upon changes that do not worsen the position of the least well off. Even apart from the other defects of this principle that we have noted, in most complex situations it is not unlikely that each of an exhaustive set of alternative legislations avoids injury to some of the worst off at some expense to others of the worst off. Other types of alternatives in other types of situations would involve still other problems.

It is by no means clear that large injuries to those who are better off are justified by avoiding injuries to those who are worse off. In a world in which expectations are real, and human personality is not entirely flexible, the damage that may be done may be irreparable. A man whose business is confiscated to improve economic distribution—even assuming that the legislation achieves its goal—may find his life in ruins, despite other opportunities technically open to him within the system, and he may be destroyed by the injury. Moreover, under some circumstances, damage to the better off may also damage those political systems within which human freedom has most meaning. We hope this choice will not confront us. But logic alone cannot exclude it.

Reducing Conflict between the Good and the Just. I certainly am not advocating a utilitarian alternative, for util-itarianism does not solve that problem either. Nor am I arguing that all such problems can be solved, for I believe evil to be an inescapable circumstance of life. I am suggesting something else, however. At a certain point the evil done to some, even if strongly justified by genuinely moral con-siderations from some points of view, may justify the resort to war by the injured. We may prevent this by superior force so that resistance becomes useless; but this has little to do with justice. We often wipe out our mistakes, and those who are dead cannot protest that evil was done to them. A failure to recognize the tensions between rules, between goods, and between just rules and various goods will likely exacerbate the problem of evil by blinding us to it.

In some cases those who are injured may regard that injury as just. If they cannot propose an alternative distributive rule for the actual society that they regard as more, or at least as equally, just, and if their identification with society is so great that they desire its good even at their expense, they may accept the sacrifice of their interest, that is, of their good.

A utilitarian might argue that this result is just because less evil is produced than alternative rules would produce. Although the argument is not entirely without merit, it does not decide the issue. Nor does it help too much to point out, as Rawls does, that on balance just institutions produce better results than institutions established according to other rules. Even if that is true, the essential point that cannot be escaped is that existential evil has been done.

Whether such evil can be opposed depends upon the force available to the contending parties. Whether it should be opposed depends upon the extent of the evil, the alternative rules that can be offered, and the harm and the good potentially to be accomplished by challenging implementation of the rule.

It may be that if the challengers can mobilize sufficient force, those in authority will recognize some justice in the protest and back down; and authority may do so merely out of prudence and in the belief that it has given in to an inappropriate claim. It may be that with relative equality of force the two sides may be unable to see any compromise between their opposed rules, and the contest now becomes one beyond the purview of justice.

I have stated the case in relatively neutral terms. However, anguish and tragedy are inescapable aspects of life—aspects that even good fortune and just rules will not enable us to evade. If autonomy is an inherent, but by no means the sole essential, characteristic of man; if, as I believe, we have a genuine interest in the human potentialities of other people; if a moral concern for justice is, as I believe, an inherent element of human nature; then we shall seek to change those aspects of our environments that produce tragic conflicts between rules, between the goods of different human beings, and between rules and goods.

Although it will be our intention to reduce the extent of harm over time, we may not succeed in this and we are surely unlikely to eliminate the occurrence of evil. However, striving toward justice—or striving to reduce injustice—is quite different from regarding justice for all as possible. Knowledge of the complexity of the process opens our minds to the fact that no single set of transitive rules has universal applicability. This knowledge may increase our tolerance in cases of true moral dilemmas and may help us find the wisdom to ameliorate them.

Thus justice is not necessarily a dominant good in the present, although, according to our assumptions, it is a regulative goal toward which we strive. And, although the concept of justice is used to regulate conflicts concerning the attainment of particular goods, their existence as goods is not determined solely by the rules of justice.

If conflicts were always between right and wrong or between good and evil—as they would be if there existed a valid complete, general, and transitive system of justice—our problems in acting justly would be relatively simple. Injury and evil would be potentially evitable. Moral dilemmas would be excluded, for the system of justice would always provide a clearly just solution within the framework of its conceptual system. However, this approach to justice mistakes the character both of the just and the good and is inherently generative of avoidable evil. The real world is one in which good and evil—at least in complex cases—are inescapably symbiotic.

Chapter 4

Political Obligation

OBLIGATION AND HUMAN NATURE

A theory of obligation would be pretentious if applied to narrowly conceived goods or interests. To say that a man is obliged to do that which is good for him is to say only that he ought to do it if he wishes to accomplish his good. The arguments of the previous chapters are designed to show that he will wish to accomplish his good, at least under the conditions of the test in principle.[1]

The problem of obligation arises in significant form when moral codes or the good of the group are opposed to the narrowly conceived good of the individual. Such moral codes may be regarded as obligatory by most people even when they conflict with important, or even vital, personal interests. Social psychologists may provide a satisfactory explanation for this state of affairs from a psychological point of view. However, its philosophical and ethical validation presents—or at least seems to present—great difficulties.

Hobbes attempted to solve the problem by establishing a sovereign whose penalties would "oblige" the individual in terms of his narrow self-interests. And, indeed, many weak "obligations" of this type do exist.

Rawls attempted to solve the problem by a hypothetical moral contract. We have seen that its content is intellectually indefensible. Moreover, to say, as he does, that moral men will observe such rules is merely to adopt a particular definition of morality. The problem still arises as to why men are obliged to be moral in that sense.

A philosophical theory of political obligation must show that at least some legal and moral norms under some conditions are goods for men in other than a narrowly instrumental sense; for otherwise it cannot explain why men should relinquish more narrowly conceived and usually clearer goods. If it can do so, then the obligations prescribed by at least that set of norms or rules become obligations of the individual.

However, more than one set of rules may meet this test. Therefore, existential conflicts of choice may arise from applications of these sets of rules, even apart from those arising from different rules of the same normative system. Each set of rules will determine a set of rights and obligations. To the extent, therefore, that these code applications conflict, there may be no determinate choice from among these rights and obligations and there will be "rightful" claims by some that can be denied "rightfully" by others. Therefore, obligation is a genuine problem that is produced by moral conflict and not merely by inadequacy of understanding or immorality of character.

The extent and content of obligation are empirical matters that vary with circumstances. Therefore, systematic empirical treatment is beyond the scope of this, or any, book. However, we can offer strong reasons for accepting its existence.

If bonding, resulting from evolutionary biology, generalizing aspects of the mind, the sense of identity, empathetic insight into other personalities, the limited plasticity of the developed personality, and other as yet unidentified aspects of human "nature" require moral rules, as I believe they do, these may be intrinsic needs and may establish "absolute"— although, under particular circumstances, inconsistent—claims upon the person. Further complications arise from the fact that although sodalities and associations may be intrinsic in general, particular memberships may be at least partly instrumental, for they are partly substitutable—but only partly, for too instrumental an approach may be destructive to the sense of identity and the integrity of the personality. On the other hand, if membership in organizations is primarily instrumental—a position I reject—political obligations are primarily instrumental as well and bind men only so long as the more particular interests of the state and of the citizens are coincident.[2]

If political and social institutions are clearly instrumental in one sense, as prerequisites for human goal seeking, and within some limits substitutable for each other, there is another sense in which I believe that our prior hypotheses indicate that they constitute intrinsic requirements in the same sense in which food, although not necessarily any particular variety, is intrinsically required. However, unlike the case of food, where the variety of choice or style of cooking is often, although not invariably, more related to taste than to nourishment, certain distinctions between types of social and political systems may ride to the heart of the difference between good and bad. It is on this latter assumption that we shall now proceed.

Obligations and "Political System"

Because political obligations have reference to political systems, let us turn to an analysis of that concept to understand political obligations. Two very powerful conceptions of the political system have been offered by Max Weber and David Easton. According to Weber the political system is that system which has a monopoly of legitimate power. According to Easton the political system is that system which authoritatively allocates values. Both of these formulations entail intrinsic difficulties. Obviously the political system does not have a monopoly of power. Fathers exercise power over children, for instance. No known political system has been able to control all criminal violence or even all revolutionary political activity. Weber's formulation depends upon the word "legitimate." In the same way, with respect to Easton's formulation, no political system has ever allocated all values. Religious values have been allocated by churches. Other values have been allocated by the family, by the economic market system, and by social groupings. Easton's formulation depends upon the word "authoritative." In *System and Process,* I describe "political system" in the following fashion:

> A political system, like many other social systems, has recognizable interests which are not identical—though not necessarily opposed and perhaps complementary—with those of the members of the system and within which there are regularized agencies and methods for making decisions concerning those interests. The rules for decision making, including the specification of the decision-making roles and the general constitutional rules governing the society, are enacted within the political system.
>
> The modern political system is distinguished by the fact that its rules specify the areas of jurisdiction for all other decision-making units and provide methods for settling conflicts of jurisdiction. It is hierarchical in character and territorial in domain. The existence of a government is an unambiguous sign of a political system since governments are hierarchical in organization and since they arbitrate jurisdictional disputes between other subsystems of the society.[3]

This conception of a political system is related directly to the systems method of analysis and, in specific, to the concepts of ultrastability and transfinite stability. The political system has the metatask capacity[4] to act as the regulator of the larger system in which it functions. It thus regulates the system by adapting it to environmental disturbances in such a way that critical values of the system are maintained. Let us now relate this formulation of "political system" to the problem of legitimacy and, therefore, to the problem of political obligation.

Note that the political system does two things. It maintains a set of institutional practices that are at least partly characterized by sets of rules; these, in turn, are justified by broader rule considerations such as justice or morality. It also engages in more specific goal prosecution and acquisition activities. These are required partly to maintain the political system and partly to satisfy subsidiary objectives of participants within the system.

Under particular sets of empirical circumstances, conflicts between these various activities can arise. For instance, during the Second World War the British government incarcerated suspected traitors under the Crown Acts. This was considered essential to prosecution of the war although inconsistent with the rules of a democratic polity. However, it was correctly believed that a return to peace would restore the set of democratic rules. On the other hand, in Northern Ireland and Palestine serious questions arise as to whether any set of political rules is capable of providing minimal levels of substantive justice for the contending parties given the specific histories of these societies, the specific self-definitions of the groups, and other empirical circumstances. Although the possibility of a satisfactory inventive solution to these problems cannot be excluded, they illustrate the necessary case: that in which formal and substantive justice may be irreconcilable or, alternatively, that in which substantive justice for competing groups may be simultaneously impossible.

Contextual Character of Obligations.   Note carefully that this conception of the problem does not entail any particular type of political system. We cannot evaluate the worth of alternative institutions except in relation to the types of task they are expected to perform and the circumstances under which they are to be performed.

No reasonable person would suggest that the operations of a modern jetliner should be subject to a vote by the passengers. This would be recognized as an absurdity. If, on the other hand, the pilot of a plane takes it upon himself to fly to Tokyo rather than to Paris, where it was scheduled to land, the passengers would feel that he had exceeded his authority. In political terms, the action would be regarded as tyrannous.

The classic philosophers distinguished between monocratic rule, where the ruler was governed by considerations of justice, and tyranny, where the ruler acted primarily in terms of his individual interests or desires. Although it is not true that every act of a tyrant legitimately can be disobeyed, a distinction to which we will soon turn, the obligations to the tyrant were of a clearly more instrumental character than were obligations to a king.

It is a well-known fact that the emergence of strong kings in the early modern ages was required to overcome feudal constraints on strong economic and social tendencies that were becoming manifest. I am not implying that strong kings were inevitable, but only that their potential was related to needs of developing subsystems within the larger social system. To have regarded monarchial rule as illegitimate because it failed to respond to the contractual necessities of the original condition would have been an absurdity.

The rise of modern representative democracy also was related to certain potentialities in social, economic, and political processes. As Marx put it, the new system was nurtured in the bosom of the old. On the other hand, no justification of political circumstances can be given entirely in terms of social, economic, and political "necessities." What emerged from the preconditions was not some preordained solution determined by a single and narrow set of constraints, but a solution based on a larger set of constraints, permitting some types of alternatives, and requiring a far more complex set of justifications, often related to correlate conceptions of the world, of human nature, and of justice.

Legitimacy

There are three layers of meaning that need to be disentangled if legitimacy is to be understood.

Actual Behavior and Legitimacy. In the first place, we have the actual behavior of people. If inhabitants of a political entity obey established authority structures, the outside observer might say that there is a concordance between the behavior of people and the putative legitimacy of the political system.

Beliefs and Legitimacy. The second level of investigation involves the mental states of the people within the system. If, from their parochial framework of knowledge, they see the authority structure as effective in maintaining control, as acting in accordance with reasonable rules of justice, as coping with reasonable effectiveness with the environmental situation as they understand it, and as not entirely inconsistent with their interests, they will tend to view it as legitimate. The type of system they view as legitimate will vary with their background, experience, stage of life, and life expectations. Under some circumstances, the divine right of kings will seem self-evident. Under some circumstances, individuals will not see themselves as rational creatures. Under some circumstances they will not conceive of themselves as political subjects, but rather as political objects.

The Context of Beliefs. The third level of examination involves self-reflexive thought about political legitimacy. If thoughtful men take into account comparative knowledge

about human nature, social science, and environmental possibility, and if the political system is adequately responsive to
these both in terms of procedural means and substantive
results, they will assess the system as legitimate. And this will
be an objective judgment although, as in the case of all
factual assessments, not necessarily correct.

Let us consider the case, however, where either the rule of
procedure or the substantive results or both are regarded as
bad—views that may be related to a particular conception of
the nature of human personality, to the extent to which man
is defined as a rational agent, or to an analysis of political,
social, or economic conditions.

In this latter case, where the regime is effective, that is,
where it cannot be replaced except at great cost, if at all,
then those who recognize the propriety of political obligation
in principle will recognize a limited duty to treat the regime
as if it were legitimate, taking into account their own needs,
their obligations to others, and the effects of their conduct
upon the potential for future change. But they will regard it
as only quasi-legitimate.

Performance and Legitimacy.   From a more pragmatic
point of view, the legitimacy of any government will come
into question whenever its constitution becomes inconsistent
with the substantive justice that important social groups
believe is their due or when its procedural rules or institutional practices are at odds with beliefs concerning the nature
of man or of the proper organization of governmental roles.
Under these conditions, claims are made against the institutional structure that can be repressed if the government has
sufficient effective force at its disposal and sufficient will
(based upon a belief in the justness of the institutions that
are being defended or the consequences to the holders of
power for not defending them) to use them. Otherwise the
attack can be deflected by buying it off, that is, by satisfying
enough of the opponents to divest the remainder of the
power to challenge the regime, or by attempting to demon-

strate that those who are challenging the regime mistake the character of their obligations.

Lawfulness and Legitimacy. The argument that the government is acting under law is not fully effective or logically impeccable. However, many people do act out of habit and there is always some cost, particularly in terms of future uncertainties, in challenging any effective system of law. On the other hand, the difficulty with an assertion of legality as ultimate criterion lies in the fact that it is often the character of the law that is under attack. Even if the exterminations in the Nazi concentration camps had been carried out under a relevant German law, no moral person would have recognized that as an effective argument for submission.

We like to believe that democracies are somehow different and that laws in substantively democratic states deserve the kind of obedience that the laws of the Nazi state did not. That, however, is hardly an argument that will be effective to a true believer. He may be convinced that he has no chance to overthrow the democratic system, but the fact that the laws have been instituted by majority voting will not impress him.

Moreover, even well-intentioned democratic laws may be injurious to particular groups. Even apart from other injustices to the Indians by the expanding American nation, the full exposure of their tribal systems to secular state organization, even under conditions of substantive equality, might well have been unjust, even if no practicable alternative existed. Their views of man and of his relation to the tribe and the universe may have been so fundamentally different from European concepts that our framework of legitimacy could become applicable, if ever, only after we had suppressed their culture, and only for a new generation of Indians.

I am not arguing that no choice is possible between competing perspectives. I agree that however "soft" our evidence, comparative knowledge does provide us with a better conception of man and of social and political organization. I do believe some comparisons are possible concerning better or worse forms of social, political, and economic organization, at least within the constraints of particular types of environmental conditions. However, there are two existential facts that must be noted. Those whose views remain different will not be convinced merely by the argument of legality. Moreover, even if our evidence were harder than it is, people are not infinitely malleable, at least within one generation. Therefore the imposition of particular institutional styles on others, even by democratic vote, may do them an unmitigated evil; and this may be true even if no compromise is possible in fact and they are in a distinct minority.

If this is the case, then those who are injured do not have an obligation to recognize authority as legitimate and they are justified in opposition. It is precisely this kind of conflict that produces existential tragedy, for if justice were purely abstract there would always be enough for everyone, and some solution related to a fully transitive and consistent set or ordering of preferences would in principle solve all our problems. In this case, with more knowledge well-intentioned and principled individuals could always find the right line of conduct that no one could justly oppose. It is the belief that this is the case that often closes our eyes to the nature of human tragedy and that inures us to the costs we impose upon others, where otherwise the conflict, though genuine, might at least be mitigated by our knowledge that we are not acting on the basis of a universal principle of justice to which all owe obligation.

The problems of political legitimacy arise differently in different forms of political systems that rest on different views of man, of political and social organization, of the world generally, and of God. Certain obvious differences depend upon whether one has the opportunity to vote for change in government or whether a king rules by divine right. Obviously the latter form of government during the Middle Ages gave rise to monkish inquiries into problems of regicide.

The distinction between formal and substantive justice, however, implies that formal justifications will not alone suffice to oblige those whose interests are severely damaged, even within democracies. Moreover, our standard continually varies with our understanding of real-life conditions.

Obligation and Contract

The obligation to support a political system—or to improve it—rests upon its intrinsic relationship to the accomplishment of good. Good is potential in social systems, in norms, and in other relationships, as well as in the consequences of more particular acts. Good also is related to the sense of identification of the personality—a subject to which I return in *Alienation and Identification*—and in the bonding between the self and some others and between the self and social systems and codes of behavior. Obligation, therefore, is imbedded in existence; it is not merely the product of a contract.[5] For this reason no political obligation exists unless an authority system is effective either actually or potentially. Whereas a similar assumption is employed by Hans Kelsen in his pure theory of law, it is an arbitrary factual element in an otherwise purely logical system. It functions here within a consistent framework. The obligation stems from the capacity of the system either actually or potentially to produce good.

Obligation, thus, does not follow merely from mutuality of will; and lawbreaking behavior by some will not justify disobedience by others, except in those cases in which the extent of lawbreaking or amoral behavior renders inoperable attempts to support this form of system, whether in the present or presumptively in the future, as a means for the accomplishment of good. The latter consideration is sufficient to remove the obligation of the individual to support institutions that would be good if they were more generally supported.

However, even in the case where the support of good institutions is general, the good of a particular group, as defined by some existential characteristic, may be at such odds with the good of good institutions that the obligation is also sundered. Note, however, that this conclusion cannot be drawn merely in principle, for it requires examination of the particular case. Individuals rationally may sacrifice themselves, although in one sense this defeats their pursuit of their own good, when their identification with institutional practices and with groups benefited by these practices is so complete that survival outside of the group is possible only in a severely damaged state. Whether this is true in any particular case depends upon the existential identifications of the person, the condition of his information-processing mechanisms, and so forth.

Thus an individual's obligations to the state may come into conflict with other obligations to himself or to other individuals or groups. Which, if any, of the obligations takes precedence cannot be determined by an *a priori* analysis that deals with only one set of considerations, that of a just political system. Analysis must be extended to the realm of praxis. Which obligation assumes priority depends upon the entire economy of the personality in the context of all its relationships to political, social, and sodality systems. Personal as well as group tragedy may be inescapable if genuine obligations are in irremedial conflict.

It is obvious that the obligation to support a bad political system may be sundered, although even this is denied by some; however, even obligations to good systems are limited, and this may be true even when, on balance, they produce good, for that good may be incompatible with the good of other groups important to the existential identity of the citizen. The good he has gained from his citizenship is only one factor that the citizen weighs in his complex moral "balance."

State-of-Nature Theory. We have seen that a theory of contract fails as a ground for obligation. This is true both of modern contract theory, as in Hobbes, Rousseau, Kant, and Rawls, and in ancient consent doctrine as in the arguments of Socrates at the end of *Crito,* where, in my opinion, the argument is deliberately specious. Modern contract theory, however, often is related to a theory of the state of nature, whether in a real or hypothetical sense. In some of these theories, it might be argued that the obligation of the contract follows not from consent but from the good that consent is alleged to produce; and, therefore, that the prior criticism does not hold.

Where the state of nature is alleged to be real, the argument fails readily. There is no historical evidence of such a state. So-called primitive societies, as anthropologists have shown, are complex and sophisticated in their social structure. Ethologists have demonstrated complex social structure among animals. And both among men and among animals the differences in social structure and behavior outweigh similarities except at such a high level of abstraction—for example, all human societies outlaw murder—that the important differences are imbedded not in the rules of behavior but in the individual societies' definitions of the terms that are included in the rules.

Where the state of nature is presumed to be hypothetical, contract theory suffers from a fatal defect: the fact that human nature does not exist in the abstract. In chapter 2, I showed that human nature is a defensible concept if it is treated dispositionally. Treated abstractly, however, it implies an identity between a representation and a real-world counterpart. I have already criticized this epistemological position with respect to such supposedly simple qualities as "red" and such complex qualities as "goods."

No such external counterparts to concepts exist. And identifications of concepts with observed qualities can be made only within the context of specified experimental conditions such as human optic systems and light from a body such as that of Sol I for "red" or a given temperature range for the inclusion of a metal within the class of hard objects.

There is no reason to believe that the requirements of association that men would perceive in a "natural" setting would be more basic or "true" than those they would perceive in a more complex setting. The behavior of humans is critically dependent on context. If man ever were in an "aboriginal" state of nature, he likely would not be capable of reason or consent in an informed sense. Monkeys raised in isolation are sociopathic, as are feral children. Therefore, it is obviously inadequate to extrapolate what an aboriginal man would prefer in a state of nature. On the other hand, for modern man to extrapolate from a hypothetical state of nature, he must base his extrapolation on his own cultural norms. Yet any slight relaxation of the standard of the state of nature immediately gives rise to behavioral and moral norms as radically different from each other as those found in the Hopi and the Kwakiutl.

A state-of-nature theory will permit the derivation of limited conclusions only to the extent that more specific assumptions are "smuggled" into the theory. Each theorist likely will "smuggle" in just those assumptions that are related to his own society in some important fashion—a theorist in libertarian societies deriving libertarian conclusions and one in collectivist societies, collectivist conclusions. He may do this in a straightforward way or counterfactually to support his preferred system by contrast.

Although such theories may on occasion illuminate the problem of obligation in a particular type of society, more often the constraints that might require particular forms of obligation in a "state of nature" will be so different from those of actual societies that no conclusions follow with respect to the character of obligations in the latter. And in some cases, one might more easily extrapolate from the describable behavior of neutrons in interstellar space to their describable behavior in the core of the sun.

"State-of-nature" theories when intended to be generally applicable are misapplications of counterfactual ideal theories, for example, motion-in-a-vacuum types of physical theory, for the latter permit approximations in certain respects whereas general theories (more accurately, concepts) of human nature do not.

No relevant social science theory employs an assumption concerning human nature that can be generalized to all other comparable theories. A counterfactual assumption, such as the profit maximization assumption in economic theory, is useful only in those economies where a prediction of its consequences is relevant to behavior. Moreover, although capitalist economic theory does not assert that all men will behave according to the profit maximizing assumption, its use within an articulated theory permits a prediction concerning contrary behavior. The failure to pay proper attention to profits produces unsuccessful competition and bankruptcy. However, the same theory fails to explain why General Motors does not maximize profits—because it would drive Ford and Chrysler out of business and invite federal intervention—and we must turn to a political explanation.

Capitalist economic theory is useless in explaining economic behavior in some types of economic systems, including those in which profit-maximizing behavior is punished by cultural sanction. Thus, no theory of natural behavior in a so-called state of nature can be assumed to provide relevant information about behavior in other kinds of systems or to establish state-of-nature conditions as preferred. If we were to conduct an experiment in which children were raised in a state of nature—presuming counterfactually that we could adequately restrict the concept so as to produce a unique set of preferences that were invariant for men, regardless of various experimental conditions that different investigators might choose—the resulting preferences might exclude or minimize the state only because of dysfunctional sociopathology, as in the case of feral children. In this case, the horizons of these "men" would be severely restricted and their choices rejected by those who have experienced some form of society and/or state.

The fact that socialization is virtually universal among animals and that acculturation is universal among primates suggests a genetic predisposition in man toward some form of altruism that is not instrumental in egocentric terms, and the terms of which depend upon the historical experiences that shape his identifications. We know from work in psychology that the development of some key potentialities in the individual—intellectual, moral, and social—are dependent not merely on certain types of environmental experiences but upon their occurrence during particular phases of the individual life history.

Even if we knew how to define what we mean by individual advantage in a way that did not beg all the important questions, an exclusively egocentric mode of analysis would be inadequate for moral theory. And it is not unlikely that the extreme individualism of much of modern society and the theories that support it are among the causes of the dysfunctions of contemporary society. Thus, even if adequate egocentric, state-of-nature-type instrumental reasons can be supplied for some of the social and political limits placed on human behavior, this form of argument at best has supportive value, for its fundamental assumption that only such derivations have merit is both unproved and in conflict with the best evidence of social science.

Furthermore, the moral irrelevance of state-of-nature or egoistic moral theories should be obvious on even simpler grounds. If altruism in some form is a genetic predisposition of man and a constraint affecting his psychological health and sense of identity, it is also an evolutionary social necessity that is reinforced by socialization and acculturation. Moreover, from a moral point of view extreme selfishness is untenable. Human accomplishments are dependent upon living in a particular society—a society the character of which was produced by the productivity of a given generation's collective ancestors. Those who accomplish more than others in that society usually benefit not only from advantages of individual genetic and social inheritance but from the fact that that society aids the development of and rewards some capabilities more than others, as the merchant would discover during the early stages of feudalism and the warrior under capitalism. Thus, whatever defects the argument for equality possesses, arguments against some redistribution are equally faulty. And attempts to derive moral theory or even a theory of economic redistribution from an atomistic individualistic standpoint are fallacious.

Philosophically, state-of-nature moral theory commits the error of seeking a single and unique moral theory that applies to all human situations and that is based on lawlike, that is, universally true, premises. Nowhere in the social sciences, where homeostatic systems are operative, are such theories available for reasons I have explained in chapter 1. Moreover, as I have argued in the previous chapters, all knowledge, including that of the hard sciences, is validated by field-dependent factors, only individual theories having the character attributed to scientific theory. However, even were theories containing lawlike statements that are true for all social systems available in the social sciences, the attempt to deduce moral theory from such a social theory—rather than to treat it as controlling the outer limits of moral behavior much as physical theory sets limits on design for building a bridge or designing an airplane—would mistake the problem of moral "theory" and of the boundary conditions under which moral rules are applicable.

In their effort to establish general principles for political society, state-of-nature theorists fail to distinguish theory—which requires counterfactual axioms as a precondition for generality—from engineering, as in the design of an airplane, where contextual variables and behavioral properties play the key roles. Choosing conditions for a society is a design or engineering problem; and it is critically dependent on behavioral parameters. Human nature, as distinguished from variable assumptions concerning human behavior that can be employed in theories explaining particular types of social systems, as in the case of the propensity to save in Keynesian economic theory, is dispositional. Therefore, it is context-dependent. We learn of its limits and of its potentialities only from comparative evidence and not by extrapolation from a hypothetical original condition. State-of-nature theories, therefore, are scientistic rather than scientific.

With recognition of this, the concept of aboriginal natural rights as a foundation for civil rights and obligations and the distinction between "natural" and "artificial" societies collapse. A dispositional concept of human nature does not require the concept of a state of nature. It suggests the use of comparative evidence concerning human behavior in articulating a theory of obligations. From this standpoint, the genesis of societies is irrelevant as a foundation for rights or obligations. Instead, obligation lies in identification with the capacity of a society—larger or smaller, depending on the state of the world—to facilitate desirable goals according to contemporary understanding. The third level of legitimation brings to consciousness an obligation to work for a better society. Thus, the correct perspective concerning "natural" obligation is norm-oriented and not state-of-nature-oriented.

Individualism and Collectivism.   My "theory" bases obligation on the individual's interest in good institutions and normative rules rather than on the fact of assent; although I agree that individuals with adequate knowledge will assent to their obligations. Because man's interest in good institutions arises out of the complex interrelationships of the individual with social systems—that is, out of his existential identifications—this theory is not atomistically individualistic. Historical man identifies with social groupings; and an essential element of his selfhood lies in this fact. On the other hand, because, as argued in chapter 3, the frames of reference are not identical, the identification of men with social groupings or with other individuals is never complete. Knowledge of this is possessed by the individual; and, on occasion, knowledge of a legitimate rupture of identification will occur. For this reason, my theory is not collectivistic either.

Both frames of reference—the individual and the social—have moral value for human beings. The determination of the principles and the tactical considerations that ought to guide moral behavior is a matter of praxis (the realm of knowledge). Therefore, statements concerning the ways in which these two sets of considerations should guide moral behavior in particular social systems depend on the character of the social systems and of their environments. Attempts to generalize that ignore the relevant considerations will lead to abstract norms that cannot guide behavior in concrete situations.

After the manuscript of this book had been, I thought, finished, a new book by Robert Nozick, *Anarchy, State and Utopia*, [6] which restates the classic libertarian position on the state, was published—too late for me to incorporate a detailed criticism of Nozick's argument in this book. I do wish, however, to note it briefly here.

It is evident that Nozick's argument will fail for a number of reasons. In the first place, as we have seen, it is impossible to devise a set of ethical rules or a governmental system that can be generalized for all societies. In the second place, contractual and state-of-nature arguments mistake the character of political and moral obligation and also of human nature, for reasons supplied earlier in this book. Furthermore, although any student of the matter will be horrified by the waste and inefficiency currently produced by excessive government regulation, the atomistic individualism assumed in libertarian expositions badly mistakes the extent to which richness of social identification is a human need and to which instrumentality in attitudes toward society is destructive of the personality.

Rich societies might do well to foresake economic efficiency in order to protect individuals from the devastating effects of business cycles (it is not clear that such economic engineering—given the instabilities that feedback produces in the economic system in contrast to what static models predict—even reduces efficiency in the intermediate run).

We have seen in this chapter that any system of distribution excludes certain types of choices. Recognition through the test in principle of the range of alternatives—and of the institutional means for permitting the manifestation of preferences within systems that provide superior opportunities—invokes moral obligations to promote such changes. *Alienation and Identification* shows how the factor of identification circumscribes the character of obligation and how it subordinates certain kinds of individual goods to certain kinds of social goods. However, the qualifiers are important, for the kind of society that is good depends upon what is good for the individual. No theory that ignores the appropriate tension between individualism and collectivism can appropriately delineate the human dilemma or the character of human obligation. Neither individualistic nor collectivistic theories are capable of this.

Avoidance of Historicism. The reader will note that the application of the three-tiered set of considerations avoids the difficulties of historicism. No examination of the legitimacy of a system can be removed from its mooring in existential, historic conditions. However, no self-reflexive judgment concerning the legitimacy of a system is restricted to an evaluation of its actual efficacy. Although recognizing that many self-reflexive criticisms may be poorly based—perhaps, for instance, related to the insecurity of young people in certain kinds of social systems—and may result from only partial perspectives on the problem, self-reflexive thought can bring to bear upon this problem the entire apparatus of human thought, including comparative knowledge of human nature and of social, political, economic, and moral institutions.

Self-reflexive thought can bring to awareness our feelings about particular roles in given institutions. We can place ourselves imaginatively in a variety of roles. We can contrast imaginatively different life styles in institutions as different as modern technological society and feudalism, for instance. Because we can examine how personality develops and becomes manifest in a variety of roles, we can escape from conceptions of man that are too greatly shaped by his embeddedness in a particular life or too abstractly denuded of concrete details, as in the case of the abstract Feuerbachian "man" against whom Karl Marx railed so vocally. It is the examination of man in his richness of being in a variety of environmental conditions both fortunate and unfortunate and in a variety of roles that reveals to us through his comparative dispositions to act the meaning of his nature and of social and political organization. Our knowledge of man and society must always be partial in some sense. Yet the original condition proposed by Rawls produces the very overabstraction against which Hegel and Marx warned us.

To what extent is man's self-reflexive agency the most important aspect of his being? To what extent must it be modified by considerations of group bonding? Medieval man would not have seen his agency as either Gewirth or Rawls does. Twenty-second-century man may have a still different view of it based upon more adequate information. Perhaps it is this very view of man as an agent, given full play in a utilitarian age, that makes him so lonely and self-destructive. If we were to come to that conclusion—which I hasten to add I do not—perhaps restrictions on democracy would be a small price to pay to achieve better social and political conditions. It is precisely because considerations of justice are closely bound to the texture of empirical conditions that our moral notions in practice, as opposed to overly abstract thought, are rich, subject to reexamination and development, and dependent upon a continual interplay between being and potentiality.

Legitimacy, Consent, and Will. Now that I have stated my position, a few brief comments may be in order over why theories of consent and will became so popular in modern

Europe. The Renaissance gradually brought man rather than God into the center of the universe. This is nowhere so graphically portrayed as in the paintings of the northern Renaissance in which the Christ shifts over time from the center to the periphery of pictures and eventually disappears entirely.

With the shift from a God-centered to a man-centered universe, a new basis for legitimacy had to be found. Methodological individualists such as Hobbes found it in consent, although Hobbes deliberately transformed his concept of freedom—which, in the state of nature, is simply absence of restraint—to include the fear of consequences in civil society, thereby, with a sleight-of-hand trick, masking the dilemma, or even paradox, of obligation in civil society that arises under his assumptions. As a consequence, society as well as God was eliminated as a source of intrinsic value and the relations of men became purely instrumental.

Modern science, the concept of fortune, and views of man as the master of nature reinforced these tendencies. Contract theory, therefore, in general became a matter of the will or intention of the parties to agreements to the virtual exclusion of matters of morals, social policy, trade customs, or changed circumstances—matters that hopelessly confounded jurisprudential analyses of contracts according to the will theory of contracts. And, as a consequence, legal theory in this form became increasingly divorced from judicial practice.

Methodological collectivists—and here I am oversimplifying for emphasis—such as Rousseau tried to find obligation not in the actual will of actual men but in the true will of Man. In a sense, these theories centered more on the right to compel that on the duty to obey, even when consent was formally introduced into the theory. Hegel's theory of trial is a complex variant of this position.

As positivism eroded the belief in a common standard for, or even the scientifically meaningful character of, the good, methodological individualism, at least in Western Europe, won out over methodological collectivism and necessarily rested its concept of legitimacy on consent. It is true that a few more sophisticated versions of this doctrine argued that consent was given on the basis of a conception of good, which, therefore, was logically prior to consent. However, this was almost always a static, individualized, and subjective conception of good that was related to an overly abstract conception of a human reason that, in turn, was detached from anything like the iterated test in principle and contextual analysis. At best, it was oriented toward a general ideal system that was so abstract that it was unrelated to real moral problems in real societies. In any case, methodological individualism tended to undercut the legitimacy of compulsion and methodological collectivism tended to undermine the legitimacy of consent. Because neither approach was complete without the formal inclusion of the unassimilable correlate concept—unassimilable, at least, within the reigning philosophical tradition—each approach produced dilemmas in practice.

The general reasons for the dilemmas produced by these approaches have already been elucidated. They are based on a view of science that is still too close to that of the seventeenth century in which laws apply to all events in a uniform manner. As we have seen, there are no general theories even for physics. And, in physics, theories containing laws are both restricted as to subject matter and subject to adjustment as their "fit" with other theories, propositions, and observations is considered within the realm of praxis. Furthermore, most of these positions are formulated within a philosophical tradition that distinguishes between "real things" and subjective representations of them. As a corollary, physical objects are viewed as objective and values as subjective. Thus, the fundamentally different status of values and of real states of the world makes the relationship of obligation to real governmental institutions highly problematic, for they are separate spheres, the relationships between which are "produced" only by consent or will. The objective and subjective are not fundamentally joined; and, in this dichotomous world, an artificial cement is required. Thus, will and consent doctrines are necessary to account for those aspects of obligation that are both observed and desired. However, they invariably fail to account for practice or to relate adequately to the observed dilemmas of obligation.

The discussion of legitimacy that is based on the conception of ethics developed in this book is not subject to these difficulties. And although obligation often becomes an existential problem because of conflicting frames of reference in real circumstances, it is no longer a philosophical problem. These existential conflicts accord with the philosophical account of a world in which facts and values and subjects and objects are not dichotomous.

Identity and Obligation

Before we turn to an examination of legitimacy in democratic systems, particularly of the American type, it may be useful to reinforce the argument that obligation and identification are factual or historical matters. From one standpoint these identifications are accidental. From another, they are a necessary focal point for the consideration of problems of justice; for they remove such discussions from the Platonic netherworld of abstractions to the real world in which real men have real interests in real goods.

By what warrant does a nation restrict its membership to the children of nationals or to those born in its territory? By the abstract criteria of John Rawls (who surprisingly does not mention this problem), nationality is as accidental as intelligence or family fortune. Why should citizenship in a nation not be open to all who wish to join it and who state their willingness to abide by its fundamental rules (a criterion, incidentally, not demanded of those who obtain nationality

by birth)? By what warrant do nations retain title to the
natural resources within their territory which they have done
nothing to create? If their greater natural wealth attracts
immigration, why is this not justified?

Obviously there is a selfish element in restriction, but is all
selfishness wrong? To repeat the aphorism of Hillel: "If I am
not for myself, who will be? If I am not for others, what am
I?" The first part of the aphorism recognizes the fact of
existential particularities that, according to wider frames of
reference, are accidental. If, from one frame of reference, we
are intelligent, rich, and American by accident, from another
frame of reference we are human by accident. Good always
has an existential referent and identification is the relevant
concept.

Rawls fails to distinguish between those claims that are
legitimized by the wider frames of references, such as being
men, and those claims that are legitimized by more particular
frames of reference. If it does not follow in logic that claims
stemming from more particular frames of reference override
those related to more general frames of reference, neither
does it follow, as Hillel's aphorism makes clear, that they are
illegitimate. No theory of justice that ignores them can be
adequate. Although Gewirth argues against Rawls that the
conception of the original condition overlooks the fact that
men are inescapably aware of these differences, the important fact is that claims based upon them have some legitimacy.

What are the claims that can serve to legitimize restrictions
on immigration? I shall not attempt to state them exhaus-
tively but only to name some. A nation has a claim to its
cultural identity. An extensive immigration that would
threaten this identity is an evil. It even has a claim to protect
the good fortune of its members, so that an extensive immigration that would drastically lower its living standards, even
if not below a tolerable minimum, legitimately may be resisted. It has some claim to doubt whether immigrants from
other cultures really understand in a judgmental sense those

things that make its institutions operate. Thus, it does not have to prove that they are a threat; it has the claim prudentially to protect against the not unreasonable possibility that they are a threat.

These claims are not absolute. Questions may be raised, even in the absence of appropriate institutional mechanisms for settling them, as to whether fortunate nations do not have some obligation to aid those less fortunate in very severe conditions or partly to open their doors to oppressed emigrant groups whose survival otherwise would be threatened. To what extent any of these claims have merit can be investigated only within the context of specific existential conditions. Similar distinctions obviously apply within nations and also within other systems and subsystems. How these distinctions apply to problems of decision cannot be answered in general form.

The Argument for Democracy

For the remainder of this chapter, I intend to examine specific types of problems concerning legitimacy as they arise in relatively democratic systems, although occasional references will be made to other forms of government. I shall conduct this examination at the most general level of analysis as I wish to clarify only some of the most obvious problems of civil obligation in a democracy. Thus, much of the relevant concrete world—work status, income level, family, social status and environment, living conditions, access to political decisions, and so forth—will be left out of account. If, instead, I were making an analysis of the problem of obligation in contemporary American society, that exclusion could not be justified. However, a complex discussion of obligation in contemporary American society would obscure my present purpose.

Before I launch this inquiry, a few words about a preference for democracy are in order. As the authors of the

Federalist Papers indicated, many of the arguments for democracy rest on pragmatic grounds. Because the democratic process permits a multitude of interests to be expressed through the political process, they cannot easily be ignored entirely. And, to the extent that such partial interests are destructive of the overriding public interest, the authors of the *Federalist Papers* hoped that they would cancel out. Thus, these authors did not view democracy as a magic device that would produce the best government or even particularly good government. It would avoid the worst of evils and protect the interests even of relatively weak groups.

Churchill said that democracy is the best of a bad lot. Other types of political systems, historical judgment suggests, might work better on occasion, but they are subject to wide variation and gross injustice. Thus, modern democracy does not have the moral basis of classic democracy, where citizenship was viewed as an important, and perhaps essential, element of man's nature.

The Unproved Case. We can hardly argue that democratic government works well. The worldwide inflation; ethnic controversies in Northern Ireland, Belgium, Canada, and Cyprus; and the racial issue in the United States raise serious questions about its effectiveness in solving the problems we face. Do these defects stem from a failure of intelligence? If so, would democracy be worth the moral price of a massive eugenics program? Is the decentralization and the pluralism of the political process the cause of its inability to solve the problem of inflation? If so, can a solution be found within the framework of democratic methods? Is it true that economic competitiveness breeds a success-orientation that is destructive of the finer feelings and productive of paranoia and personality abnormality? If so, would we be willing to demolish democratic institutions?

I mention these problems primarily because I shall have to burke, that is, fail to do justice to, them in the discussion below. However, let us be honest enough to admit that we do not know enough about the requirements of democratic self-government under modern conditions, about its impact upon human personality, upon its consequences for political decision making, and so forth. Despite my own belief in democratic forms of government, I do not view their success or their consistency with good or justice as self-evident. The arguments for democracy are hypotheses with some empirical evidence to sustain them. The strongest argument for democracy is negative: evidence concerning the inequities and failures of all other types of political systems.

A Moral Foundation for Democratic Belief. A belief in democracy as the virtuous form of government does entail a belief in human autonomy. A partial argument for this position is made in *Alienation and Identification,* where I attempt to show how respect for autonomy in others is related to one's own sense of identity and authenticity. However, the argument, although persuasive, goes beyond what can be proved in the current state of social science. Although my argument does not legitimize the sometimes excessive individualism that is found in societies that adhere to primarily instrumental standards, it does emphasize individual autonomy as an aspect of appropriate social cohesion.

The democratic state—as a good form of government rather than as the best of a bad lot—cannot be disinterested in the education of its citizens. Intelligent, creative, inquiring minds—indeed, morally educated minds responsive to the autonomous needs of others—are required if democratic systems are to work in a moral sense. If, as I believe, a moral, as opposed to an instrumental, belief in democracy is related to a particular view of human nature, it entails more than formal institutional requirements; it entails also a program for educating citizens who are adequate to the institutions one is trying to build. Such citizens must be responsive to the needs of the democratic system.

The invisible hand of Adam Smith and Mandeville's fable of the bees are interesting, and under some circumstances such devices can be made to work. But it is dubious that such motivations will sustain a democracy in periods of trial, for a disposition to protect good institutions is as required as is moral behavior in the example of the water shortage given in chapter 3.[7] Behavior that is appropriate in the economic subsystem may not be appropriate in the political subsystem. This is not a theorem, but it seems to me a commonsense observation that we ignore at our peril.

A democratic system also requires the other prerequisites of democratic citizenship, including self-respect, productivity, and so forth. The existential conditions implied are sufficient income to maintain these other values, access to information in order to operate as autonomous persons and to keep the political system under control, and the long-run maintenance of only those inequalities necessary to sustain the overall system at some optimal level of operation.

RESPONSIBILITY IN A DEMOCRACY

"Representation" and Accountability

Serious problems attend all contractual theories of government and are reflected in the controversy over the term "representative." Edmund Burke made his classic choice for the representation of the interests of the electors rather than of their opinions. The contrary position, of course, is that the representative. is there to represent the opinions of his constituents.

Neither view is adequate. Few of us would vote for a representative who merely mirrored our opinions. On the other hand, few of us would vote for a representative whose view of our interests differed remarkably from ours. The issue is misconceived when we ask what it is that our representatives represent, for they are chosen as our governors and not as our representatives. As governors, they are accountable and their fate is decided at the next election by our satisfac-

212   *Justice, Human Nature, and Political Obligation*

tion with their performance in office. Apart from the way the problem arises from concern over the source of political obligation, it is related to an earlier view of modern democracy as a special form of the town assembly in a simple society. Where few issues arise, where they are relatively simple to understand, where the relationship between the interests of the constituents and the resolution of political debate are relatively clear; then in those situations in which the problem of numbers interferes with the gathering of the entire population, the conception that the representative is a surrogate for the general population makes some sense. It still entails all the difficulties of the will theory of contract, but at least it is understandable in terms of the presumed functioning of the system. In a complex age in which few can understand with any profundity even a single issue, let alone the entire range of issues on which government is based, and in which the legislature has difficulty in competing with the executive with respect to the understanding and mapping of policies, this view of the "representative" process becomes inapplicable and the idea that a "majority will" should decide each issue is an absurdity.

The function of our governors is not to mirror our opinions or wishes but to enact and execute policies that remain within some tolerable area of consensus and the consequences of which receive our balanced approval at the time of accountability. We may judge fairly or unfairly, for those undesired consequences that result from the duress of harsh circumstances may be attributed to a failure of the policies of the incumbent, while those successes that result from accident may be regarded as evidence of statesmanship. Nonetheless one essential aspect of the "democracy" of modern democratic procedures lies in the accountability of the governors to the people.

Accountability and Obligation. In short, the Arrow paradox is an irrelevant mathematical teaser. It is not the function of democracy to maximize some social utility schedule or to establish a univocal set of majoritarian preferences. This is not to deny that such would be interesting if they existed or to argue that preferences and majorities are entirely irrelevant. However, the choice of democracy rests upon a preference for a general set of procedures and a belief in a relationship between these procedures, human nature, environmental constraints, and alternative choices. What we support is a system that gives play to human autonomy in the most fundamental institutions of society—the individual, the family, and the polity—by permitting a reasonable level of initiative and competition. As long as this system also produces a tolerable level of more particular goods, including a reasonable level of social solidarity, most of us will prefer it to systems that restrict individual autonomy more. If it is challenged successfully at the philosophical level, as opposed to a revolutionary seizure of power, it will be because we assess its costs in terms of other human desiderata—a sense of belonging, perhaps—as too high. Therefore, with respect to the performance of political office-holders, we can afford to reserve judgment until the time of accountability. Our choices are not between an imperfect reality and an abstract general will but among real historical alternatives. Our interest in this real historical process, when it exists, is what obliges us to support it and to accept, within limits, its results.

The Obligations of Governors

I do not mean to suggest, however, that there is no check on the actions of governors apart from consitutional responsibility, legality, and accountability. Governance of a modern democratic nation requires continual public support, not only as a sign of likely success at the next elections, but also as a means of motivating the various branches of government effectively to implement government policy and of reducing resistance to its requirements. The executive, for instance,

requires cooperation from the legislature and also understanding cooperation from the bureaucracy.

Political obligation entails the responsibility of the citizen
toward authority but it also entails the responsibility of
officeholders toward the political system. If modern democracies operate as I suggest, then those who hold office have a
political obligation to behave in ways that provide public
support.

The President.   If the political system serves moral as well
as other purposes and if the executive has a responsibility in
making ceremonially manifest important system roles, the
president has a duty to emphasize publicly his moral role. His
obligations extend beyond the success of individual policies
to a responsibility for public belief in the fairness and morality
of national institutions and for a moral concern for fellow
citizens and even for those in other nations as well.

The actual expectations of the public may not accord with
the content of the previous paragraph. If the public view of
the human personality is that it is basically selfish and if its
view of institutional practices is that these operate on the
basis of corruption and dishonesty, then these will be regarded as among the rules of the game. Indeed, if this
assessment is correct with respect to both actual behavior and
future possibility, then the previous paragraph is factually
incorrect and the president has no ceremonial moral obligation, for behavior that accorded with it would lead only to
frustration and disillusionment. Such attitudes clearly would
underline the instrumental character of politics. Thus, they
would legitimate the citizens's selfish behavior in reducing his
identification with the political system and in protecting
himself when his interests are threatened.

However, if such selfish public expectations are related less
to human potentialities than to some aspects of current
behavior, the executive does a disservice to institutions when
he reinforces these attitudes by behavior and expressions that
confirm them. This becomes gross malfeasance in office.

The political obligations of the government are complex. There is a responsibility to make the government work as a system. There is a responsibility not to stray too far from popular understanding of policy. There is a responsibility to protect the basic values of the nation as well as its physical existence. These goals are not always compatible and the means of implementing them cannot always be public.

Important negotiations with foreign governments, for instance, sometimes must be kept secret, for premature publicity might harden bargaining positions or, even worse, create circumstances that produce a rupture of the negotiations. For example, a premature announcement concerning the Chinese-American rapprochement might have frustrated its achievement; yet it is recognized as highly desirable. President Franklin Delano Roosevelt took enormous risks to aid the allies before the Japanese attack at Pearl Harbor that brought the United States into the Second World War. The measures that he took were not fairly or honestly presented to the public and would not likely have been supported by the public had he done so. Although some recent historians believe that he was protecting no essential national interest—a judgment with which I disagree—their assessment is irrelevant to the example in stipulated form. If the president firmly believed on the basis of extremely solid evidence that maintaining the institutional values of the United States required running these risks, was he justified in his deception? Clearly he should exercise humility in reaching such a judgment, and he should search for alternatives. But, in the final analysis, if he really believes that this is the only way in which he can protect national institutions, would it not be a violation of his mandate to defer to the uninformed public view? This stipulated case exemplifies a circumstance in which the president must exercise the theory of accountability to its fullest limits. Unlike many of our other examples, this would be a case in which the direct relationship between the assessment of the evidence, the goal to be reached, and the effective responsibility of the decision maker does not entail megalo-maniacal assumptions.

There are other aspects of the situation of the executive in the modern age that support the principle of accountability against that of representation. The president is at the center of national communications. He has access to information from the public media and from all intelligence agencies. Particularly with respect to international policy, no authority can be substituted for his. In many cases, there will be no time for public debate. Regardless of whether one agrees with the actions of President Kennedy during the Cuban missile crisis, a national debate would have changed the character of the available alternatives; and it would have precluded the actions that took place and that did work. It does not require much imagination to foresee the possibility of a nuclear catastrophe in "locking" the hands of the executive.

The recent (1974) debate in the United States somewhat weakened the authority of the executive in the conduct of foreign relations. This, however, had only a marginal effect, for the public is aware of how small the world has become, of how intimately our fate is interwoven with that of other nations, and of how the exercise of force anywhere entails some risk, even if not necessarily an extraordinarily high risk, of nuclear conflict.

The vast power inherent in the presidency does not legiti-mate arbitrary use of that power. On the contrary, that power places an especial responsibility upon the holder of that office to legitimize the actions he takes. From an ex-ternal point of view, the fact that the final decision is the decision of one man, even though it may have been produced by large-scale consensus within the government, raises a prob-lem of democratic legitimacy that is a counterpart to the legitimacy of illegal dissent.

The existence of power and authority does not legitimate each exercise of it. The classic writers understood the distinc-tion between aristocracy and tyranny. The tyrant may have had as much formal authority as the aristocrat, but the tyrant exercised his authority in an arbitrary or lawless manner. Whatever power the president may have, the educated public certainly does not expect him to use it in a tyrannical fashion. Although the president will be accountable for his action at the end of his term of office, this does not mean that there are not forms of interim accountability. The degree of support that the president has for ongoing policies constitutes a quasi-referendum on the legitimacy of his exercise of authority.

The authority the president exercises is his by the nature of his political role, not by the nature of his individual personality. Thus he has an obligation continually to make manifest his appropriate public performance of his role. Where time and conditions permit, the public has a right to be taken into the president's confidence in terms of the ends he is trying to achieve and the means he is using. Where time and conditions do not permit, it has a right to a reasonable explanation at an appropriate time of the relationships between the actions taken and national and international goals. The president does not need to win a national debate as to the rightness of his course of action provided that he establishes a reasonable consistency between it, desirable objectives, and justice.

If the president appropriately exercises his role, the occasional lie that is necessary in the public interest will be accepted by the public without engendering excessive cynicism if eventually it becomes known. If he does not appropriately exercise his role, he will call into question the legitimacy of governmental policy. Manifest dishonesty in the president's conduct will produce cynicism concerning moral values. In addition to the cynicism it would generate, and the pervasive consequences of this cynicism for the general conduct of public affairs, public recognition of a general presidential right to behave dishonestly would also serve to legitimate extensive self-serving, and eventually self-defeating, exercises in dishonesty throughout the polity.

The Executive Establishment. The executive establishment is an exceptionally complex instrument. There are conflicts over policy within it and sometimes sabotage of policy. During the Cuban missile crisis, for instance, President Kennedy discovered that the Jupiter missiles—which he had twice ordered removed from Turkey—remained there as an embarrassment to him during this crucial period. Officials who considered the president's policies incorrect had frustrated them by refraining from carrying them out. Yet these officials were not accountable in the same way as was the president, even though with respect to specific issues he is accountable in principle only and not in practice.

There are, however, more subtle ways in which an administrative apparatus can preclude the proper devisement or exercise of policy—ways that are legal but administratively improper or administratively proper but morally presumptuous. For instance, civil servants or bureaucrats may carefully filter the information that goes into the executive hierarchy or that goes to Congress. Such actions may be rationalized on the grounds that full conveyal of information would lead uncomprehending executives to wrong decisions. Or they may be carried out to protect a favored line of policy. Negotiations may be bungled to prevent an undesired outcome. Or they may be facilitated to advance some private interest. Military officers may hide their supplies of manpower or weapons. Or they may deliberately precipitate an action to preclude military or even diplomatic decisions to which they take objection. Or information may be leaked prematurely to block executive policy.

These actions are all taken by lawful authority. On the other hand, the exercise of that authority is clearly contrary to political obligation. These individuals are acting under the cover of legitimate authority to do that which they lack legitimate authority to do. These derelictions of duty would be difficult to prove before courts-martial or civil service boards. Yet they corrupt legitimate authority and the democratic process.

These examples of usurpation of authority within the government are not dependent on particular political ideologies. A civil servant with opinions in the moderate spectrum of politics may object strongly to a particular policy, perhaps in the tax area. Someone of leftist persuasion may believe it important to stop a drift toward the use of force, toward war, or toward an arms race. Someone with a right-wing bias may believe it important to prevent detente with the Communist powers or to weaken the authority of those who, in his opinion, are weakening the military force of the United States.

When officials leak information, they may believe that they are merely carrying their case to the public. However, what they are often doing in these instances is undermining the authority of the accountable officials. They are making the great beast of government even more unwieldy and even less accountable than it normally is, for it soon loses its sense of direction and the focus of control is blurred, even the president believing that government has escaped his control. Coherence in policy is undermined, the intentions of elected officials are frustrated, the presentation of policy is confused, collegial confidence within the government is undermined, and the transmission of information and communication within the government is interfered with; all of these consequences being injurious to the modern democratic process.

The lower-ranking official cannot put himself on the same basis as those of superior authority—disputing in his own mind over policies to be adopted and attempting to interpose his own viewpoint—without unsettling the democratic process. Officials should be aware of the different types of assumptions that apply to officials at different levels of authority. Just as the ordinary citizen must require a higher standard of proof before engaging in illegal dissent than is required of the accountable official in making policy in an uncertain world, so the lower-ranking official, before attempting to interpose himself between appropriately determined policy and its implementation, must set an extremely high standard of information. Moreover, he must be able to distinguish between blocking policy and changing it, between blocking or confusing policy and substituting some other but more desirable policy. And he must also consider the precedent-setting consequences of his usurpative behavior. The presumption must always be against such obstruction. The higher the procedural requirements that inhibit the exercise of such obstruction, the less damaging its precedent-setting value within the system.

On the other hand, it is important to distinguish between sabotaging policy and making the system work. Modern political, social, and economic systems are extremely complex. The rules formulated at high levels of authority set broad and abstract standards that sometimes do great substantive injustice to particular individuals or interests. Responsible administrators know how to violate general policy rules to adjust legitimate interests. The case of the slowdown under the rules during the Italian postal strike of 1972 illustrates the fact that large administrative machines will not run at all if the "book" is strictly followed.

If public officials have an obligation not to sabotage policy declared by legitimate authority, at least in good political systems, this does not mean that they must implement it automatically. They also have a responsibility to the good of the system. This may entail delaying the implementation of policy sufficiently to force its reexamination. Resistance of the bureaucracy in the face of executive decision genuinely may reflect an awareness of particularities of the case of which the executive is unaware. Such a complex system probably cannot function adequately without resistance. Resistance forces attention upon potential areas of strain within the system. Admittedly there is a fine line between resistance that is eufunctional for the system and illegitimate sabotage of authority.

Every subsystem within the political system has self-serving reasons, related either to personal interests or to function maintenance, for resisting particular implementations of policy. The attempt to bound these conflicts by a system of rules is certain to be self-defeating. The limitations of stipulative language and of formal procedures for deriving conclusions from premises restrict our ability to compose a coherent and complete transitively ordered set of rules, even one related to specified environmental conditions. This is an area where judgment necessarily plays a substantial role. It can be illuminated by examples, as I shall attempt below, but the clarity of the examples depends upon skill in the selection of the existential conditions that are admitted to consideration. Real-world examples most often do not fit so neatly into categories.

Let us begin our case examination with examples related to regimes most of us would regard as illegitimate. Were the assassination attempts against Hitler just? Even if they were likely to fail, the risks to the individuals carrying them out would likely have been among the factors they took into account with respect to their own moral judgments. However, even if they neglected the risks to themselves, they would have a duty to consider the consequences of failure for other individuals.

If, in its fury, the Hitler regime would mercilessly step up its extermination campaign, perhaps the efforts were not justified; but this decision would be made in purely instrumental terms vis-a-vis Hitler. On the other hand, perhaps the example of the attempt would serve an important moral function in calling the legitimacy of the regime into question. In this case, perhaps we would come to the opposite conclusion despite the other evils stemming from the attempt.

The exterminations within the concentration camps were so clearly outrageous to anyone with a decent moral sense that sabotage of these efforts within the camps seems clearly justified. Here, there is a direct and clear relationship between the end to be achieved and the means that are employed. On first examination, the starting of a nuclear war would seem as evil as the exterminations within the concentration camps. Thus, morality would seem to require a conscience-based refusal to cooperate with such efforts. Consider, however, a case in which American intelligence has learned that the Soviet Union intends to carry out a nuclear first-strike against the United States. After careful calculations in the Pentagon, it is decided that the United States is capable of carrying out a high-risk, but potentially successful, preemptive attack against Soviet missile squadrons. The president orders it. However, two Minuteman squadron commanders decide the order is immoral and refuse to implement it, thereby insuring the failure of the preemptive attack, but not its prevention.

Do we really wish military officers to make such decisions on the basis of their conscience? In answering this question, we must keep in mind, in addition to the facts of the example stipulated above, the fact that different consciences come to different substantive conclusions. Consider the case where three SAC officers decide that American policy is immoral and is risking world conquest by the Communist powers. They believe that they must make one last attempt to force a showdown before it is too late. They carry out an unauthorized nuclear bombing mission against Moscow.

Consider another stipulated example that is not meant to be historically accurate. Suppose when General MacArthur was supreme commander of the UN forces in Korea that he believed on the basis of sound historical evidence that the fate of the world for the next ten thousand years would be settled in that area. Suppose he believed that the president was stupid and the Joint Chiefs of Staff pusillanimous. Suppose he believed that a precipitous retreat under Communist attack would force the United States into a condition of war with Communist China that would enable the United States to solve the problem of world primacy while it still retained the power to do so. In this example, General MacArthur would lack legitimate authority for the course of action pursued. On the other hand he would be in a situation where he was potentially capable of substituting his policy for that of the president.

Suppose that his evaluation is carried through with remarkable objectivity. In this example, the case for usurpative authority would be strong. I resist the conclusion because my reading of history leads me to doubt that the presumption of evidence in a case of this specific kind could ever be strong enough to justify this type of action by an official who is not properly accountable. However, even if one agrred with the moral appropriateness of this exercise of usurpative authority, it would still be illegal. The general would be subject to court-martial and punishment if his offense could be proved, and appropriately so, as the formal legitimation of the rule he followed would reverse the ordinary presumptions underlying our constitutional order. It would, sooner or later, threaten civilian control of the government, and it would likely lead to anarchic self-serving implementations of the rule by other military officers.

The cases cited, few as they are give some indication of the richness of detail that must be taken into account with respect to administrative sabotage of executive policy. It is clear that substantive conscience is not sufficient. Those who act need to understand the difference between their role responsibility and that of those higher in the political hierarchy: the difference between officials who are accountable to the electorate and those who are not. They need to understand the limitations of information on which their decisions are based and the possible self-serving interests their attempts at sabotage may be implementing. They must have some conception of the limitations of their own moral conscience. (Many too easily assume that those who disagree with them are either stupid or immoral.) They must also understand the dangers inherent in assuming a univocal, transitive order of values, the interpretation of which is fully clear to their consciences. These procedural due-process requirements cannot eliminate the ambiguities of different existential situations, but they can illuminate the political obligations of the actor in a way that more simpleminded analysis does not.

The reader may wish to provide other illustrations for himself. I do not intend more detailed discussion here, for my methodology entails the fact that conclusions will depend upon contextual differences. Thus, at best I can provide an orientation toward the factors relevant for the examination of the problems of political obligation. More than this would require us to move from brief orienta-require us to move from brief orientational statements to a thorough examination in context of particular cases.

The Citizen. If the obligation of the citizen toward the state can be impaired, then, it is important to be aware of the conditions under which limitations of identification occur and the relationship of such limitations to the general prob-lem of political authority and legitimacy. Rawls suggests, for instance, that if civil disobedience is seen as a political act addressed to the sense of justice of the community, then it should be limited to instances of "substantial and clear in-justice, and preferably to those which obstruct the path to removing other injustices."[8] Thus he contends that restric-tions on civil rights are serious infringements of his first principle of justice and that this justifies civil disobedience designed to remove them.

The problem with his position on civil disobedience is one that attends his entire theory of justice. Because he has a univocal, transitive system, there is only one just position. However, what is a clear and substantial injustice to one person is not to another; and their rights—and more certainly their beliefs about their rights—may well be in conflict. Because these differences of views may be related to different views of human nature and of human possibilities, Rawls's argument lacks the rational *a priori* character he attributes to it.

Moreover, although Rawls's criteria have some significance for a reflective conscience, it is dangerous to attempt to legitimate illegal dissent by the procedural requirements he establishes for it: good-faith appeals to the conscience of the majority have failed; the courts have not been of assistance; the political parties have been indifferent or unwilling to aid; protests and demonstrations have not worked; thus, if "past actions have shown the majority immovable or apathetic, further attempts may reasonably be thought fruitless."[9]

The difficulty with Rawls's position is that the very same procedural requirements could be met by the defenders of school segregation, for instance. They tried in their local legislatures and won. They were overruled in the national legislature. They tried to reverse the decision there and failed. They appealed to the courts and the courts were unresponsive to their claims. The injuries to them were real. They saw their children being sent to inferior school systems. Often, they had moved to segregated areas at higher cost in order to insure better schools for their children.

It is not clear that their position runs counter to Rawls's two principles, although he believes it does. But even if their argument does run counter to Rawls's two principles, those two principles have the defects we have already noted. Moreover, in any case, those who disagree with the two principles, even if they are wrong, will note only the procedural elements their position has in common with his.

It may be the case that both various minority groups and the segregationists have a legitimate interest in civil disobedience; but the political system cannot accept this justification. Rawls is not entirely unaware of this danger although he does not give it sufficient attention.

Rawls fails to distinguish between the appropriate moral claim of the members of a persecuted group to engage in disobedience—and concerning which the exercise of procedural requirements does play an important role in justification, either in moral terms if there is some degree of first-order identification with the larger group, or prudentially if there is not—and the recognition of that claim within the political system. The two are not proper corollaries, but his theory of justice does not permit this distinction. Although it does place prudential limits on the exercise of the right to disobedience by groups contemplating civil disobedience, it recognizes no right of action against those opposing the law but only the pragmatic fact that such actions will be taken.

The Socratic Parallel.   The heart of the dilemma of civil disobedience is that we are confronted with two ultimately irreconcilable moral rules, neither of which is clearly preferable to the other: "Unjust laws do not establish obligations" and "No man may place himself above the law." This is the Socratic problem in Plato's *Crito* and *Apology*. The Athenian Assembly, which accuses the Platonic Socrates of subversion, intends only a slap on the wrist that is designed to moderate his future conduct. Socrates had not intended to engender disobedience to the law as a consequence of philosophic discourse in his school. Yet, if he accepts the slap on the wrist, he denigrates the value of his philosophic teaching according to which all particular theologies are false. Thus, by his contemptuous treatment of the Assembly, he forces it to escalate the penalty against himself, ultimately to that of death.

Yet it was customary in the Athens of Socrates for those condemned to death to escape jail and flee to another city. Therefore, Crito, the friend of Socrates, comes to assist his escape. However, Socrates, the "corrupter of youth and defiler of the gods," refuses the customary escape and drinks the hemlock instead.

The message of these two dialogues is very complex, and certainly it is subject to dispute. Nonetheless, it seems clear that Socrates does not intend the simpleminded implication that all laws should be obeyed. He is concerned with the problem of justice and particularly concerned with the laws and gods of Athens. He has been convicted of the crime, which he has admitted, of calling these laws into question. How can it be, therefore, especially since he regards the law as unjust, that he fails to utilize the customary route for escaping the penalty: a penalty that the Assembly never really intended to be carried out in any event?

His death clearly is a claim upon the attention, the minds, and the hearts of those who reflect upon it. The defiler of the law has shown a deeper respect for the law than the ordinary citizen and a love for the City that is rare. At the same time he establishes his identity as a citizen of Athens who loves the city so deeply that he cannot contemplate living in exile (the elements of particularity) and who respects the laws so much that he is willing to accept the ultimate penalty of death (the elements of generality and universality inherent in legal and moral systems). The propaedeutic lesson in the Platonic dialogues rests on the resolution by Socrates of his dilemma of conscientious choice; it does not provide a clear and unambiguous determination of right conduct for other individuals, nor is it likely intended to do so. The ambiguity in the dialogues is a creative ambiguity because it forces our attention onto the antithetical elements of the problem.

The Lesson of the Socratic Parallel. Willingness to accept a penalty is not an essential element in the justification of civil disobedience. Acceptance of a penalty may play a justificatory role where the objector has a wider interest in the basic rules of the system, which he publicly reinforces by his acceptance of the penalty. In other cases, where this commonality does not exist, where it is attenuated, or where the penalty for the individual overweighs (in his view at least) the contribution to the harmonious workings of the community that his punishment would produce, there may be a fundamental conflict between his good and that of the community, which results from punishing him. In such cases it is quite licit for him to disobey the law—and in extreme cases disobedience may even be morally obligatory—while attempting to evade punishment. And it may be appropriate for the community to punish him, even though it may take extenuating circumstances or character into account.

There is a difference between substantively just and unjust laws even if no univocal standard exists and even if our ability to make determinations with respect to laws depends upon the state of our information. Yet, even if the law is unjust, its public violation threatens its impartial application. This is probably true of all systems of law, as opposed to tyrannies, although the problem becomes particularly poignant in those cases in which the political methods for changing the law are in general just. At least in those cases in which those who violate the law attempt constitutional change, that is, to change the system of substantive law determination for the better, it can be argued that they are attacking not the impartial application of the law but the system whereby law is determined. Where, however, the system of law perhaps can be improved marginally, but not radically, in terms of the justice of its procedures, and where those who protest the law fail to convince others of the justice of their claims, a consequent disobedience may injure a just system of government to obtain a (possibly deserved) good for a particular group.

Here, as in the Socratic example, no firm answers can be offered. Is civil disobedience, or even violent resistance to the law, justified in such cases? From the standpoint of the protesting group, it may very well be, depending upon the particular case and the degree of the group's interest in maintaining the general system of procedural justice. From the standpoint of the polity, it can hardly be justified, for the community's interest in the good of the smaller group is limited, even if real, and its interest in the system of procedural justice, both with respect to the making of law and its application, has overriding importance.

We cannot reduce the contestants to shadows thrown upon the wall by conceptions of universal and general rules of justice. There is an inherent element of particularity in the process. The resolution of this conflict, however, is bounded, even if not fully determined, by considerations of law and justice. Earlier we referred to the fact that all claims ultimately have some particular element. However, to the extent that these claims are based upon what is an accidental disadvantage from the standpoint of a larger identity grouping—

misfortune in birth, for instance, as contrasted with the general aspects of human being—or where the claims are based upon new perspectives on social or political systems according to which existing principles of distribution or representation are less than optimal, the conscience of those resisting these claims is influenced and their will to defend them is weakened. This does not mean that their claims to defend their interests are without legitimacy or that they will not be defended; but it implies that the will to defend them will be reduced and that the character of the social, economic, or political equilibrium will be changed over time.

This process works through the understanding of people; and because this understanding is imperfect, it may respond more to distorted conceptions of what is right or just than to more objectively determined versions. Guilt may be dysfunctional and harmful rather than eufunctional. I am not arguing that change is better, but rather that our systems have floating equilibria responsive to potentially improved and widened conceptions of justice as these enter human awareness.

Methods of Challenging the Law. The system of law may be challenged in numerous different ways. The constitutional test case is in fact a challenge not to the law so much as to the current interpretation of the law. Thus, for instance, the initial sit-ins in the South provided the Supreme Court with an opportunity to apply changed and presumably more enlightened standards to the interpretation of the Constitution, at the risk for those who participated in the sit-ins that the Court would disagree with them, with the penal possibilities that might ensue from this. Challenges of this kind assist the system of law by enabling it to respond to changed conceptions of human personality and agency. Except where the claimant substitutes it for a preferable but infeasible forcible challenge, this type of challenge is based on an implicit recognition of the common interest of the contending parties in the eufunctioning of the institutions of the society.

Civil disobedience also may make a distinction between coercive and non-coercive methods. Non-coercive methods are intended to change the minds or hearts of others by example. Carrying a placard in a picket line or waving a bloody flag may have this purpose. Coercion, however, may occur even where physical force is not employed. For instance, social ostracism is coercive even though not violent. Other activities may shade into violence, such as physically blocking entrances. Other examples might include violence against property, such as in the destruction of a lifetime collection of research notes belonging to a professor. These all involve some degree of war against the opposing parties; and, conversely, violence is not inconsistent with the changing of minds. Islam was imposed by the sword and the Albigenses were removed from history by the sword.

Some challenges are made not with the expectation that the system will reinterpret the system of law in a more enlightened manner but with the expectation that the cost of meeting the challenge will encourage at least partial submission to the demands that are being made. Challenges of this type often resort to force or violence. But they are coercive in nature and, to this extent, imply either a lack of mutuality of interests or, at the minimum, a fundamental conflict in the perception of interests.

Sometimes, however, resorts to force or violence in fact awaken some individuals to awareness concerning the injustice of social or political institutions in a way that peaceful protest cannot. The character of the violence, in addition to alarming people, makes them aware for the first time of the extent of the felt injury and brings them, perhaps for the first time, to an examination of the equities of the case in a disinterested manner. It would be dishonest to ignore the extent to which improvement on the racial front in the United States resulted from a resort to violence.

On the other hand, the polity usually cannot accommodate much violence and it can ill afford to legitimate it. Thus, there may be a common interest, both among those who had formerly supported the status quo and those who supported change, in the prosecution of those who committed the violence, even though situationally it was justified from the standpoint of the group advocating change. Clearly this introduces a harsh dilemma for those who start the violence.

Those who argue for imposing their ideas by violence when all procedural remedies are exhausted and others will not adopt their view may not mistake the wider good in every case. However, the argument that all procedural remedies have been exhausted can hardly ever be completely true, for the political contest within democracies at least can be refought and the composition of the Supereme Court changes over time. These remedies, therefore, remain available, except in those cases where the injury is irreversible and so massive that their availability is purely hypothetical. If violence is all that will prevent the majority from exterminating a certain group of individuals or dispensing with basic human liberties, I agree that violence is a good: certainly for the threatened group and perhaps even from a more enlightened consideration of the interests of the larger group. However, this remedy depends upon force where rational argument has failed. To legitimate such remedies in principle may lead those who lose the political and legal contests to regard it as legitimate to impose their opinions by force. And this might be the end of democracy as we know it. Thus, the larger system cannot safely legitimize violence.

The Political System and Challenges to It

What is viewed from the standpoint of the protester as an act of conscience against an immoral system is a usurpative act from the standpoint of the political system. Where the usurpative act is egregiously overt and contrary to a clear public consensus, the problem of the legitimation of the usurpative does not arise. The legitimacy of the system is reaffirmed by the conclusiveness with which the rebellious act is repressed. On the other hand, many actually usurpative acts—such as the private declassification of governmental papers—are not obviously usurpative to large numbers of people, who confuse the putative good these acts accomplish with the legitimacy of the actor in carrying it out. Other acts, even though clearly usurpative, respond to more or less widely felt needs, as in the private witch hunts against governmental employees or the use of illegal means by government investigators during the McCarthy period.

In these cases, great care must be exercised. Too much acclaim for the usurpative acts threatens the basis of legitimate authority within the system. However, too much repression of them may have similar consequences because of the injury to the public sense of substantive justice. Although it is important to avoid engendering a sense of cynicism by producing an expectation that felonies will go unpunished if they are in accord with popular feelings, there will also be a sense of injustice if the perpetrators of deeds generally ·regarded as good, even if illegal, pay too heavy a penalty.

How Protest Is Absorbed.   Political systems require some degree of ambiguity. If the end is believed to be good but the means is egregiously illegal, then perhaps the government can move promptly to support the same end by other, and more appropriate, methods. This tends to blur the substantive justification of those who illegally pursue the consensually accepted substantive ends and to isolate them morally. Such a response confirms the public sense that the system functions with justice. In other cases, administrative devices can be used to obscure the extent to which illegitimate means are employed to achieve desired ends. This partakes of hypocrisy and, pursued beyond appropriate limits, could produce cynicism. However, within limits, it is essential to the equilibrium between the objective of maintaining the sense of substantive justice and that of avoiding patently illegal acts.

No political system is likely to persist if either objective fails to be met. Yet, since all known systems sometimes strongly offend the sense of justice, all at one time or another, and some more frequently than others, motivate usurpative actions that can be reconciled only with difficulty with the maintenance of legitimate procedures.

Revolutions. Revolutions always involve conflicts of interest that are not reconcilable according to an unequivocal or univocal standard of justice for reasons that have been stated previously. Presumably the revolutionaries have some specific claim that is being pursued through the use of force. The history of revolutions and the failure of human expectations establish an obvious requirement for a sense of humility in making the judgment to resort to force. However, individuals conceivably might feel that a particular judgment in favor of revolution is based upon a sound examination of the circumstances of the particular case. In some cases, revolutionary circumstances may exist independently of the activity of the revolutionaries, with the major question being whether they will organize and lead it or allow it to proceed in an anarchic manner.

One special case that must be distinguished from the ordinary case of revolution requires further discussion. It involves that case in which the revolutionaries believe that they must change human nature to produce a just society: a goal that involves wholesale social, economic, and political reorganization. Whatever claims the revolutionaries make to lead "the people," they are asserting at best the claim of a future generation against the present generation and at worst their claims against the rest of the population. They are therefore at war with virtually the entire population of the political entity that is to be conquered by the revolution (although their slogans may be deceptive in this respect).

This case needs to be distinguished from that of an ancient society in which freedom for some was purchased at the expense of servitude for the many. In that case, there was at least a partial war between the elite and the masses, and the good to be achieved by revolution was a present one, and understandable on the basis of then-current knowledge.

The revolutionaries of whom we speak demand radical changes in every aspect of the current situation. Social science provides no warrant for believing that they will succeed. History provides no example of a success in this type of endeavor. The rights of the current generation—and these are genuine—are to be scrapped.

The claims made by such revolutionaries have no warrant of any type that we have previously mentioned, for they are based neither on considerations of justice common to the contending parties nor on existential prescriptive rights of a particular type. They are formulated *ex nihilo* in the minds of the revolutionaries. Hitler once attempted to base the legitimacy of his regime upon the existence of all Germans past, present, and future. Revolutionaries of the type of which we speak rest their authority on hypothetical future generations whose interests can be represented only in their imagination in an extremely abstract form. There is no check on such constructions other than the imaginations of those who make them.

Marx once sardonically said that Hegel constructed the world out of his head—a form of subjective idealism that Marx knew Hegel did not accept. In effect, this form of revolutionary activity is a form of extreme subjective idealism that treats politics as if it were literature or the theater, and a particularly unstructured type of literature or theater at that. The elite who take this position wish to use the masses as a potter might use a never-hardening clay to shape and to reshape it into the images that meet his desires as they appear to his imagination. As such, it is fundamentally destructive to any unity that might exist among humankind. It denies any common humanity or moral agency to any but the revolutionary elite.

The Problem of Service. Does the political system have the right to call upon individuals for service? According to John Rawls, personal service may be required by a nation only when this is necessary to protect the liberties of its citizens. This judgment is to be made by the individual. Therefore, although Rawls does not explicitly take the most extremely individualistic view of the relationship between the individual and the community, the balance is weighted heavily in favor of individualistic judgment. The particularistic bonds between the individual and the community, both of a substantive and ceremonial character, are attenuated by this point of view.

A view of human nature implicitly underlies this distinction, and it is one that I think entails large costs in terms of the human personality. If the state is merely a contractual network, and if it is only instrumental, the bonds between it and the citizen can be dissolved if an unfavorable calculation is made. As I understand the human need for identification, membership, and ceremonial fulfillment, this view of the relationship is destructive. In personality systems which, in addition to their biologically emotional needs, employ information as essential elements in governing their own activities, this view of the relationship may set up a positive feedback cycle that serves still further to attenuate the personality. Although I would not deny that the bonds between the citizen and the state can—and under some circumstances should—be ruptured, Rawls's analysis makes what should be a last-resort alternative too easy for the good of either the individual or the society. Rawls evades this problem by failing—fallaciously, as we have shown—to admit the possibility of conflict between a good individual and a just society.

To preserve their institutions, nations require effective forces, bases, allies, and many other instrumentalities. Their allies cannot always be chosen on the basis of the political acceptability of their domestic institutions, and the outcomes of alternative foreign policies are often debatable and rarely clearly or directly related to such an abstraction as liberty. To restrict the obligations of the citizen to those foreign policies having a clear relationship to the liberties of the nation or to forbid the government to pursue policies not clearly related to them would insure ineffectiveness in the actual world.

Rawls argues that a person may conscientiously refuse to enter the armed services during a particular war "on the ground that the aims of the conflict are unjust."[10] The grounds may be that the objectives sought are economic advantage or national power and these ends cannot be justified under Rawls's principles. But economic advantage or national power may help to defend national liberties or even the liberties of other people.

Threats to the survival of the state, to its liberties, and to its security are rarely demonstrable in any fully satisfactory way. So, in evaluating the extent of his obligation, which involves possible harm to himself, and therefore a partially independent frame of moral reference, the citizen will perceive his obligation as weakened under Rawls's criterion. If we tell him the choice is his, we do damage to the public interest.

How seriously should we take Rawls's conclusion that a citizen need not aid his nation in an unjust war? His rules seem applicable, if at all, to contemporary problems. (I will ignore the problems of medieval or classical wars, for they are even more difficult to relate to his rules.) Therefore, let us take a case from contemporary history the details of which we deliberately change to obtain a stipulated example. Let us stipulate that the democracies had actually initiated the war against Nazi Germany for aggressive purposes. Let us stipulate also that the fire bombing of Dresden and Hamburg were war crimes and that the Nazis committed no crimes directly related to the war (as contrasted with internal crimes against humanity). Should British and French citizens have refused to support their governments' war activities and German citizens loyally supported theirs?

Perhaps Rawls might counter that the British and French should oppose their governments until their countries were invaded and that the Germans should support theirs as long as the attacks were in their territory; but this is a fine line that is difficult to draw in practice, for the first stages of war may determine the outcome of the latter stages.

Conceivably one might argue that the superordinate value of liberty takes precedence over all other considerations and therefore should lead the German citizen to oppose the Nazi state and the British and French citizens to support their states when the enemy is Nazi Germany, regardless of who started the war or why it was started. But this is not consistent with what Rawls says in his discussion and could be consistent with unjust motives.

Rawls says that if a nation violates the laws of wars, one has a right to resist service on the ground that he may not be able to resist the demand to obey and thus may be forced to act contrary to his natural duties. Indeed, he says, if the likelihood of receiving "flagrantly unjust commands is sufficiently great one may have a duty and not only a right to refuse." This makes the situation even more difficult.

Rawls fails to take into account that the failure to run this risk may threaten the liberties of citizens in a war in which the fate of the nation and the freedom of its institutions are at stake. He does not consider the possibility that a citizen may have an obligation to serve and also an obligation to refuse unjust orders.

The discussion by Rawls reveals the implicit extreme individualism of his position, for it is fear concerning personal virtue that produces his conclusion, not concern for moral duty. I say this with some feeling. I enlisted in the Second World War but surreptitiously turned my back when the oath was given because I was aware that my conscience might forbid me to carry out some possible orders. I acted surreptitiously because I was aware that my enlistment would not be accepted if I served public notice that I would not take the oath. At one time during the war in the Pacific, we were under orders from our general to cooperate in actions that were distinctly offensive morally and where resistance to those orders could not possibly affect the conduct of the war. Although threatened with punishments that would have impaired life or liberty, a number of us continued to sabotage these particular orders. We did so surreptitiously, even though the fact of our doing so was known, because to have done so openly would have constituted a direct affront to command authority that would have left it with no alternative but to carry out the threats: a consequence that we obviously did not desire for personal reasons but that also would have prevented us from continuing actions that we considered morally right. This type of behavior seems more consistent with the political obligations of the citizen than that recommended by Rawls.

Rawls fails to distinguish between the moral duty of an individual and the obligation of the citizen within a political system. Most human activity is complex and ambiguous. Few wars are fought for simple objectives that are easy to understand. Even if we agree that it is illicit to wage a war against the liberties of others, it does not follow that each citizen has the right to make this judgment for himself. We have established procedures and elected officials whose duty it is to make these determinations.

It is misleading, and it can be self-serving, to state that the citizen has a right (and perhaps even a duty) to refuse service when these terms ordinarily imply that the political system has a correlative obligation to recognize these rights. If anything, the contrary is the case; the citizen has an obligation to give important weight to the choices made according to the appropriate procedures of the political system, even though he disagrees with them or doubts their justice. If a war still seems particularly outrageous to him, after giving due weight to every appropriate consideration, he may morally refuse service, but he has no right that requires recognition within the political system. More than this, public recognition of such a "right" would encourage others to make self-serving interpretations of the facts of the case and would produce invidious distinctions between those "square" enough to serve and those sophisticated enough to evade service. Such a situation would threaten the moral sentiments that hold a nation together.

The Government's Responsibilities. Governments also have a responsibility to consider the consequences of their activities. It is a fact that it is hard to serve in a war when the rest of the nation is at peace and pursuing profit. Remote wars fought for limited objectives under justifications that are poorly explained to the public produce enormous difficulties with respect to legitimacy.

States will often be ill advised to act in ways that weaken a citizen's sense of identification with the justice of its cause. We do not wish to carry this argument too far, for we are all familiar with national hysteria in which the justice of the cause is assumed by the citizen. However, that was more true of the late nineteenth than of the mid-twentieth century. So, at least within the contemporary period, the hypothesis that the perception by the citizen of the justice of the state's cause is an important element in maintaining its security and the freedom of its citizens has merit. Yet, given the ambiguity of judgments in the international arena, do we wish to reinforce a conception that each citizen is the judge of his country's cause? It is a confusion to rationalize the objections that poorly justified wars give rise to as fundamental principles of political philosophy.

The Problem of Clarity. There is an even more fundamental question that Rawls has not asked. If the war is fundamentally and clearly unjust, why is the community pursuing it? Can't it recognize that it is unjust? Although in principle we must admit that some people cannot recognize injustice, this surely raises an issue as to whether the argued "clarity" of the case may not say more about the "eye" of the objector than about the facts of the case. If, on the other hand, the community is willfully pursuing a war it recognizes as unjust, is it likely to recognize the right of objection?

Rawls's system does not permit a distinction between a moral duty of an individual and the rights and obligations of a citizen. Because he insists upon a univocal transitive order affecting all moral behavior, conflicts of this kind cannot arise; and, therefore, the issues, as he discusses them, bear little relationship to the existential problems that claim our attention.

THE INTERNATIONAL SYSTEM

The type of procedure that accords with justice, or the extent to which justice can be applied to a particular framework of activity, depends upon the type of system we are talking about. Moral behavior was an unreasonable expectation in the south Italian town of which Banfield wrote. On the other hand, income tax violations by some Americans do not justify them by others, for the system maintains a reasonably effective system of income tax laws, even though we may disagree about the justice of particular provisions of that law.

The international system, for instance, differs in fundamental ways from those of domestic systems. It has no specific government that settles political disputes among the participants. The effectiveness of the norms within the system depend in the last resort upon self-help by the members of the system. In many cases, violation of existing rules is the only way of legislating new rules, and it is perhaps less resorted to than would otherwise be the case precisely because of its self-serving character and the difficulty of drawing lines. There are rules to the system and they are reasonably well maintained. Moreover, there is a difference between the norms appropriate to a "balance of power" system and those appropriate to a loose bipolar system.[11]

These two systems differ not only from national systems but also from each other with respect to the extent to which a system of law is applicable. Thus, for instance, the principle of non-intervention applies far more clearly to a "balance of power" system than to a bipolar system. An international systems analysis can be employed to explain why the outlawry of force, which some believe was attempted by the United Nations Charter, was not a practicable objective in a bipolar system, although controls on the exercise of force and the justifications that are acceptable for its use are possible.

Systems such as the international system are called subsystem-dominant.[12] This means that their equilibrating processes are more like those of an imperfect than a perfect market. Equilibria exist but they are subject to shock; under some circumstances, a particular nation, if not opposed in time, may change the character of the entire system—a result that is less likely within modern national systems.

The Problem of Violence

During the Vietnamese war, some argued that violence against the war inside the nation was justified because the nation used violence outside of its borders. Whatever good arguments might have existed against the propriety of the war, or whatever good arguments might have been used for violence within the state, this was not one of them. Within a democratic nation there are not entirely unreasonable procedures for legislative and judicial readjustments of inappropriate states of affairs. This is a good reason not to resort to violence domestically. No similar procedures existed in Southeast Asia that would have guaranteed either the initial unfettered choice of the populace—that is, a choice without actual violence or the threat of it, with respect to the types of institutions that would be adopted—or a continuing set of choices in this respect. The international system is not necessarily defective in this respect, for to call it defective implies that some alternate mechanism exists that would enable it to follow appropriate democratic procedures that would be consistent with the substantive interests of the actors within the system. As this is not the case, the use of force may be the only effective remedy where substantive injury occurs. The analogy, therefore, is quite inadequate.

Promises and Agreements

The differences between national and international systems have consequences for a variety of cases including the binding character of promises. It is not true that promises absolutely bind even within domestic systems, for legal practice, particularly with respect to personal service contracts, recognizes exceptions to this. International practice has two fully coordinate rules: one that treaties must be observed and the other that circumstances change cases. This recognizes the fact that no state can be expected to observe a treaty that, under changed circumstances, is inconsistent with its national values, its security, or especially its survival.

Self-determination

I have spoken of the absence of institutions in Southeast Asia that would permit genuinely free choice by the inhabitants of that area. Rawls argues that we do have an interest in the liberties of others and that in the international area this involves the principle of self-determination. There are two major problems with this view of the matter. In the first place, it is too abstract to suggest that we have a clear and definite interest in self-determination in other nations. I do not suggest that we do not, but conceivably it could be the case that self-determination by some is inconsistent with self-determination by others. Under some circumstances such self-determination might increase the probability of nuclear war or some other catastrophe or might reduce the resources available to those nations with free and just institutions to resist the encroachments of others. Again, I do not suggest that this is the case. It is important to note, however, that too abstract a discussion of this issue loses sight of such possible interrelationships.

A second problem arises with the concept of self-determination. What is self-determination? Even if we leave out of account national systems that are obviously too small, too poor, or too weak to be genuinely self-governing in the present world system, and if we recognize that political organizations, as is true of individuals, are subject to external influences, there are still serious questions as to what the term means. Is a successful revolution by a small group of determined revolutionaries in a colonial area self-determination? What of the great mass of individuals who have been passive in the process and who were not consulted during it? Is there less self-determination under a colonial regime that permits some democratic parliamentary procedures than under a totalitarian domestic dictatorship? Does majority voting on Cyprus constitute self-determination when a substantial minority, the Turks, with some justification consider themselves to be oppressed by a cohesive majority? Was self-determination denied when Mozambique was part of metropolitan Portugal? Did the fact that only a few blacks had been franchised in Mozambique matter if the franchise were genuinely open to all blacks who qualified and if qualification were reasonably open to all who aspired thereto? Does rule by one group over another become imperialistic when both groups, or only one, regard the groups as fundamentally different according to some "important" characteristics, for example, skin color? Could a situation become imperialistic that was not previously so? Could the racial issue in the United States partake of this character in time? These questions suggest the complexity of the issues and their impermeability to simple, abstract considerations.

Intervention and Values

As in the domestic system, our consideration of appropriate rules for the international system depends upon the characteristics of that system and the consequences of the alternative rules. Consider the argument against intervention and for self-determination. Clearly a "nation" may constitute a basis for identification. Interference by others often is resented and counterproductive. Often it is self-serving, based on ignorance of local conditions, and destructive of constructive forces in the area. A presumption against intervention and for "self-determination" is, therefore, perhaps justified. Yet would it have been wrong if a foreign nation had intervened to throw Hitler out when he came to power? Is there not a potential conflict between "self-determination" in any particular instance and interventions designed to reinforce the long-term success of democratic institutions? What if a nation engages in deliberate genocide or drugs its people? Perhaps we do not wish to intervene if this means nuclear war. Yet, surely at some modest price, only the hard of heart would refuse to intervene. Is this inconsistent with self-determination?

The situation is more complex even than this, for our framework of values is based upon our view of human nature and sociological possibility. Many of those who take a non-interventionary view with respect to other areas of the world explicitly assume that democracy—or freedom in our sense—may not be appropriate everywhere in the world or within the framework of social or political possibility for certain areas. Thus, it is viewed as a mere ethnocentrism for us to seek to extend our system of liberties to these areas. Whether this view is right or wrong does not depend upon an examination of the original condition but upon an analysis of human personality and biology and social, political, and economic conditions as they operate within cultural frameworks. Rawls's discussion of this issue is somewhat troubling, for he is not against intervention; yet his views on conscription and just war seem to have far more in common with the views of those who doubt the capacity for freedom of people in certain areas of the world than they do with his own first principle.

The difficulty with general formulations—apart from previously mentioned inadequacies of stipulated languages and of deductive theory—lies in the fact that they treat as first principles those considerations that are at best orientational devices for the consideration of problems, and, even then, only within the framework of particular historical periods.

EPILOGUE

By now the neo-Hegelian implications of the argument have become clear. Justice does not exist in the abstract. It is called into being by human activity. Its scope is dependent upon the particularities of being. It represents a tendency to become, that is, to enter into a greater fullness of being. Justice, as does wisdom, takes wing with the owls of Minerva only when evening has fallen.

Hegel called history the realm of accident, but regarded necessity as working itself out through accident. In my view, the close connection between accident and necessity that is essential to the Hegelian pattern breaks down. A tendency need not actualize itself. The patterns that occur in history and the ends toward which we grope are not foreordained. Accident may deflect us. It may corrupt or pervert us. It may set off dysfunctional informational mechanisms that become inconsistent with wisdom.

If, however, there is an existential gamble to life, it is only an element in the process. The ideas we have are not free-floating subjectivities; they are not choices made in a vacuum. We may stake our life upon faith, but it is a grounded faith; it is grounded in a knowledge of being, whatever derailment accidents may entail.

We are conative, value-producing systems. We rise from the ooze and slime of history to build institutions that have inherent worth. We can never eliminate all conflicts between the well-being of different people or groups or between the good and the just. But we can change the world to minimize those things that cause injustice and, in anticipation, those things that might cause future injustice, insofar as our inadequate ability to foresee the future allows us. As we manifest these aspects of our being, we move, in Marx's phrase, from the realm of necessity into the kingdom of freedom.

Appendix 1

Knowing and Communicating

When we say that science is objectively communicable, we really mean that it is communicable to those capable of understanding it. The number "two" may be the square root of "four," but apparently there is no way of demonstrating this to a swallow or to a human moron. Comparatively few people are capable of understanding the implications of relativity theory. This, in part, accounts for so many of the errors in literary works in which the authors refer to relativity. Thus, although science does provide for objective communicability, if only in principle, this communicability is restricted to instruments capable of recognizing its truths.

THE WITTGENSTEIN/TOULMIN DISTINCTION

According to Allan Janik and Stephen Toulmin, in their book *Wittgenstein's Vienna,*[1] the Wittgenstein of the *Tractatus* distinguished between a world of scientific natural facts that were subject to experimental evidence and a world of values that were subject to intuition and imagination. This is an only partly valid disjunction.

Wittgenstein's early position overstates the clarity of natural science and understates the extent to which ordered knowledge is possible in other areas of inquiry. Quine's conception of science as a field, which is summarized in appendix 2, explains some of the problems of natural science better than Toulmin's version of Wittgenstein's views. Consider, for instance, the problems that I. Langmuir had with the Davis-Barnes experiment:

> Well, in the discussion, we questioned how, experimentally, you could examine the whole spectrum; because each count, you see, takes a long time. There was a long series of alpha particle counts, that took two minutes at a time, and you had to do it ten or fifteen times and you had to adjust the voltage to a hundredth of a volt. If you have to go through steps of a hundredth of a volt each and to cover all the range from 330 up to 900 volts, you'd have quite a job. (Laughter) Well, they said that they didn't do it quite that way. They had found by some preliminary world that they did check with the Bohr orbit velocities so they knew where to look for them. They found them sometimes not exactly where they expected them but they explored around in that neighborhood and the result was that they got them with extraordinary precision. So high, in fact, that they were sure they'd be able to check the Rydberg constant more accurately than it can be done by studying the hydrogen spectrum, which is something like one in the 10^8. At any rate, they had no inhibitions at all as to the accuracy which could be obtained by this method especially since they were measuring these voltages within a hundredth of a volt. Anybody who looks at the setup would be a little doubtful about whether the electrons had velocities that were fixed and definite within 1/100 of a volt because this is not exactly a homogeneous field. The distance was only about 5mm in which they were moving along together.[2]

The properties at issue were defined by physical theory—not merely by simple observation—and the supposed identifications were unlikely according to a specific accepted theory, Bohr's theory of the hydrogen atom. Thus Langmuir was led by theoretical considerations to a rejection of observational identifications that had been made by Davis and Barnes and to an explanation of their mistake.

This example indicates the extent to which expert natural scientists mistakenly can identify observational data; and Langmuir's pamphlet has many more examples. However, even to call all conflicts in such matters mistakes is to misperceive the epistemological problem. Knowledge is a field and our ability to perceive or to characterize observational data depends on that field, including its theoretical elements, as Quine has shown. The extent to which this is so helps explain some of the dogmas of current science in which contemporary experimental "results" are reified into an absolute picture of the universe that excludes phenomena inconsistent with current beliefs concerning the laws of nature.

Part of the problem arises from preconceptions involving inadequate accounts of observation and proof. Because we expect our perceptions to mirror a corresponding external reality and because we believe science is strictly deductive, we deemphasize the extent to which the field of knowledge (praxis) structures our perceptual coding and our receptivity to the legitimacy of particular types of explanations and the illegitimacy of others. Our accounts of the field of praxis are objective but do not take the same form as our accounts of specific theories or propositions. Consistency, partial relatednesses, and "fit" constitute the key criteria. Thus, as we move farther from the "center" of the field, the more likely it is that variations in our accounts of the field are equivalently plausible; and the looser relationships between the elements of the account become. At some point, the factors that account for our perception of "fit" and consistency become significantly less communicable, and hence objective, and more dependent on the remarkable neurological scanning capacity of preconscious mind. Somewhere in between, we can communicate some of the elements of the account—for instance, that a thief was six feet tall, weighed two hundred pounds, and had red hair—in a manner that excludes a range of "fits" but that does not determine it uniquely.

The foregoing distinctions are relevant to scientific discovery, which evades a full accounting and which does not operate according to any known procedure. We can demonstrate the dependence of Einsteinian relativity theory upon the Michelson-Morley experiment and the Lorentz equations. But neither these nor some exhaustive set of preconditions will account fully for Einstein's discovery. Indeed, the greatest natural scientists of the theoretical type are usually the most "intuitive," not the most precise.

Discovery involves recognition of patterns and "fits." However, we cannot fully explain how we recognize that elements fit in particular classes. This is an art that involves partly preconscious facilities of mind. In realms involving great variability, such as statesmanship, the art of recognizing similarities in relationships is only partly communicable. One major difference between Churchill and Chamberlain, for instance, lay in their respective abilities to recognize certain aspects of Hitler's personality rather than in differences in their ability to reason about the positions they took.

PRAXIS AND KNOWLEDGE

The Limits of Language

Much of human knowledge involves recognition of "fits," differences, metaphoric relationships, and so forth. Many of these are finely structured, so finely structured that our verbal faculties are inadequate for their communication. This is true for much of scientific endeavor where we are concerned less with experimental formalities than with the link between our so-called protocol sentences and experimental results—a link that is not based upon one-to-one identities.

We know far more than we can express within the range of logic. Just as Aristotle knew that if horses are animals, the heads of horses are the heads of animals, even though he could not express this within his form of syllogism, much of our communication depends upon types of knowledge that are not—and that to some extent perhaps cannot be—communicated objectively.

Taste and Ethics

Although Toulmin is correct is stressing the importance of reasoning in ethics, it is important to recognize that much moral conduct will depend upon taste, that is, upon a recognition of appropriateness that cannot be expressed within the framework of rules. The ability we have to sense and to respond to differences in situations far exceeds our ability to justify our actions in an objectively expressible manner. Indeed, the compulsive individual who is too restricted by rules will fail to respond to those differences in the real world that require moral discrimination.

However, the difference here is not between value facts and other types of facts but between facts that are amenable to the framework of our currently available formal techniques and those facts that respond to more intuitive types of identifications. The sensitivity of the moral instrument is an essential feature of the beauty of the moral music it makes.

The Complexity of the Knower

John Rawls argues for an increased complexity of the perceiving apparatus as a desideratum,[3] although, in his system, the good is subordinate to the just. He offers as evidence for the value of such complexity the observation that those who acquire a taste for good music are unwilling to give that taste up and regard it as superior to a taste for more popular forms of music.

The difficulty with this form of argument is that it is divorced from an examination of the character of the perceiving system. Apart from the fact that the observation is not universally accurate—some who know symphonic music prefer popular music—it could be objected to on grounds of a theory of dissonance. According to Festinger's theory of psychological dissonance, an individual will acquire a belief in the desirability of an objective on which much time and effort is spent. An appreciation of good music requires much time and effort. Beyond this, one would hardly argue that the addictive property of opium proves its desirability.

If one goes back to the *Yellow Book* period in English arts, to Pater, J. A. Symonds, and Coleridge, for instance, one finds what can only be called an excessive addiction to highly discriminating sensual aspects of life. Pater's proposed sensorium, for instance, an organ designed to produce permutations of odors, is an illustration of this form of excess.

If, on the other hand, one turns to a conception of the perceiving organism, then one might argue that those increases of perceptual ability that respond to important differences in the environment, but that do not take on an excessive life of their own, in terms, for instance, of stunting other essential elements of the organism, are desirable. Presumably, for instance, we might be able to develop a theory of esthetics, more variable in nature than ethics for obvious reasons, that is related to a systemic pragmaticist conception of the human situation.

Regardless, however, of whether or not this is correct, it at least points to the essential problem: that of relating observations to at least an explanation sketch of the system we are talking about. In the absence of such an explanation sketch, the observation is capable of supporting contradictory hypotheses.

The Knower and Communicator

The ability to communicate about aspects of reality depends upon recognition that is based on preexisting knowledge. We cannot move from sense to knowledge, as Locke did with his tabula rasa, for experience can neither be cognized nor communicated except within a framework of preexisting knowledge. This process may involve negative feedback and certain self-correcting features, so that the realm of knowledge is extensible. However, our demonstrations require a state of knowledge and cannot be communicated in its absence. A computer that was programed to identify incorrectly inputs from the external world could never acquire information about that world. This is the restricted sense in which Leibniz's conception of the windowless monad makes some sense. Communication depends upon a prior "coordination" of communication systems, although "coordination" can increase as initial communications involve resettings of their internal programs. There is an inevitable partial circularity in reason. Communication can occur only between at least partly kindred minds.

The experimental methods used to confirm propositions or theories assume replicability. Even if repeated experiments show no exception, the conclusion that a hypothesis is confirmed assumes that the universe that has been sampled is representative. This, however, is what can never be known. Any theory of selection of evidence itself makes assumptions about the characteristics of the universe from which the selections are made. However far we carry this process, there is some metalevel at which the assumptions are untested. We can never be certain—indeed we can never assign any absolute probability number to our level of confidence—that all our observations are not taken from some temporary kink in some particular part of the universe that for some obscure reason follows the lawlike behavior we have observed. The events in it may be of vanishingly small probability in some larger and more representative sample, and our repeated experiments may only sample more adequately this unrepresented sample in which we live. It is in this sense that Charles Sanders Peirce remarked that the laws of the universe may themselves be changing and asserted that when a gambler follows the odds he is placing his faith in what happens to the entire community of gamblers.

Objectivity requires public communicability in Dewey's terms. Objectivity refers to those aspects of the field of knowledge that can be communicated, at least in principle, in publicly replicable ways to others or to the "self." It thus requires some form of language; and the recursive aspects of language produce the illusion of a transcendental ego that is not encapsulated in the field of experience. The divorce of language from the contextual conditions that make its reference to experience adequate produce the illusions of a subject/object dichotomy (rather than a self/other distinction) and of a fact/value dichotomy. Many of the generalizations of social science that divorce us from the real problems of the world also arise from the same kinds of language reifications.

Appendix 2

The Two Dogmas of Empiricism

As Quine has shown,[1] the absolute distinction between synthetic and analytic knowledge breaks down. This point is so fundamentally important that we will attempt briefly to reproduce Quine's argument. As Kant conceived of an analytic statement, it attributed no more to its subject than is already conceptually contained in it. His formulation has two shortcomings. In the first place, it was limited to statements of a subject-predicate form. In the second place, the notion of "contained" was left at a metaphorical level. Therefore, attempts were made to redefine Kant's concept of analyticity. It was asserted that a statement is analytic when it is true by virtue of its meaning and independently of fact. However, meaning and naming are not identical. "Evening star" and "morning star" and "Scott" and "the author of *Waverley*" illustrate that terms can name the same thing and differ in meaning. As Quine notes, "nine" and "the number of planets" name one and the same abstract entity but must be regarded as unlike in meaning, for astronomical observation was required, and not merely inspection of the meanings of the words, to determine the identical character of the entity in question. The same conclusion follows with respect to general terms or predicates. The terms "creature with a heart" and "creature with kidneys" are probably alike in extension but are different in meaning. Rationality is involved in the concept of man but not in the concept of "featherless biped," although man is the only featherless biped.

Quine has also analyzed those cases that appear to be logically true, for instance, "No unmarried man is married." If this sentence is logically true, it remains true under any and all reinterpretations of "man" and "married." On the assumption that there is a prior inventory of logical particles, a logically true statement is one that is true and remains true under all reinterpretations of its components except for the logical particles. However, Quine points to a second class of analytic statements such as "No bachelor is married." This can be turned into a logical truth by putting synonyms in place of the original statement. In this way, by replacing "bachelor" with "unmarried man," the second statement is transformed into the first. Thus, the concept of analytic truth is saved only by introducing the concept of "synonymy." Unfortunately this concept, as Quine states, is "no less in need of clarification than analyticity itself."

Carnap, therefore, tried to explain analyticity by appeal to state descriptions. A state description is an exhaustive assignment of truth values to the atomic, or non-compound, statements of the language. All other statements, according to Carnap, are constructed of their component clauses by familiar logical devices so that specifiable logical laws determine the truth value of any complex statement for each state description. A statement is then regarded as analytic when it is true under every state description. However, as Quine notes, this version of analyticity works only if the atomic statements of the language are, "unlike 'John is a bachelor' and 'John is married,' mutually independent." If this were not true, there would be a state description that assigned truth independently to each statement and it would have the consequence that "No bachelors are married" would be synthetic rather than analytic under the criterion.

Thus Carnap's criterion of analyticity in terms of state descriptions works only for languages devoid of extralogical synonym pairs, such as "bachelor" and "unmarried man." Therefore, Quine says, the criterion in terms of state descriptions is a reconstruction of a test of logical truth, "not of analyticity."

For this reason, an attempt has been made to assert that analytic statements of the second type reduce to those of the first type, the logical truths, by definition. In the example used, "bachelor" would be defined as "unmarried man." But how do we know this, Quine asks? Are we to appeal to a dictionary and accept it as law? Dictionaries are not put together as sets of analytic truths. Lexicographers attempt to record antecedent facts and they presume the synonymy from usage.

There is a variant type of definitional activity that Carnap called explication. Here the purpose is not merely to paraphrase the definiendum into an outright synonym but to improve upon it by refining or supplementing its meaning. However, even though in this case one does not merely report a preexisting synonymy between definiendum and definiens, the conclusion rests on other preexisting synonymies. What happens is that explication preserves "the usage of . . . favored contexts while sharpening the usage of other contexts." Thus, although some previous usages are excluded, the process rests upon preexisting synonymies. Only in the case of the explicitly conventional introduction of novel notations for purposes of sheer abbreviation, Quine says, is "the definiendum . . . synonymous with the definiens" and this is so simply because it has been created expressly for the purpose of being synonymous with it.

Quine discusses the attempt to solve the problem by means of extensional concepts. The argument is too complicated to be reproduced here, but essentially he shows that it depends upon working with a language rich enough to contain the adverb "necessarily," this adverb being so construed as to yield truth when and only when applied to an analytical statement. However, as he shows, to condone such an adverb is to suppose that sense has already been made of the concept of "analytic." Therefore, although the argument is not flatly circular, it is very close to it. Quine shows that interchangeability is no assurance of cognitive synonymy of the desired type in an extensional language. For this reason, the attempt to explicate analyticity through the concept of synonymity fails.

Those writers interested in this attempt then attempted to define analyticity directly, in this case through the use of semantical rules. The most consistent attempt of this type was made by Carnap. However, the problem arose that his rules contained the word "analytic," which we do not yet understand. The semantic rules of Carnap permitted us to understand to what analyticity was attributed but not what the attribution asserted. For this reason, one might prefer to view the so-called semantical rule as a conventional definition of a new and simple symbol. However, although such statements do explicate what makes statements analytic for a particular language, they still do not explicate "analytic" or "analytic for."

Thus there was a further retreat to the statement that "such and such statements are included among the truths." However, this merely substitutes a new difficulty for the old; the statements are true according to the phrase "semantical rule," but we do not know what "semantical rule" means.

As Quine points out, it should by now be obvious that truth in general depends both on language and extralinguistic fact. The statement "Caesar crossed the Rubicon" would be false if the world had been different in different ways, but it also would be false if "crossed" happened to mean "ate." This leads to the supposition that the truth of a statement is somehow divisible into a linguistic and a factual component. If this is so, it might appear reasonable that in some statements the factual component should be absent and that such statements constitute the class of analytic statements. But, although seemingly reasonable, a boundary between analytic and synthetic statements has not been drawn in fact. It is merely a metaphysical dogma of empiricists, Quine says, that such a boundary exists.

Carnap therefore attempted to solve the problem by a radical reductionism that employed not words but statements as units, setting himself the task of specifying a sense-datum language and showing how to translate the rest of significant discourse, statement by statement, into it. Roughly summarized, the plan was that qualities should be assigned to point-instants in such a way as to achieve the simplest world compatible with our experience. "Carnap did not seem to recognize, however, that his treatment of physical objects" failed to complete the reduction in principle and not merely through sketchiness. "Statements of the form 'Quality q is at point-instant x; y; z; t;' were," according to Carnap's canons, to be assigned truth values so as to maximize and minimize certain overall features. The truth values were to be revised with experience. Quine says that this was a good schematization (although deliberately oversimplified) of what science really does; but he says that it does not provide even the sketchiest indication of how a statement of the form "Quality q is at x; y; z; t;" could ever be translated into Carnap's initial language of sense data and logic. The connective "is at" is undefined in the system. The canons tells us how to use it but do not eliminate or illuminate it.

The difficulties of the position led Carnap in his later writings to abandon the translatability of statements about the physical world into statements about immediate experience. Radical reductionism was surrendered.

According to Quine, the dogmas of reductionism and analyticity are identical. However, he notes how stubbornly the distinction between analytic and synthetic has resisted any "straightforward drawing." He states that he is "impressed also, apart from prefabricated examples of black and white balls in an urn, with how baffling the problem has always been of arriving at any explicit theory of the empirical confirmation of a synthetic statement." He concludes that it is "nonsense . . . to speak of a linguistic component and a factual component in the truth of any individual statement." Science is dependent upon both language and experience; but this double dependence cannot be referred back to "the statements of science taken one by one. . . . The totality of our so-called knowledge or beliefs, from the most casual matters of geography and history to the profoundest laws of atomic physics or even of pure mathematics and logic, . . . impinges on experience only along the edges." Contrary experiences at the boundary of the field occasion readjustments in the interior of the field. "Re-evaluation of some statements entails re-evaluation of others, because of their logical interconnection." Logical and mathematical systems are simply part of the system of knowledge, further "elements of the field." The totality of knowledge "is so underdetermined by its boundary conditions, experience," that contrary single experiences provide us with considerable latitude in reevaluating our beliefs. Particular experiences are linked with less direct beliefs only "indirectly through considerations of equilibrium affecting the field as a whole."

Although in principle explanation involves laws that sustain counterfactual and subjective conditional statements, our understanding of what a law is and of its appropriately determined boundary conditions rests on the general equilibrium of which Quine speaks. Therefore our understanding of whether an explanation is adequate always transcends the statements that can be given in such deductive form, although it can never violate them and remain an explanation.

That I find Quine's viewpoint felicitous is not surprising in view of our common pragmatic background. In an earlier work, before I had read "Two Dogmas," I wrote: "Knowledge and communication depend upon closure. The world of knowing is open, the world of the known is closed. The world of knowing is the world of continuing interaction. The world of the known is the world of closed scientific explanations and of analytic truths."[2] The world of knowing is what Quine calls the loose equilibrium of science as a field, the "totality of our so-called knowledge or beliefs."

Appendix 3

Means-Ends Rationality

The belief that values are subjective or that they are merely preferences—and that, therefore, they cannot be evaluated according to public standards—is consistent with the distinction Max Weber made between instrumental rationality and intrinsic rationality It also accords with the beliefs of some psychiatrists that even psychotic behavior is not irrational in instrumental terms: that it merely responds to goals and beliefs that are highly idiosyncratic.

Initially, at least, Weber's distinction seems to accord with recognizable differences in the real world. If a man wishes to ride in his automobile and if the gas tank is empty, it is consistent with common sense to assert that it is rational to fill the gas tank with gasoline and irrational to fill it with water. In this type of strictly demarcated case, there are clear criteria for the distinction between means and ends, and hence for means—ends rationality. The goal is given and the means for achieving it are clear. Is the world divided into means and ends, in which case we can treat the latter as "givens" and examine the former in terms of efficiency? This clearly does not work.

Suppose we ask why the man wishes to ride in the car? The answer might be that this is instrumental to still some other activity, such as meeting his boss. If this kind of examination produces a chain of ends, whether an end is intrinsic or instrumental depends not so much on the real status of values as upon the phase of the problem under consideration. Although there is no absolute distinction between means and ends in this case, an analytic distinction nonetheless would permit each phase of the problem to be considered independently, thereby permitting us to treat every problem in instrumental terms without raising seemingly insoluble questions concerning intrinsic rationality.

The foregoing hypothesis rests on an assumption that goals fall into a linear hierarchy. Let us examine a hypothetical example, however, and see whether this is really the case. Let us return to the man who wishes to ride in the automobile. Perhaps he wishes to travel to meet his boss. We can now ask whether riding in the car is rationally adapted toward that end. However, in this case, it might be possible for him to walk, to take a cab, or, if the distance is longer, to fly. Suppose that we ask why he wishes to see his boss? Perhaps he wishes to ingratiate himself so that his pay will be raised. However, the same time might be spent looking for another job that pays better. Suppose we ask why he wants more pay? It may be that he wishes to be able to afford more cultural activities. However, he might now begin to consider the trade-off between money and leisure. If we ask why he wishes more cultural activities, he might answer that this is related to his desire to live a life in which he can take some pride. However, in this case, he might begin to ask whether his occupation forces him into such undesirable practices—for instance, the business may be one that emphasizes ruthless competition—that it might be worthwhile to take a job that paid less and provided him with less leisure time, provided that the ethics of the work situation were more consistent with his image of what he wants to be. On the other hand, if he has a family dependent upon his income, there may be a trade-off here as well.

The illusion of the simple example lies in the belief—never validated by actual practice—that objectives can be placed in a linear hierarchy such that lower-ranking objectives are always validated by those higher in the hierarchy. We have seen from our example that this does not work. Moreover, the hierarchial view does not apply to values, even when they are considered abstractly, let alone when considered in terms of concrete ends. The illusion that values lie in a hierarchy—in effect that each level of values contains fewer categories than the next lower one and that the highest level has one category only—produces a supreme value inconsistent with or irrelevant to lower level particularizations. This illusion underlies formal theories of law, ethics, and also of science.

Theories do have deductive form, a fact made clear by elegant theories of physics. However, their application in science always requires standards of evidence not contained in the theory. Indeed, evidence that ordinarily might be acceptable sometimes is not if a theory is inconsistent with numerous other theories for which there is evidence.

Because we treat the rest of the realm of knowledge as if it were a direct statement of reality (and therefore unproblematic) when we attempt to validate a theory, we treat the process as if it were entirely deductive, whereas in fact the criteria determining proof depend on the equilibrium of the whole realm—a matter not subject to exclusively deductive methodology. However, what is axiomatic in one theory may be deducible from another and vice versa. And what appears to be a valid measurement may be inconsistent with still other scientific results. Whether an axiom, a theorem, a conclusion, or a criterion for measurement is acceptable is related to its consistency with the realm of praxis. There is no general theory or philosophy of science that predetermines any of the foregoing possibilities.

The problem of distinguishing between the form of a theory and its application in specific circumstances takes highly tangible form in the social sciences and philosophy. An abstract hierarchy of values available for application to a particular case would exist only if a valid general theory were possible. Yet, in abstractly formal general theories in philosophy and the social sciences—for instance, Kelsen's theory of law with its fundamental norm of legality—the ultimate norm or value is always either vacuous or definitional. Kelsen's ultimate norm of legality is vacuous because it is consistent with all legal systems and therefore constrains none, although it does distinguish legal systems from other types of systems. Yet, only if there were a substantive general theory could an abstract hierarchy of values or norms exist.

With respect to means-ends rationality, therefore, we may be able to specify a reasonable relationship between values for a particular problem, class of problems, or type of society. Other information is always assumed as the weight of evidence changes. Moreover, as the problem or the circumstances of application change, the prior ordering of values may become more or less appropriate. New sets of alternatives may create new empirical relationships among values.

What is a means and what is an end is relative to the character of the problem that requires decision. The linkage between elements of the problem is determined by the conditions of the case and not by a prior system of classification. There is a multiplicity of ways of arranging means and ends depending on what questions are asked and how they are analyzed. Because of the multiplicity of questions that can be asked and because of the ways in which the questions branch out rather than narrow—as in our earlier example—when we attempt to trace the chain of ends, the distinction between means and ends becomes less clear in general the more important the question that is asked. And this is not a simple matter of the means transforming the end. Therefore, it is impossible to make a purely instrumental analysis in any except the most arbitrarily circumscribed case. The more significant and broadly ranging the question asked, the more the analyst is forced to investigate problems of intrinsic value. In its broadest sense, this leads to an investigation of the nature of man and the character of society.

Thus, the critique of the Weberian dichotomy between instrumental and intrinsic rationality leads back to the psychiatric distinction. The assertion of irrationality in the case of a psychotic is an assertion not that his means may be disproportionate to a single end, but that the relationship of that end or value to any reasonable constellation of ends or values can justly be called irrational. Although the psychiatric attribution of instrumental rationality may be correct in one sense—the intended end of action may be better understood when we apprehend the delusional system—the behavior remains irrational in the broader sense.

The argument against a simple means-ends dichotomization becomes even clearer in game and bargaining problems. In game-theoretical analysis, for instance, there is no single standard of rationality but a variety of standards adapted to particular types of games. Some of these seem more compelling than others. Some seem quite strong and some weak. In each case, however, the criteria impute certain characteristics to the psyche of the individual who holds them. For instance, he may desire to minimize uncertainty, in which case the minimax criterion may seem rational. Alternatively, he may desire to minimize the loss he would sustain if he decides incorrectly about the states of nature, in which case the minimax regret principle may seem more appropriate.

However, a very simple analysis will show that one's fundamental attitude toward risk is dependent upon life situations as well as upon psychic characteristics. For instance, the risks involved in gambling may be minimal for the rich person but devastating for the poor one (except when he makes an occasional small bet in a lottery, where winning could change his life style). I do not intend to examine how differences in a person's circumstances can lead to different preferences for risk orderings—which, as von Neumann made clear in his utility axioms, are essential to the conception of utility—but merely to show that what is taken as given for one purpose, for instance, evaluating a specific game problem, is usually problematical from another standpoint: an entire life. From the larger standpoint, therefore, risk preferences are not a fundamental axiom of choice but a variable that changes, depending upon the other aspects of the realm of praxis.

Perhaps one might argue that although an absolute disjunction between means and ends cannot be made, the realm of ends is still one of subjective preferences. A satisfactory answer to this objection is given in the first two chapters of this book. However, that answer is reinforced in the present inquiry. If preferences existed in a single-ordered hierarchy, perhaps the objection might hold. But they do not exist in that form. The very order of preference, as well as the very order of risk-bearing willingness, depends upon the entire concatenation of circumstances. And this means that we cannot investigate the order of preferences without investigating the conditions of life, including our understanding of human character and social life in general as well as of individual human character in diverse social settings. Thus, we are immediately thrust from the abstract to the concrete and from "subjective" to objective considerations that are subject to public communication. The interdependence is such that the linkage is intimate and that investigations of questions of value, except in the artificially limited case, can never be carried out by a purely instrumental analysis. The Weberian point of view transforms a limitation of inquiry into a substantive distinction. Whatever the practical necessity of recognizing such limitations in thinking about particular cases, the inferences of a more general kind made from them are clearly non sequiturs.

The more basic defect lies in the subject-object dichotomization that is inherent in the Kantian tradition and its positivistic successors. By positing an external world about which mental reports are given, the "objects" of knowledge are reified and divorced from the process by which knowledge is achieved and communicated. "Real" colors or other "real" qualities of objects are contrasted with mental images and subjective values, whereas the characterization of reality—as the first two chapters of this book make clear—invokes a relationship between a knower with specified empirical characteristics and the known. The characteristics of objects do not simply "exist"; they are produced by an interactive process. This is true of both angstrom waves and values. The Kantian and positivistic approaches render inadequate accounts of reality, of philosophy, of scientific method, and of value theory.

Notes

Preface

1. Stephen Toulmin, *Reason in Ethics* (Cambridge: At the University Press, 1950); John Rawls, *A Theory of Justice* (Cambridge: Harvard University Press, Belknap Press, 1971).

2. See W. Ross Ashby, *Design for a Brain* (New York: John Wiley & Sons, 1952).

3. Morton A. Kaplan, *System and Process in International Politics* (New York: John Wiley & Sons, 1957), pp. 279-80.

Chapter 1. The System

1. In Herbert Butterfield and Martin Wight, eds., *Diplomatic Investigations* (Cambridge: Harvard University Press, 1966), pp. 149-75.

2. In my theory of international politics, for instance, the essential rules of the system would fall into this category. We may also include system step functions: for instance, the system transformation rules. See *System and Process*, pp. 9-10, for a discussion of essential and transformation rules.

3. Although demands and supports are processed through personality systems, as well as political and social systems, what the personality perceives as a demand, and what it offers as a support, depends on

its perception of its alternatives in context. In the United States, for instance, the discontents of blacks were not presented as demands to the political system in the 1930s, and indeed were not perceived as such by most blacks. Thus, although empirically it may be possible to state that a particular system is potentially unstable and that its level of support is low because many demands are unsatisfied, the existence—and the level—of the demands is not independent of the system in which they occur. Neither the categorization of real-world elements as demands or supports nor their measurement can be determined except insofar as they have consequences within a particular type of system. No covering laws utilizing measures that are valid across different types of systems are available to the social scientist.

Although much integration theory, for instance, rests on transfers across system boundaries, for which there are empirical measures, these are less illuminating in the absence of contextual analysis than is sometimes thought. The general process of integration is well known. Metals are bonded when strong relationships exist between many individual elements of different metals. However, bonding also occurs when fungi spread throughout a system. Whether such transfers produce an integration in which the uniting elements are preserved, whether one is absorbed by and transformed into the other, whether both are destroyed, or whether the process reverses itself at a certain point cannot be determined in the absence of qualitative contextual analysis in which the system properties of both the combining elements and the new overarching system are examined.

4. Ashby, *Design for a Brain*, p. 99.

5. Willard van Orman Quine, *From a Logical Point of View: Nine Logico-philosophical Essays*, 2nd ed., rev. (Cambridge: Harvard University Press, 1961), p. 47.

6. The general position that we start with knowledge and not with sense impressions is classical. More recently, as Morris R. Cohen pointed out in *A Preface to Logic* (New York: Henry Holt, 1944), the string-of-marks theory runs into difficulty because it provides no means of recognizing the identity of the same symbol in different places. Cohen's attack on conceptual jurisprudence is informed by this same non-reductionist viewpoint. However, the best discussion of this subject appears in Quine, *From a Logical Point of View*, pp. 20-46. It is so important to the objections raised to Toulmin in chapter 2 and Rawls in chapter 3 that the argument is summarized in appendix 2.

7. Ashby, *Design for a Brain*, pp. 153-65.

8. John von Neumann, *The Computer and the Brain* (New Haven: Yale University Press, 1958), pp. 90-92.

9. See "A Nightmare" in Morton A. Kaplan, *Macropolitics. Essays on the Philosophy and Science of Politics* (Chicago: Aldine Publishing Co., 1969), pp. 197-205, for a pessimistic scenario involving dehumanization as a consequence of incremental choice.

10. Edward C. Banfield and L. F. Banfield, *The Moral Basis of a Backward Society* (New York: Free Press, 1958).

11. See Morton A. Kaplan, *On Historical and Political Knowing* (Chicago: University of Chicago Press, 1971), pp. 4-12, for a discussion of this problem, including the phenomenon of pathological science.

Chapter 2. The Good

1. For Toulmin's discussion of the objective, subjective, and imperative approaches, see pp. 10-60; of physical and moral reality, pp. 130-43, and of limiting questions, pp. 144-63.

2. Toulmin, *Reason in Ethics*, p. 18.

3. Ibid., p. 28.

4. C. L. Stevenson, *Ethics and Language* (New Haven: Yale University Press, 1944).

5. Toulmin, *Reason in Ethics*, p. 38.

6. A. J. Ayer, *Language, Truth, and Logic*, 2nd ed. (London: Gollancz, 1946).

7. Toulmin, *Reason in Ethics*, p. 145.

8. Toulmin's conception of limiting questions appears related to Bertrand Russell's distinction between vicious and non-vicious regressuses. Russell pointed out that we can inquire into the cause of any particular thing but that we cannot ask what is the cause of this world. The first inquiry in principle leads to an infinite regressus that is empirically meaningful. That is, for any event, no matter how remote, we can always, in principle at least, inquire into its cause. This is what Russell means when he says that the regressus is non-vicious. It is a regressus of implications only, whereas the second regressus is vicious because it is a regressus of meanings. It asks a question that cannot be answered within the same framework of analysis and, in effect, gives rise to a pseudoquestion. Thus, Toulmin seems to put himself within the framework that Russell proposes and to dismiss certain types of ethical questions as pseudoquestions that mislead us because of their form.

9. Toulmin, *Reason in Ethics*, p. 40.

10. See Kaplan, *System and Process*, pp. 271-80, reprinted in *Macropolitics*, pp. 156-67. The only similar position I have come across is in Alan Gewirth, "The Normative Structure of Action," *Review of Metaphysics* 25, 2 (December 1971): 238-61.

11. This method of evaluation was employed by my former associate Donald Reinken in determining the utility schedules for nations in a "balance of power" system as played out on a computer model. The utilities were oriented toward the institutional framework of international politics and specific policies were evaluated on the basis both of their impact on that institutional framework and on the specific fortunes of the nations considered separately. (See Donald L. Reinken, "Computer Explorations of the 'Balance of Power': A Project Report," in Morton A. Kaplan, ed., *New Approaches to International Relations* [New York: St. Martin's Press, 1968].) This procedure is different from that imposed under the von Neumann utility axioms. To be employed in my test in principle, it requires a recursive metatechnique. Given our point of focus, something could be a good for one person and an evil for another, or a good for a person and an evil for a social system and vice versa.

12. *Macropolitics*, pp. 42-43.

Chapter 3. The Just

1. Paul Kecskemeti, *Meaning, Communication, and Value* (Chicago: (Chicago: University of Chicago Press, 1952), pp. 314ff.

2. Rawls, *A Theory of Justice*, p. 11.

3. Ibid., p. 12.

4. Ibid., p. 37.

5. Ibid., p. 13.

6. Ibid., p. 60.

7. Ibid., pp. 62-63.

8. Ibid., pp. 76ff.

9. Ibid.

10. Ibid., pp. 541ff.

11. Game theory is a mathematical theory designed to produce optimal rules for choice in situations in which players have at least partly opposed interests. The zero-sum game, for which there is a general solution, is one in which the gains and losses of the players add to zero. There is no general solution for the non-zero-sum game, and a

variety of decision rules for them, depending upon the matrix of the individual games. The terms employed in the games have strict technical meanings. The numbers employed in the payoff boxes are utiles and represent the players' preferences for outcomes conceived as "gambles." Bargaining theories are employed for some problems that are not completely amenable to game theoretic analysis and employ criteria of "fairness." For a longer discussion, see my following writings: *System and Process*, pp. 169-241; *New Approaches*, pp. 483-518; *Strategic Thinking and Its Moral Implications*, (Chicago: Center for Policy Study, University of Chicago, 1973), pp. 13-38. See *New Approaches*, pp. 489-94, for a discussion of rationality.

12. Those familiar with the methodology of *System and Process* will recall that three sets of equilibria exist for the models of chapter 2: within the set of essential rules; between the essential rules and other system variables; and between the system and its environment. These are subject to theoretical analysis, although the transformation rules that account for system change are not derivable from an overall theory. The essential rules of a system are those rules that describe the characteristic role functions of actors in a system. In a monogamous family system, one man is married to one woman. In the American congressional system, tax laws are initiated in the House. In more traditional systems, the young defer to the elders. However, Rawls's two rules of justice are not similar to essential rules, for they are not related to other system variables. Therefore, they cannot function determinatively even in a simple game or bargaining model.

Whereas the essential rules of my international system models vary with the states of the other variables and of the environment, Rawls has attempted to generalize by abstracting from such considerations. As a consequence, contradictory rules are consistent with his assumptions. Because his rules thus have no articulated theoretical relationships to other relevant systemic factors—for his level of abstractness excludes this—there is no theoretical ground even for considering how a change in circumstances would lead to variations in the rules. See *System and Process*, pp. 9 and 25ff., for a discussion of essential and transformation rules and the three sets of equilibria. See *Macropolitics*, pp. 234ff., for a discussion of how a theory that does apply in an articulated fashion to a particular type of social system can explain what rule changes will accompany other system or parameter changes.

13. Rawls, *A Theory of Justice*, p. 153.

14. The prisoners' dilemma is a case in which two players produce their jointly least desired outcome as a consequence of rational choices that are made without knowledge of the other's choice. This results

from the peculiar nature of the game matrix, in which each player is better off individually by following a non-cooperative strategy regardless of what the other player does. For a discussion of the prisoners' dilemma, possible solutions to it, and related problems, see *System and Process*, pp. 199ff.; *New Approaches*, pp. 494ff., and *Strategic Thinking*, pp. 15ff. I was able to show some fifteen years ago that the prisoners' dilemma could be used to prove the necessity of moral rules in society. See also the discussion on pp. 157-159 and note 34 below.

15. The attempts to avoid this outcome by resort to metastrategies are theoretically unsound. See John C. Harsanyi, review of *Paradoxes of Rationality* by Nigel Howard, *American Political Science Review* 67 (June 1973): 599-600 (Also the Howard-Harsanyi communications in vol. 68 [June 1974], pp. 729-31). See also Kaplan, "Strategy and Morality," in *Strategic Thinking*, pp. 16-17. Incidentally, a moral rule does not solve the prisoners' dilemma as Rawls believes; it transforms it into a different problem.

16. See footnote 27 below.

17. See R. Duncan Luce and Howard Raiffa, *Games and Decisions* (New York: John Wiley & Sons, 1957), pp. 199ff.

18. See *New Approaches*, pp. 513ff., and "Strategy and Morality," *Strategic Thinking*, pp. 13ff.

19. See Rudolf Stammler, *Theory of Justice*, Husik (New York: Macmillan, 1925), pp. 19-76, for his discussion of the community of free-willing men and concentric circles of obligation.

20. For a discussion of Pareto Optimality, see Luce and Raiffa, *Games and Decisions*, pp. 127, 193, 339, 350, 364-65.

21. Rawls, *A Theory of Justice*, p. 217.

22. Ibid., p. 169.

23. Ibid., p. 204.

24. Ibid., pp. 20ff.

25. The St. Petersburg paradox is a game in which a fair coin is tossed and in which one player will win $\$2^n$, where n is the toss on which heads appears. Query: How much should one pay to be allowed to play this game? Mathematically, the value of the game is infinite. Therefore, in arithmetic terms, one should be willing to pay any finite sum, no matter how large, to play it. This obviously does not accord with our preferences. For a discussion of the von Neumann utility assumptions, see Luce and Raiffa, *Games and Decisions*, pp. 19ff. For a discussion of some problems in utility analysis, see Kaplan, *System and Process*, pp. 208ff., and *New Approaches*, pp. 492ff.

26. A Nash bargain is one in which a unique point is selected according to Nash's axioms at the outer limit of the bargaining space. This outer limit represents the best set of solutions for both players jointly and in the absence of which at least one of the players will be worse off without making the other better off. For a discussion of the Nash bargain and of some of its problems see *System and Process*, pp. 195ff., and *New Approaches*, pp. 199ff.

27. In a seminar at the Center for Advanced Study in 1956, Howard Raiffa argued that the $50/$5 Nash point division would be rejected by the player on the $5 axis because he could hold out until each player had the same dollar amount to lose, which occurs at the $9.09, $9.09 point. I argued that the player on the $5 axis would then be rejecting a sure $5 for a potential additional $4.09 if he accepted Raiffa's argument, while the player on the $50 axis would risk only $9.09 by rejecting this alternative bargain in the hope of obtaining an additional $40.91 if he insisted on the Nash solution. See *System and Process*, pp. 197-99. Raiffa agreed no solution had clear precedence.

28. Rawls, *A Theory of Justice*, pp. 131ff.

29. Ibid., p. 135.

30. If realistic theories of jurisprudence threaten to denude legal theory of explanations involving the use of rules—an element of legal activity required to distinguish it from political decision making—conceptual jurisprudence detached law from its reliance upon social circumstances, a development that received its apotheosis in Hans Kelsen's remarkable work. Kelsen's theory rested upon a fundamental assumption, that of legality. Yet this assumption was consistent with many different proposed or actual substantive systems of law. Kelsen was finally forced to assume that the ultimate principle of law applied only to those systems that were made effective by political authority—a ground that was unsatisfactory for explanatory purposes because it was unrelated to his theoretical system.

31. Rawls, *A Theory of Justice*, p. 345.

32. Alan Gewirth, "Moral Rationality," The Lindley Lecture, University of Kansas, 1972.

33. Ibid., p. 21.

34. See J. C. C. Smart, "Extreme and Restricted Utilitarianism," *Philosophical Quarterly* 29 (October 1956): 344-54; Morton A. Kaplan, "Some Problems of the Extreme Utilitarian Position," *Ethics* 70, 3 (April 1960): 228-32; J. C. C. Smart, "Extreme Utilitarianism: A Reply to M. A. Kaplan," *Ethics* 71, 1 (January 1961): 133-34; and Morton A. Kaplan, "Restricted Utilitarianism," *Ethics* 71, 4 (July 1961: 301-2.

35. See John C. Harsanyi, "Can the Maximin Principle Serve as a Basis for Morality?: A Critique of John Rawls's Theory," Working Paper No. CP-351, Center for Research in Management Science, University of California, Berkeley, May 1973; Harsanyi, "A Further Note on Rawls's Theory," Working Paper No. CP-363, Center for Research in Management Science, University of California, Berkeley, July 1974; Kenneth J. Arrow, "Some Ordinalist-Utilitarian Notes on Rawls' Theory of Justice," *Journal of Philosophy* 70 (May 1973): 254; John Rawls, "Concepts of Distributional Equity: Some Reasons for the Maximin Criterion," *American Economic Review*, Papers and Proceedings (May 1974), pp. 141-46.

36. Banfield and Banfield, *The Moral Basis of a Backward Society*.

37. Rawls, *A Theory of Justice*, p. 58.

Chapter 4 Political Obligation

1. If he acts contrarily, he may say that he cannot control his impulses.

2. Hobbes's argument for obligation was based on conservative premises. Thus, to make it "binding," he deliberately changed his definitions in midstream. See Morton A. Kaplan, "How Sovereign is Hobbes' Sovereign?" *Western Political Quarterly* 9, 2 (June 1956): 389-405.

3. *System and Process*, pp. 13-14.

4. See *System and Process*, pp. 94-95, for a definition of metatask capacity. It is essentially the capacity to organize a system to perform particular tasks.

5. After all, a contract cannot establish an obligation unless it is a good that takes priority over other goods or unless a normative system makes it obligatory. Therefore, contracts themselves are subject to moral analysis.

6. Robert Nozick, *Anarchy, State and Utopia* (New York: Basic Books, 1974).

7. Even where it is in their long-term interest to assist the state, "every little payment appeareth a great grievance; [citizens] are destitute of those prospective glasses (namely, Morall and Civill Science) to see a farre off the miseries that hang over them, and cannot without such payments be avoided" (Thomas Hobbes, *Leviathan*, ed. Pogson Smith [New York: Oxford University Press, 1952], p. 141).

8. Rawls, *A Theory of Justice*, pp. 372-73.

9. Ibid., p. 373.

10. Ibid., p. 381.

11. See Morton A. Kaplan and Nicholas de B. Katzenbach, *The Political Foundations of International Law* (New York: John Wiley & Sons, 1961), especially chapter 2.

12. See my *System and Process*, pp. 16-18, for an explication of this concept.

Appendix 1. Knowing and Communicating

1. Allan Janik and Stephen Toulmin, *Wittgenstein's Vienna,* (New York: Simon & Schuster, 1973).

2. I. Langmuir, *Pathological Science,* edited and transcribed by R. N. Hall, General Electric Technical Information Series, Report No. 68-C-035, General Electric Research and Development Center, April 1968, pp. 2-3.

3. Rawls, *A Theory of Justice,* pp. 426ff.

Appendix 2. The Two Dogmas of Empiricism

1. Condensed from Quine, *From a Logical Point of View,* pp. 20-46.

2. *On Historical and Political Knowing,* pp. 144-145.

Index